Publisher and Creative Director:
B. Martin Pedersen

Chief Visionary Officer:
Patti Judd

Design Director:
Hee Ra Kim

Designers:
B. Martin Pedersen
Hee Ra Kim
Hiewon Sohn

Associate Editor:
Sara Gonzalez

Editorial Interns:
Summer Buffin
Amanda Farrell
Anayaé Holmes
Alyssa Micalizzi

Japanese Advisors:
USA: Toshiaki & Kumiko Ide
Japan: Taku Satoh
Sakura Nomiyama

Chief Executive Officer:
B. Martin Pedersen

Financial Officer:
Arna T. Pedersen

Legal Counsel:
John M. Roth

Cover Art:
"Bobby Roaché Design"
Photo by Athena Azevedo

Published by:
Graphis Inc.
389 Fifth Avenue, Suite 1105
New York, NY 10016
Phone: 212-532-9387
www.graphis.com
help@graphis.com

Distributed by:
National Book Networks, Inc.
15200 NBN Way
Blue Ridge Summit, PA 17214
Phone: 800-462-6420
customercare@nbnbooks.com

ISBN 13: 978-1-931241-90-8

In this COVID pandemic, just about everyone in our profession is sadly economically affected.

Design and Advertising agencies may now have clients who are reducing staff and also giving out less work. To maintain business, most of us are likely working virtually to cut expenses with staff many can barely afford but are in need of to survive.

Photographers are in a much tougher situation with rare assignments since social distancing restrictions have made location and studio work with models almost impossible to achieve.

At Graphis, we are working virtually on our books and journals as well as developing new ideas for our future. Since many bookstores have closed due to the pandemic, and previously due to the retail giant Amazon, Graphis now survives mostly on direct sales.

As anyone who sells through Amazon knows, sales have slimmer profit margins since we also have to pay for the shipping costs. The securities and exchange commissioners whose jobs it had been to prevent monopolies to take place have sadly allowed this to happen.

For all of us, especially illustrators and photographers, it may be an opportune time to recharge and dig down deep with renewed creativity to further develop new work in your portfolios.

Below we present established talents whose work deserves to be seen, and whose equally important philosophies should be read for inspiration.

Design: **Michael Osborne** (US), one of the famous Michaels from San Francisco with years of award winning work. **Underline Studio** (CAN), a branding design agency that elevates client brands to new levels, and **Uwe Loesch** (DE), AGI member and Professor whose posters are perfectly unconventional.

Advertising: **John Fairley** of Curious Productions, a UK-based agency that is always on the hunt for innovative and creative solutions in advertising.

Photography: **Athena Azevedo** (US), an in-house photographer at IF Studio who defines beauty and luxury in every shot. **Vincent Junier** (FR), whose stunning still life and commercial photography have given him worldwide recognition.

Art/Illustration: **John Mattos** (US) and his retro-style illustrations that have made an impression on illustrators and designers alike.

Education: **Mel White** (US), Advertising Professor at Syracuse University, The Newhouse School, who continually drives her students to success, developing award-winning ads.

Products: A single-occupancy vehicle called the 2021 ElectraMeccanica SOLO, a Solar Charged Jacket by Vollebak (USA), and modern chair designs: sChaise by Smarin (France), and the Neotenic Lounge Chair by JUMBO NYC (USA).

Architecture: Stage of Forest by META-Project (CN), the Cocoon House by Nina Edwards Anker (nea studio) (US), and the "Most Dynamic Library" Deichman Library by Lundhagem Architects and Atelier Oslo (NO).

B. Martin Pedersen
Publisher & Creative Director

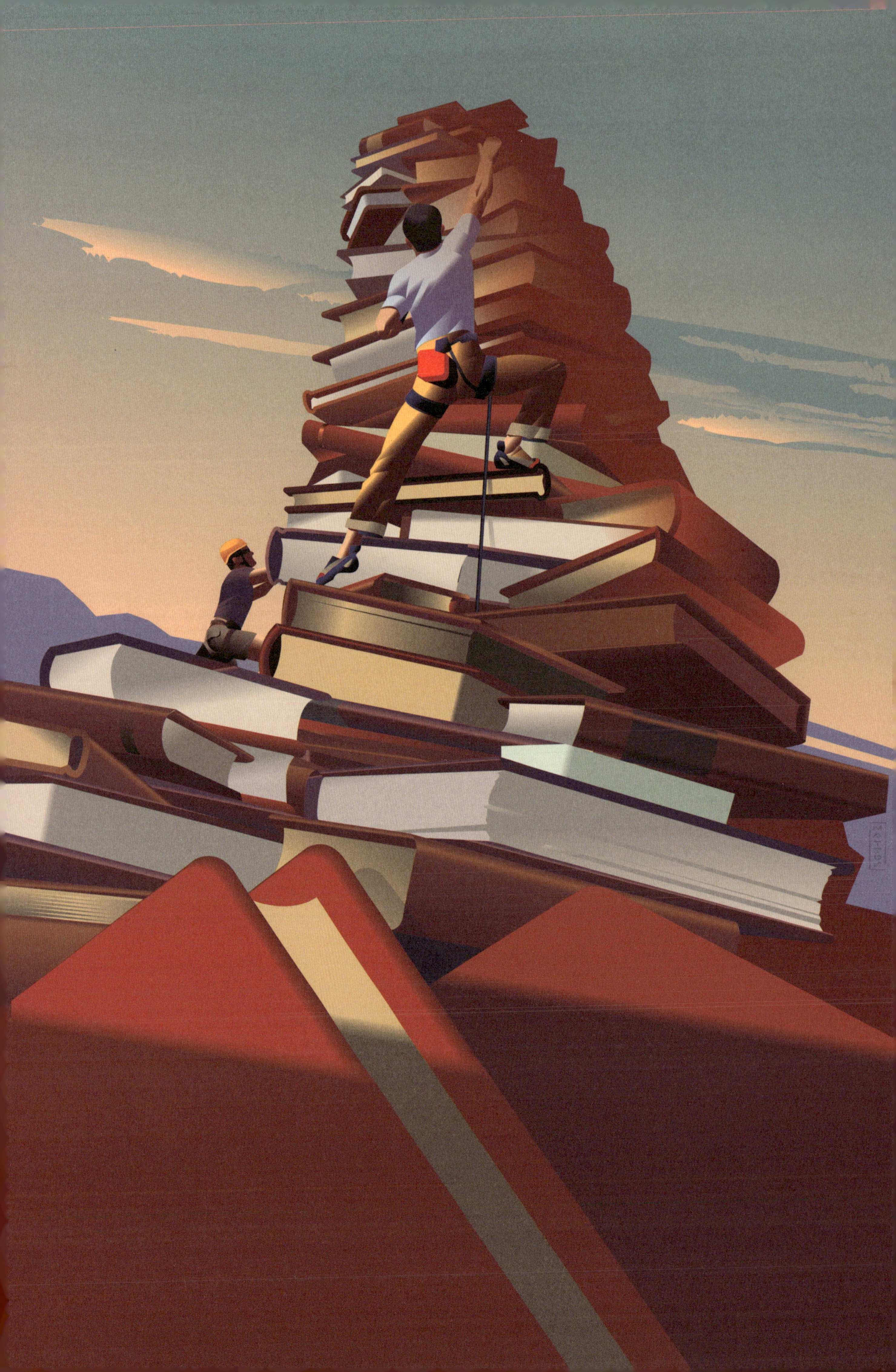

Contents

(Opposite page) Salesforce and Learning: Illustrator: John Mattos

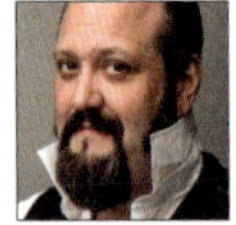

John Fairley is Design Director of Curious Productions in London. In a career spanning more than twenty years, he's created an enviable body of work in the worlds of advertising and design. That work has been consistently awarded and exhibited across the globe for its boldness, originality, and near-obsessive devotion to detail. John's philosophy is very simple: 'Make great creative work. Collaborate with the very best people, and be genuine and kind in the process'. ■ His illustrious client list includes: American Express, the BBC, Estée Lauder, Nike, Rolls Royce, Sony, Universal Pictures, and the Warner Music Group. He's developed strong and fruitful relationships with all of them, and they keep coming back for his knack of creating imaginative, impactful and emotionally engaging campaigns.

Introduction by Deborah Goldweis

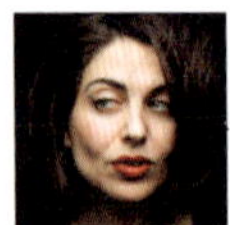

Athena Azevedo is a Graphis Photography Master and works as the Associate Creative Director and in-house photographer with the Graphis Design Master's Toshiaki and Hisa Ide at IF Studio, an award-winning branding, and graphic design agency. ■ Athena is also the founding Executive Director of the International Brazilian Opera Company (IBOC). She received her BA in "Cultural Construction and the Narrative Image" from the University of California, Berkeley, and found her passion for Brazilian culture and arts during a year abroad program to Salvador da Bahia and Rio de Janeiro. She lives in NYC with her husband and daughter.

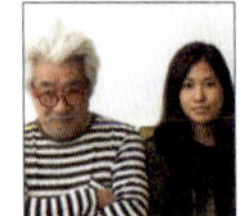

Introduction by Toshiaki and Hisa Ide (Graphis Masters)
Toshiaki and Hisa Ide are an award-winning father and daughter team leading the creative vision at IF Studio. After Hisa graduated with honors from SVA in 2010, she joined Toshiaki, the Creative Director and Co-founder of IF Studio. The pair have won numerous publications and awards since. Toshi's 30 years of experience with agencies such as Wells Rich Greene, Grey Advertising, and Bates USA on accounts including Estée Lauder, Olay, IBM, AT&T, and American Express, are complemented by Hisa's fresh and sophisticated aesthetic as Design Director.

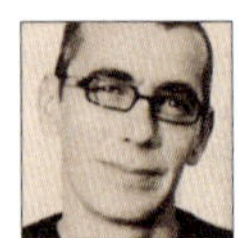

Born in 1964 and inspired by his friend's father, a still life photographer, Vincent started practicing photography very early at the age of 17. For several years he specialized in portrait and still life photography for press and magazines. In 1993, he decided to pursue a new path: switching to graphic design within the press industry and, later-on, further elaborating his conceptual skills as a creative director for communication agencies. For the past 5 years, he's finally decided to come back to his first passion — still life photography. By developing ways to play with the lighting and his unique ability for proportions and compositions, Vincent turns whatever he captures through his lens into a desirable object. As a self-taught photographer, most of his qualities derive from not being constrained by school-taught rules. His work combines artistic simplicity and a fresh aesthetic, often with a touch of oddness.

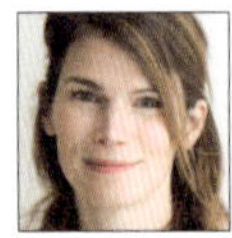

Introduction by Laure Bouvet
Starting as an art buyer and TV producer for major French advertising agencies, like Young & Rubicam, and Fred & Farid, Laure then led the Art buying department of La Chose in Paris for 7 years. Laure gained a unique experience diving into thousands of books and selecting artists, among which many are photographers, for a large number of national and international advertising campaigns. Laure knows what makes a portfolio catch the eye of creative directors and clients. ■ Laure founded Well Done John (welldonejohn.com) in 2018. At Well Done John, Laure is not only an art buyer, but also a coach for photographers. As a coach, she provides a personalized service to help photographers develop their activity. Aware of the profound changes that are occurring in the photography industry, Laure advises photo artists on their approach and their interaction with agencies. Issues like the role of social media, the use of video, shrinking budgets and new legal practices are part of her expertise. Laure helps photographers build a portfolio with a strong identity, adequately use social networks and gain precious know-how in legal and financial negotiation.

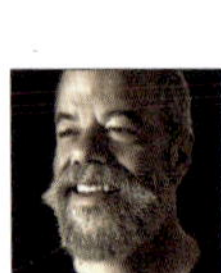

John Mattos was born in California's Central Valley. He graduated from Art Center College in 1975, traveled in Western Europe for 2 years, Then began his freelance illustration career. ■ Currently based in San Francisco, John has been honored with over 100 awards for graphic excellence, and has work included in the Eli Broad Museum of Contemporary Art in Los Angeles, and the new George Lucas Museum of Narrative Art, also in Los Angeles.

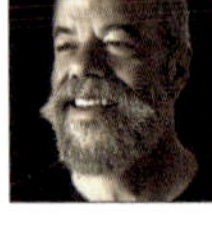

Introduction by Charles E. White III
Charlie White III has been at the forefront of experiential art for many decades. During the 70's, a young Charlie White III reached iconic status as an illustrator and concept designer who pushed thought-provoking boundaries in album covers, annual reports, and art and advertising concepts for a diverse range of clients such as *Playboy*, and *New York Magazine*, as well as National Lampoon, Lockheed Warner Records etc. He spent the next two decades storytelling with an immersive environment for the entertainment industry, providing unique and astonishing solutions. More of his clients around the world include: Universal Studios CityWalk, Disney California and Tokyo, Treasure Island Las Vegas, Atlantis Bahamas and Dubai, and Ushaka South Africa. Charlie brings the "what if" factor that can lift a project to the extraordinary.

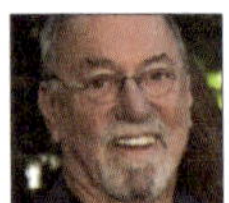

(Opposite page) Read, Top 10 Books Read in 2019, Poster, 2019, Underline Studio

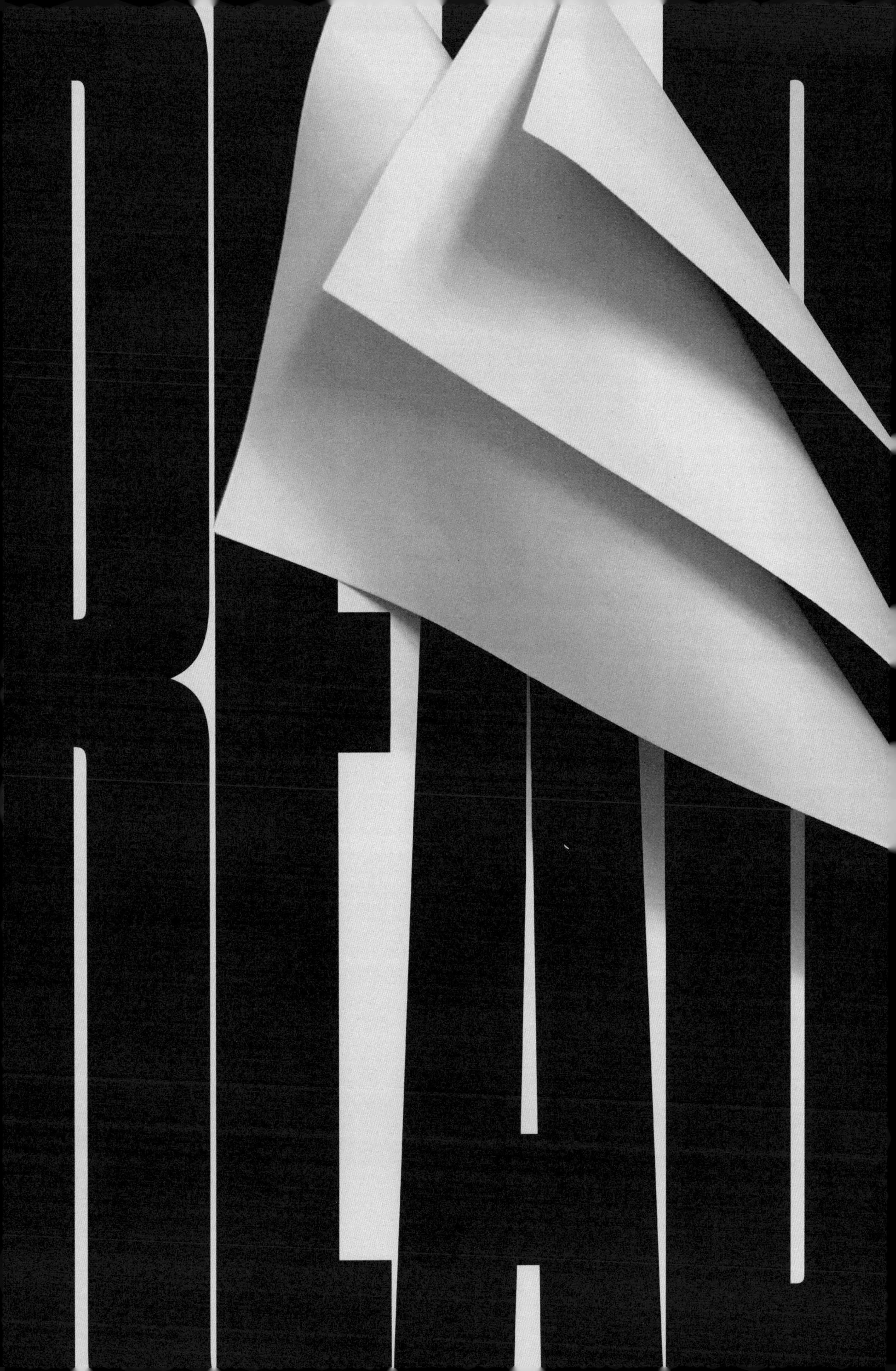

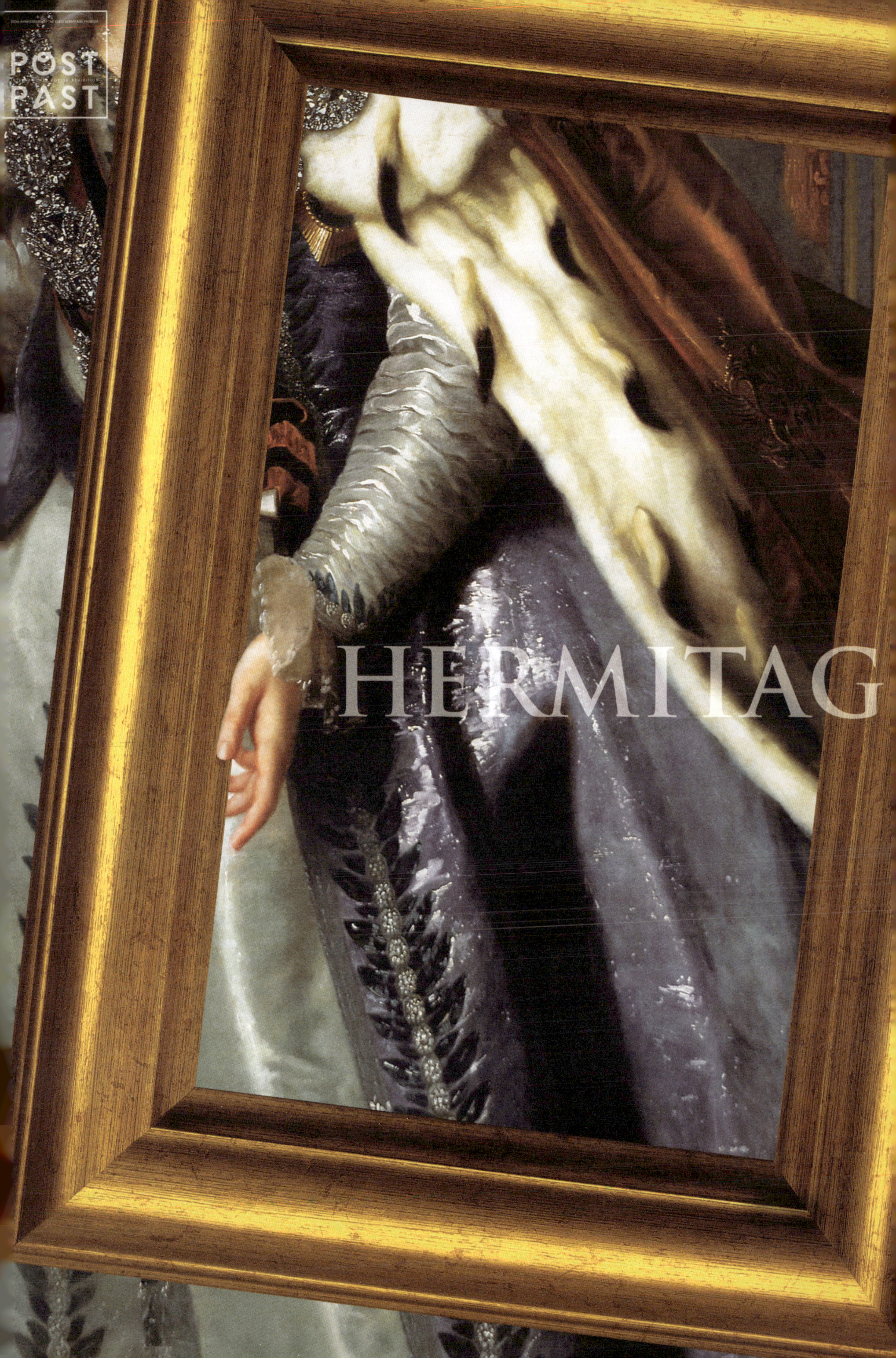
POST
PAST
HERMITAG

(Opposite page) Hermitage, 250th anniversary of the State Hermitage Museum St. Petersburg, 2013

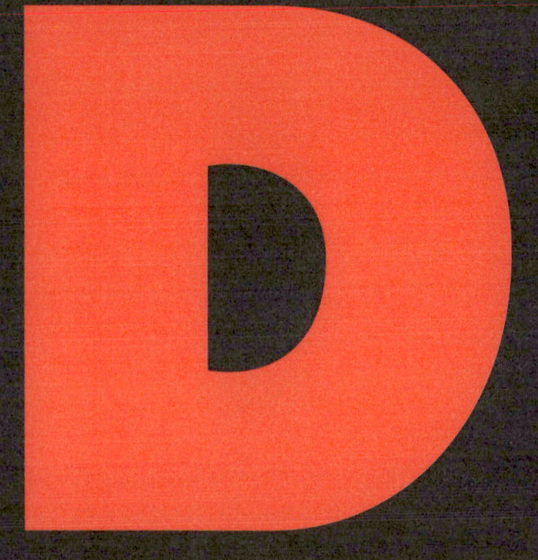

DESIGN

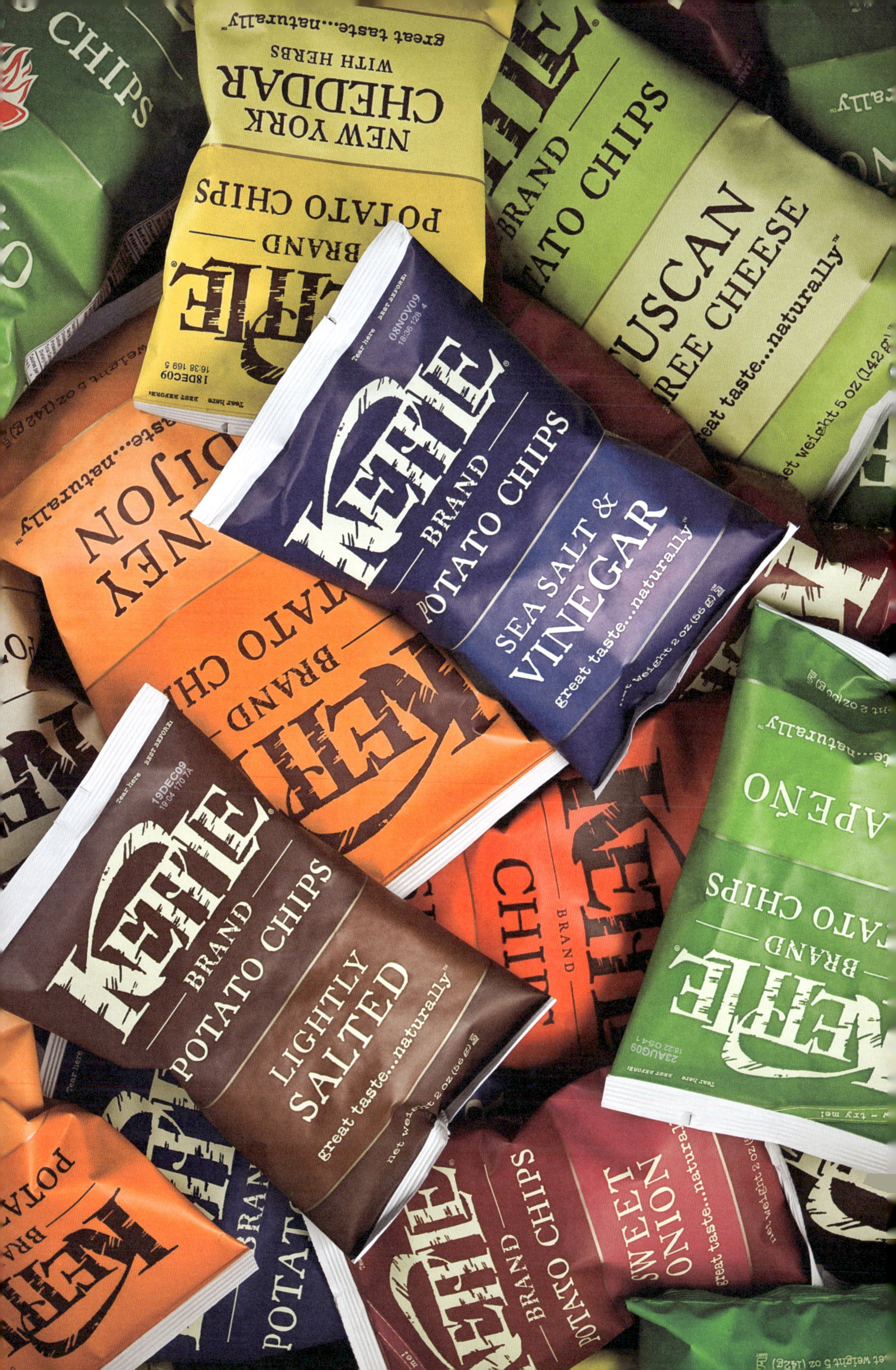

HIS APPROACH TO HIS WORK AND LIFE, AID HIM IN SOLVING A RANGE OF CHALLENGES FROM NON-PROFIT CLIENTS TO MAJOR CORPORATE PROJECTS. HE STILL FINDS THE ENERGY TO TEACH THE NEXT GENERATION OF DESIGNERS.

Kit Hinrichs, *Principal and Creative Director, Studio Hinrichs*

MICHAEL IS SMART, GOOD, CAUSE-ORIENTED, PERSONABLE, FUNNY, AND HAS DEEPLY FOCUSED PASSIONS THAT MAKE IT INTO HIS WORK.

Michael Cronan, *Partner, Cronan*

WHEN HE WANTS TO DO SOMETHING, HE APPROACHES IT WITH HIS ENTIRE HEART AND SOUL, NEVER STOPPING TILL THE VISION IS REALIZED. HIS WORK—THOUGHTFUL, PURE AND POWERFUL—WILL STAND THE TEST OF TIME.

Mary Scott, *Chair, School of Graphic Design*

THE STUDIO'S WORK PUTS OUT DESIGN THAT IS EASILY DIGESTIBLE BY THE MASSES (PUN INTENDED), AND AT THE SAME TIME SATISFIES THE PALATE OF DISCRIMINATING DESIGNERS WITH ATTENTION TO TYPE, PATTERN AND COLOR.

Marc English, *Designer, Marc English Design*

(Page 9) Potato chip packaging. Client: Kettle Brand; Design: Michael Osborne/Alice Koswara / (Opposite page) Photo: Christopher Irion

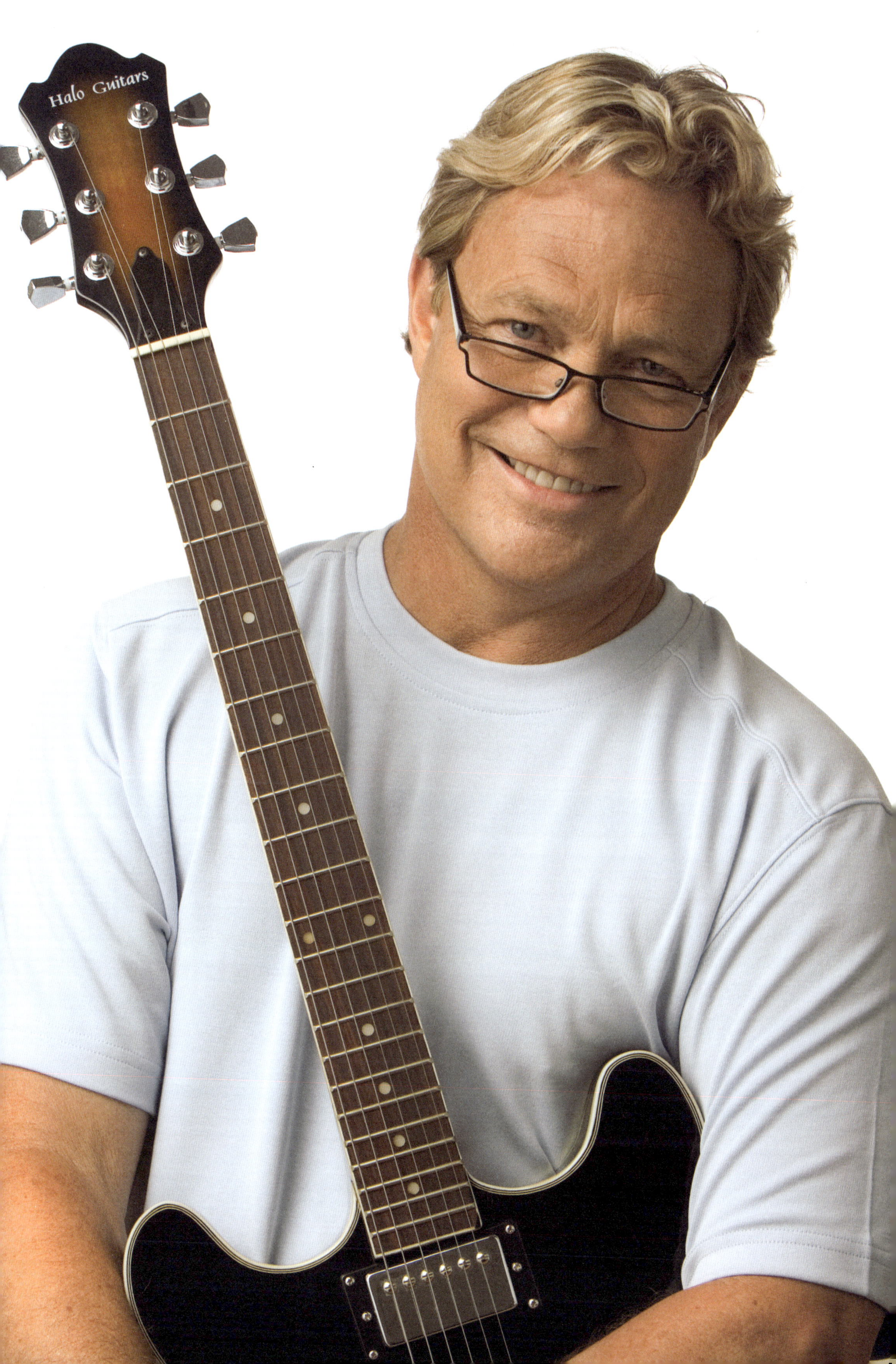
Halo Guitars

Walking into Michael Osborne's San Francisco atelier and gallery, you witness an inviting display of the visual arts. Client projects and his personal art engender a spirit of aesthetic cooperation between the fine arts and graphic design. Included in this industry of things is Michael at work with a talented staff of bright, young designers and interns from the Academy of Art, where he finished a Masters program. Some days he was teaching, other times you might find him in his letterpress print shop, or perhaps working in the garden and at times in the kitchen inventing a unique edible. The now retired artist and designer was at his work and play. It's a Renaissance stance: An American boy of Indian ancestry from Art Center, from the Vietnam conflict, from tragedies and hiccups of financial struggle, a maker of fabulous stamps for the United States Postal Service, and a San Francisco community servant designing exquisite visual projects, who still looks like a handsome 38-year-old center fielder for the San Francisco Giants. Michael is a kindred spirit, who knows that many of us are creative schizophrenics with internal demands that allow us to work as artists for ourselves and as creative graphic designers for global commerce. Some have it all.

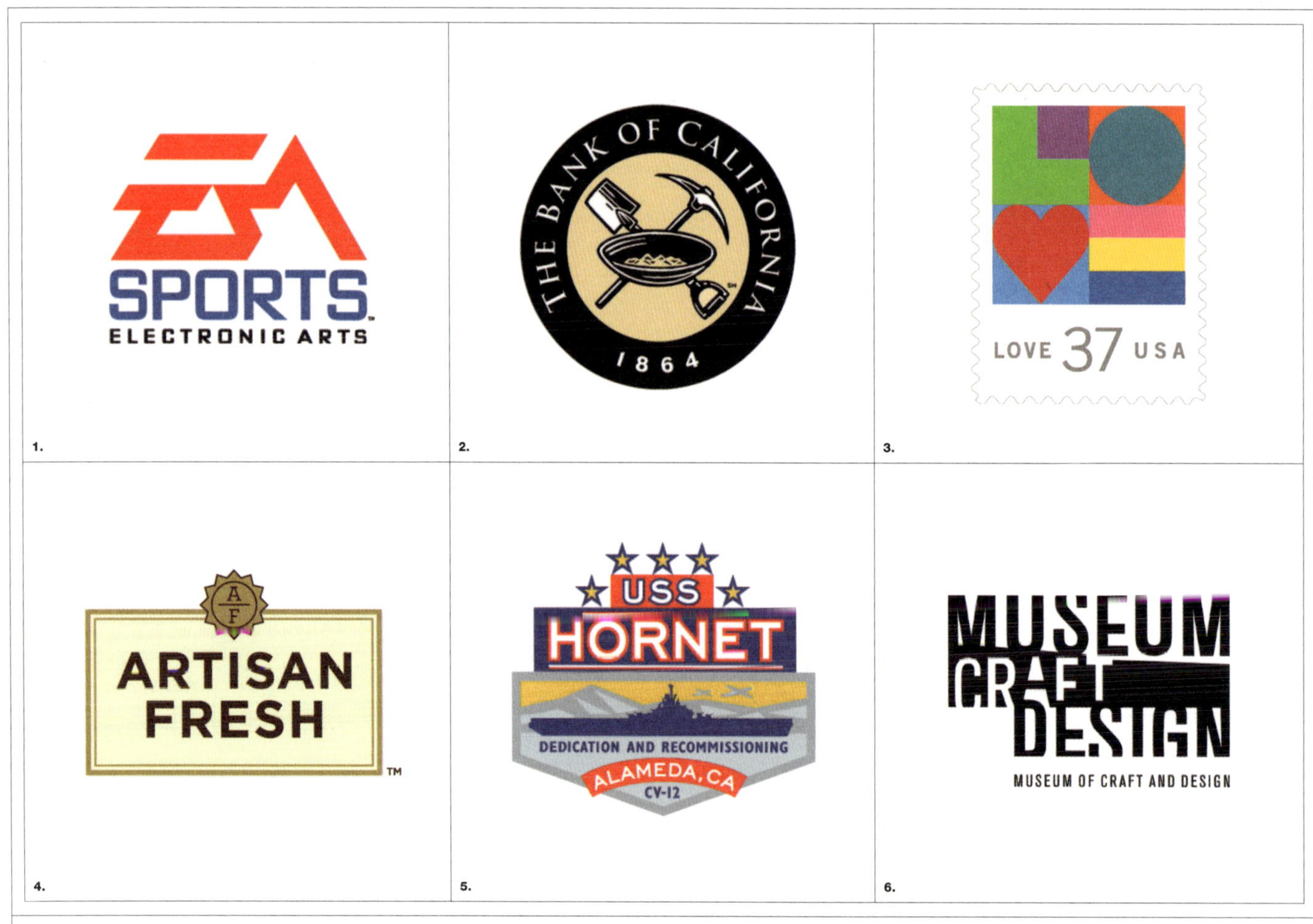

1. *EA Sports identity. Client: Electronic Arts; Design: Michael Osborne.* **2.** *Bank identity. Client: Bank of California; Design: Michael Osborne.*
3. *2002 Love stamp. Client: USPS; Art Director: Ethel Kessler; Design: Michael Osborne.* **4.** *Artisan Fresh brand identity and packaging. Client: Sam's Club;*
Design: Michael Osborne/Alice Koswara. **5.** *USS Hornet dedication identity. Client: USS Hornet Museum; Design: Michael Osborne.*
6. *Museum identity. Client: Museum of Craft and Design; Design: Michael Osborne.*

HIS WORK IS DISTINCTLY ORIGINAL AND EXECUTED FLAWLESSLY WITH EXQUISITE TASTE. TO ME, HE IS CLEARLY ONE OF THE FIVE TOP MICHAELS WHO PUT CALIFORNIA ON THE MAP. **B. Martin Pedersen,** *Designer*

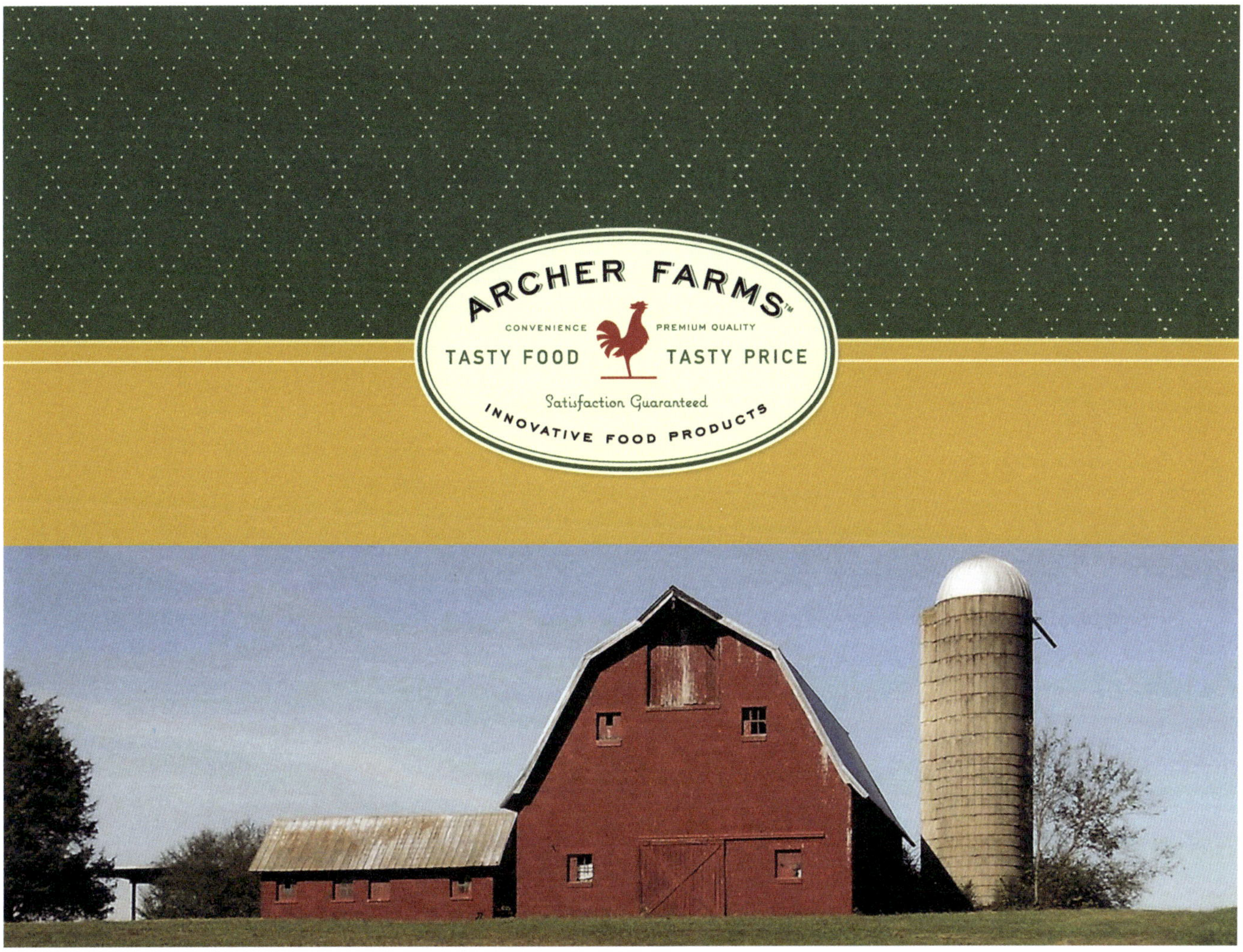

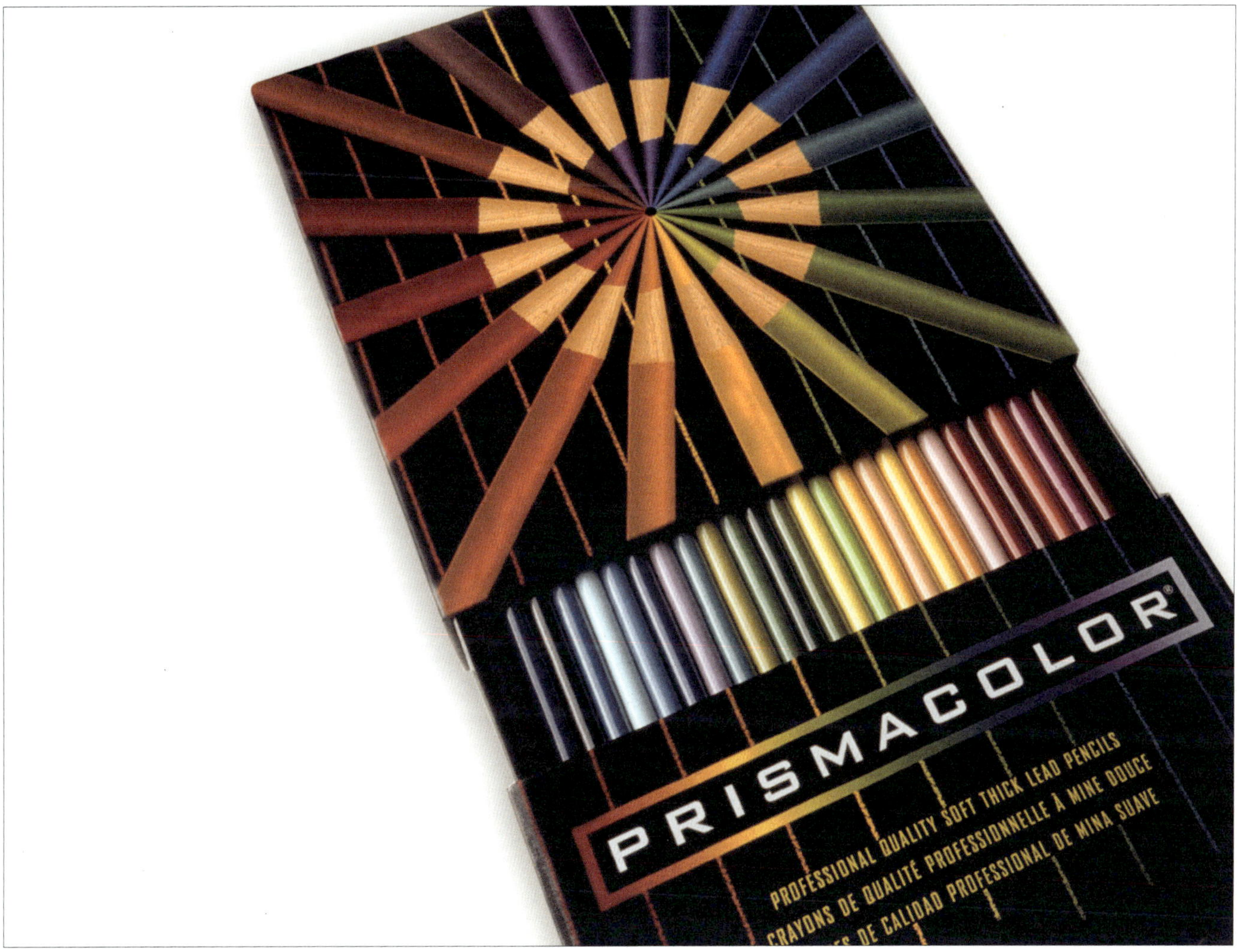

(Top) Archer Farms identity and packaging. Client: Target; Design: Michael Osborne / (Bottom) Prismacolor identity and packaging. Client: Berol Corp.; Design: Michael Osborne

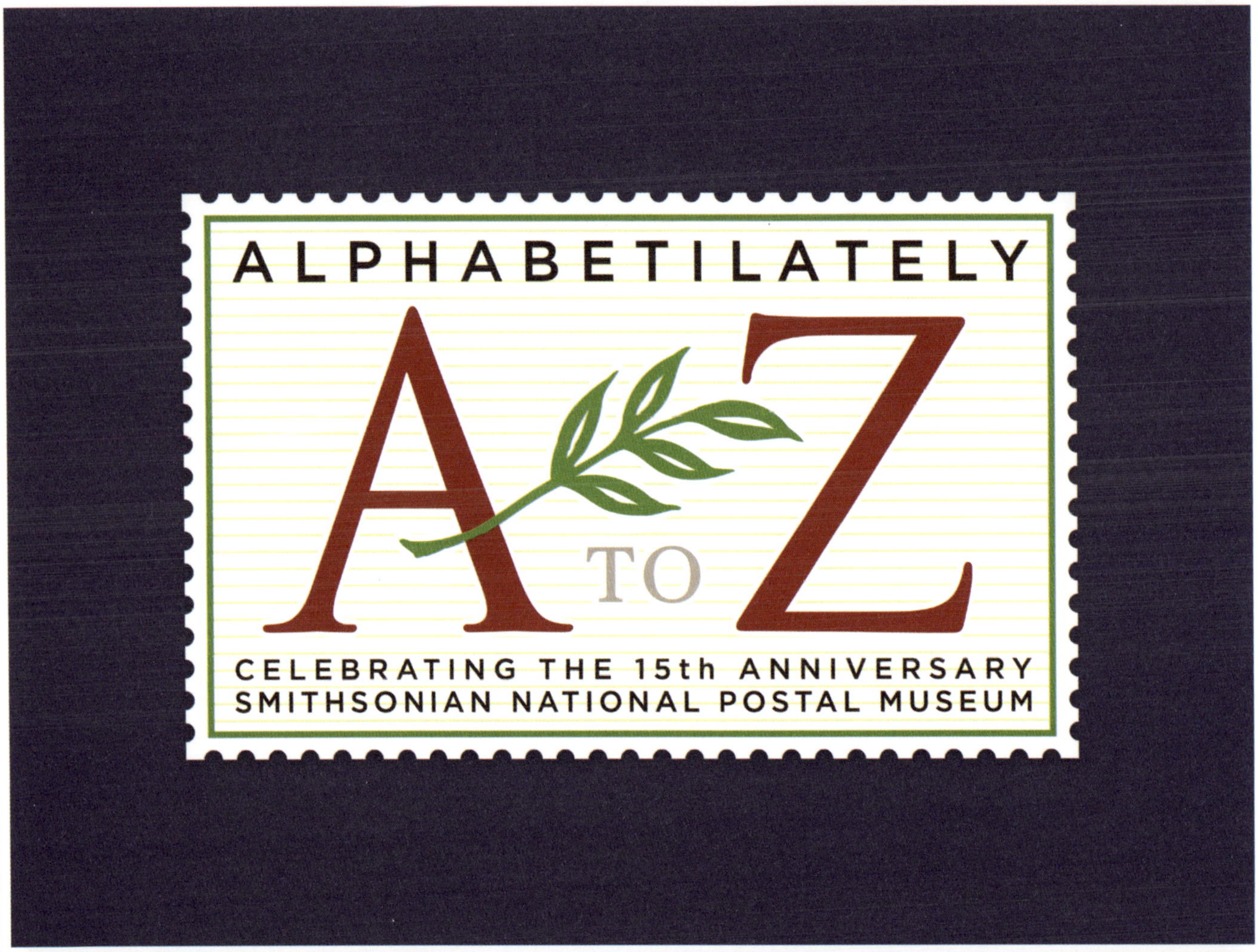

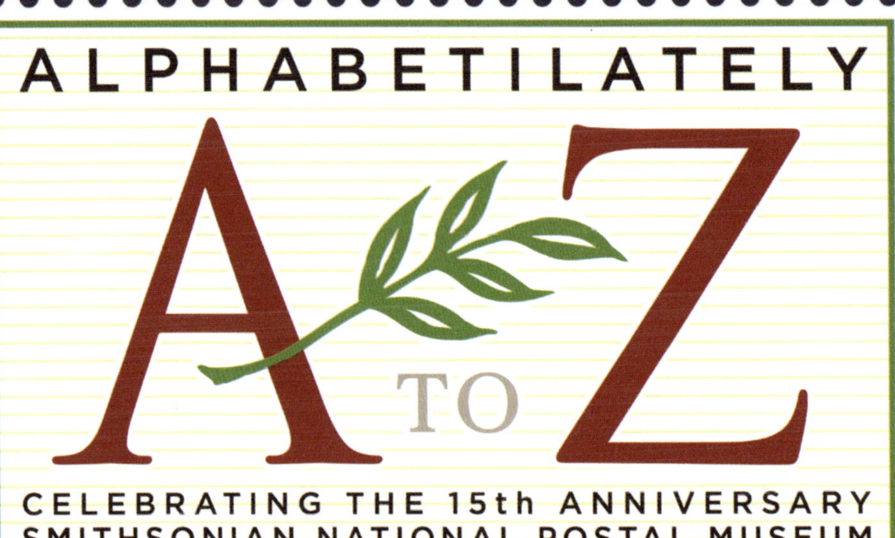

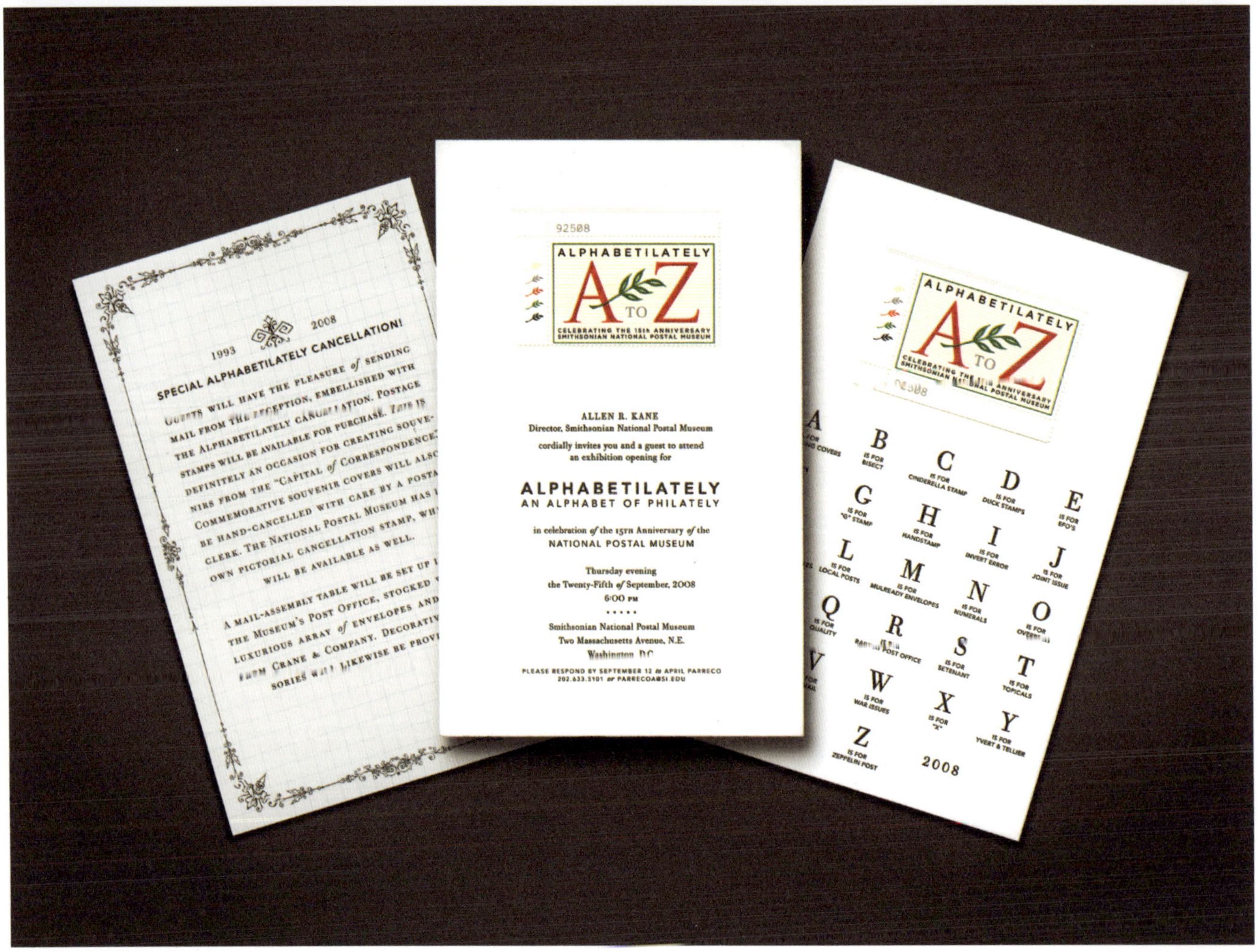

(Above) Anniversary identity stamp and invitation materials. Client: Smithsonian National Postal Museum; Design: Michael Osborne; Letterpress printing: One Heart Press
(Opposite page) Vodka label and bottle structure. Client: Square One; Design: Michael Osborne/Alice Koswara

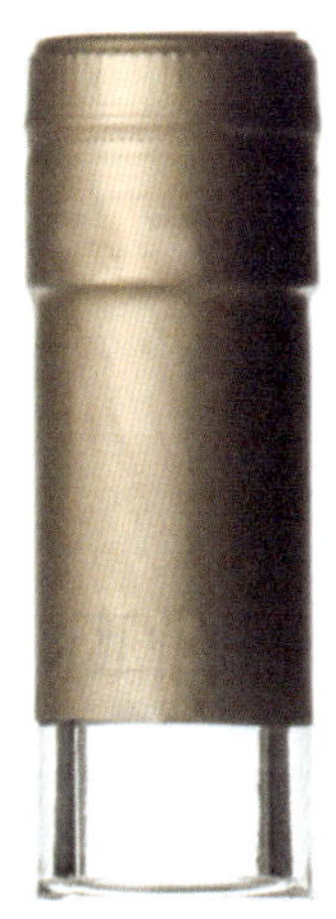

SQUARE
ONE ORGANIC
VODKA
100% MADE FROM ORGANIC RYE
DISTILLED & BOTTLED BY SQUARE ONE
ORGANIC SPIRITS, RIGBY, IDAHO
40% ALC. BY VOL. (80 PROOF) 750 ML

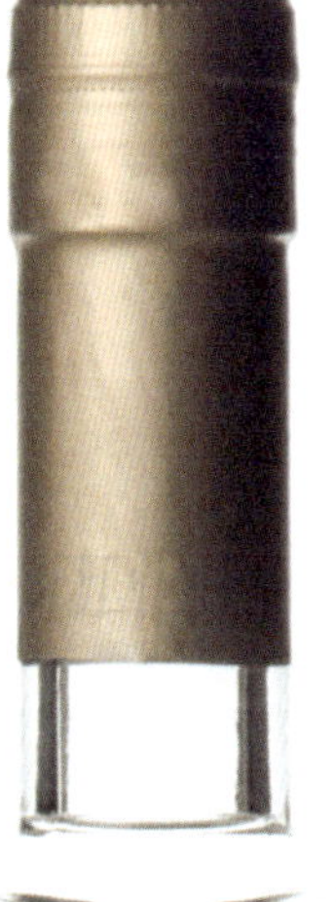
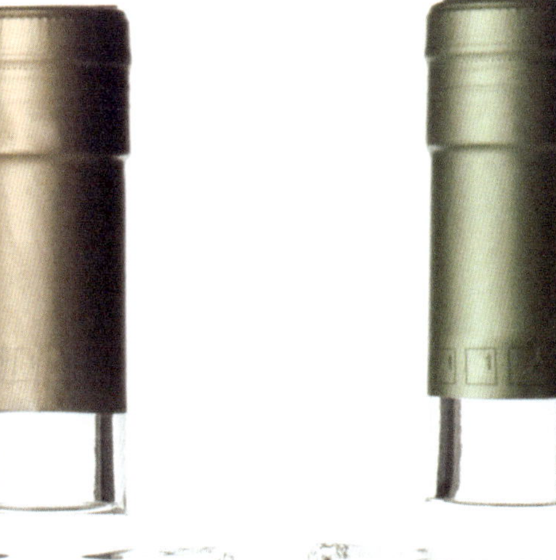

SQUARE
ONE CUCUMBER
100% MADE FROM ORGANIC RYE
ORGANIC
CUCUMBER FLAVORED VODKA
DISTILLED & BOTTLED BY SQUARE ONE
ORGANIC SPIRITS, RIGBY, IDAHO
USDA ORGANIC
40% ALC. BY VOL. (80 PROOF) 750 ML

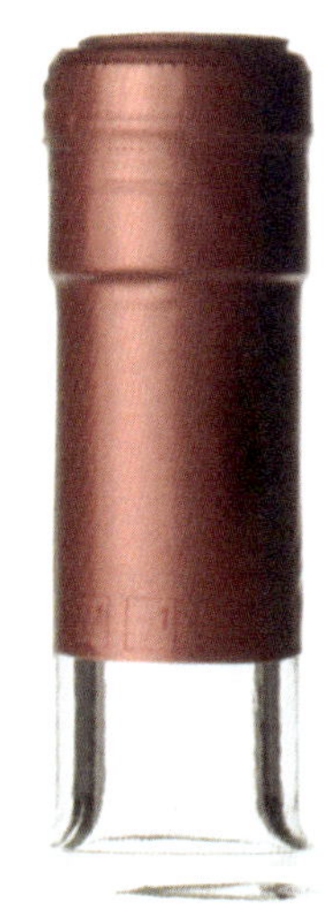

SQUARE
ONE BOTANICAL
100% MADE FROM ORGANIC RYE
BOTANICAL ORGANIC SPIRIT
RYE NEUTRAL SPIRITS WITH NATURAL
ORGANIC FLAVORS
USDA ORGANIC
45% ALC. BY VOL. (90 PROOF) 750 ML

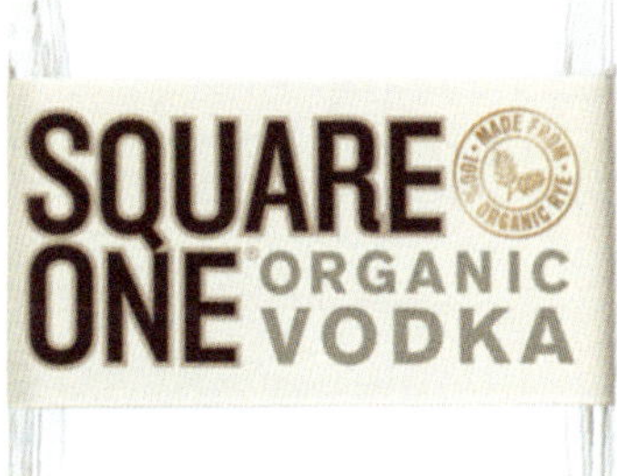
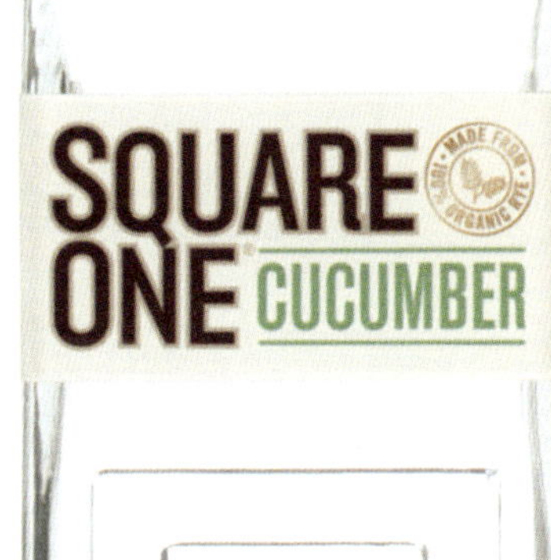

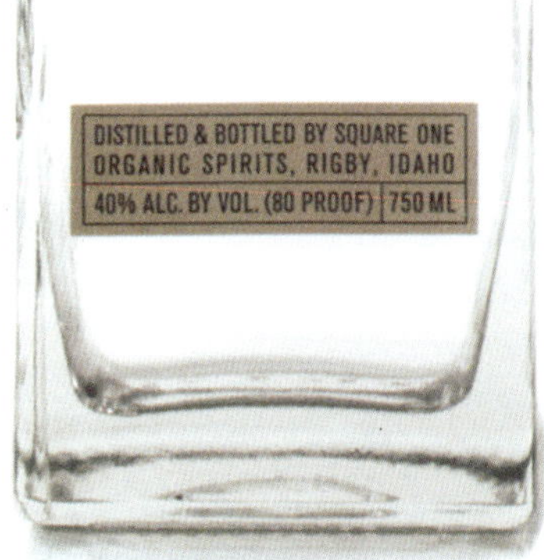

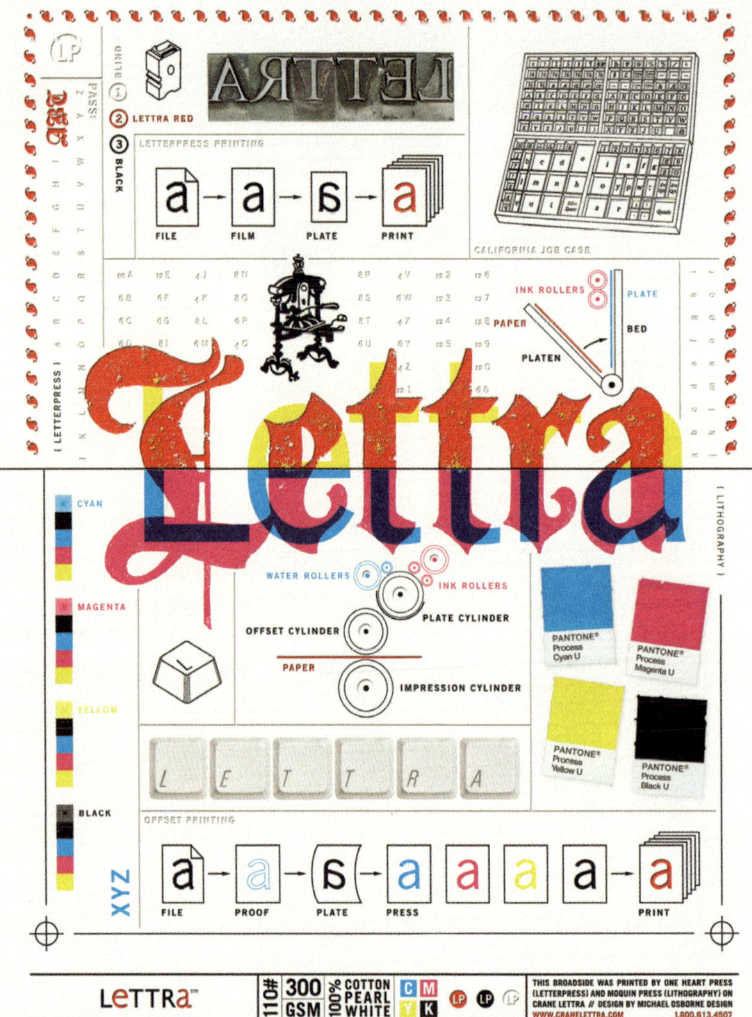

LP
PASS:
BLIND
LETTRA RED
BLACK
LETTERPRESS PRINTING
FILE
FILM
PLATE
PRINT
[LETTERPRESS]
CALIFORNIA JOB CASE
INK ROLLERS
PLATE
PAPER
BED
PLATEN
Lettra
CYAN
MAGENTA
YELLOW
BLACK
WATER ROLLERS
INK ROLLERS
PLATE CYLINDER
OFFSET CYLINDER
PAPER
IMPRESSION CYLINDER
PANTONE® Process Cyan U
PANTONE® Process Magenta U
PANTONE® Process Yellow U
PANTONE® Process Black U
[LITHOGRAPHY]
L E T T R A
OFFSET PRINTING
FILE
PROOF
PLATE
PRESS
PRINT
XYZ
LETTRA™
110# 300 GSM 100% COTTON PEARL WHITE CMYK LP LP LP
THIS BROADSIDE WAS PRINTED BY ONE HEART PRESS (LETTERPRESS) AND MOQUIN PRESS (LITHOGRAPHY) ON CRANE LETTRA // DESIGN BY MICHAEL OSBORNE DESIGN
WWW.CRANELETTRA.COM   1.800.613.4507

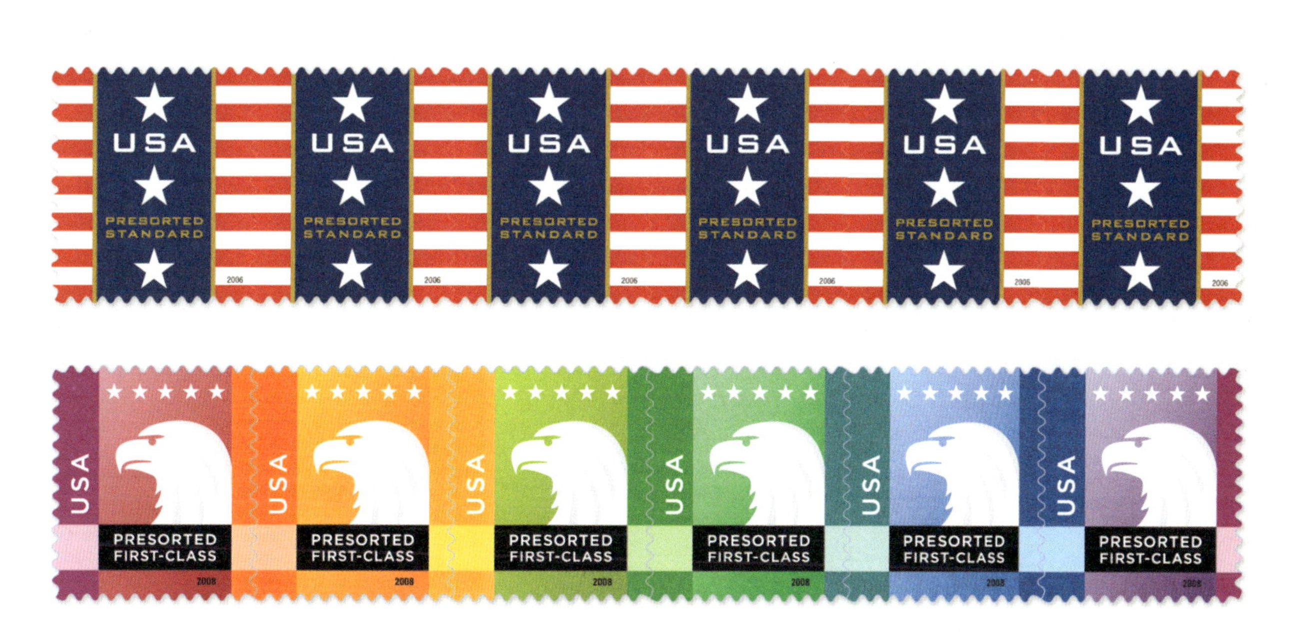

(Top) Presorted Flag stamp, Presorted Spectrum Eagle stamps; (Bottom) 2006 Christmas stamp. Client: USPS; Art Director: Ethel Kessler: Designer: Michael Osborne

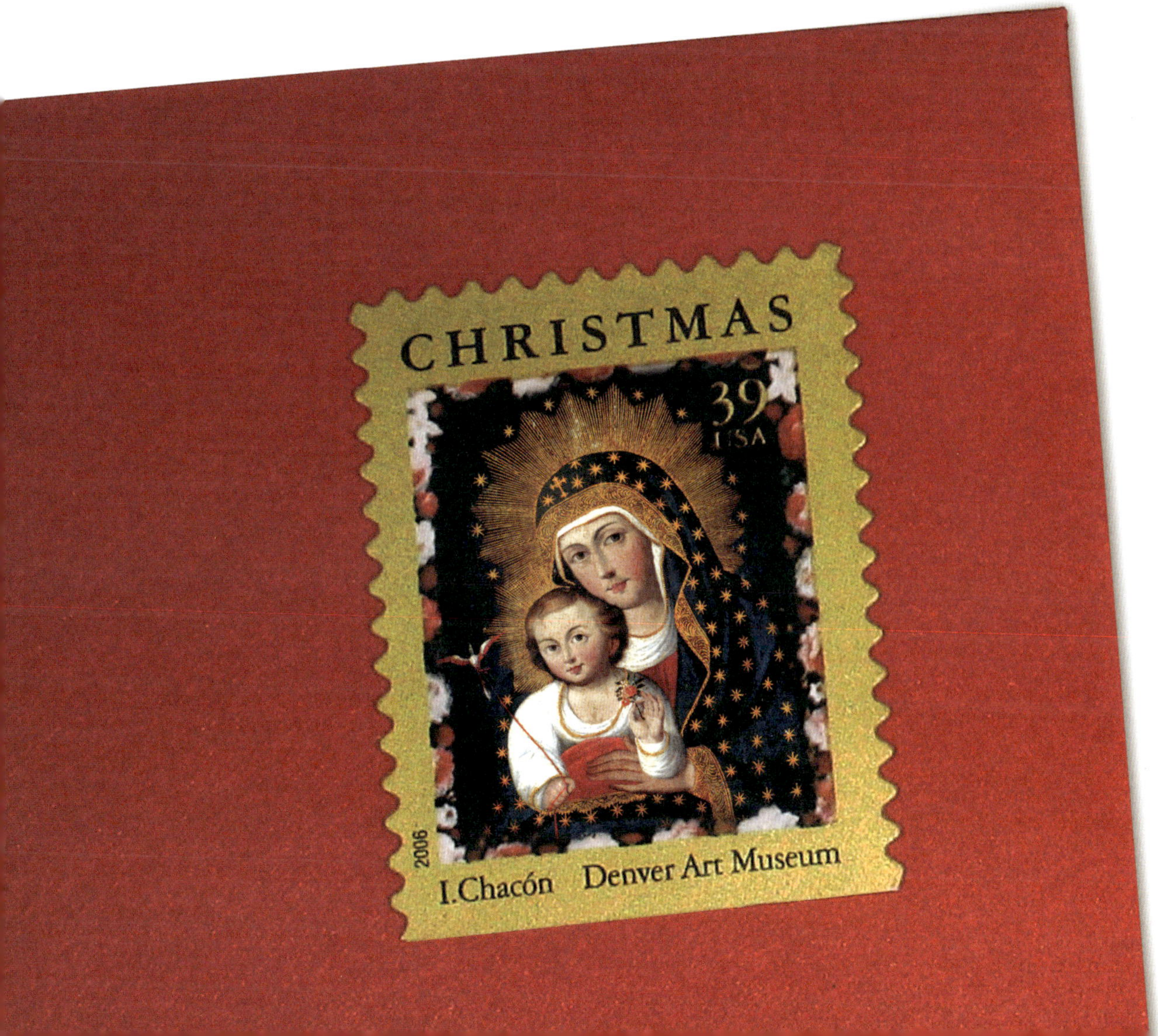

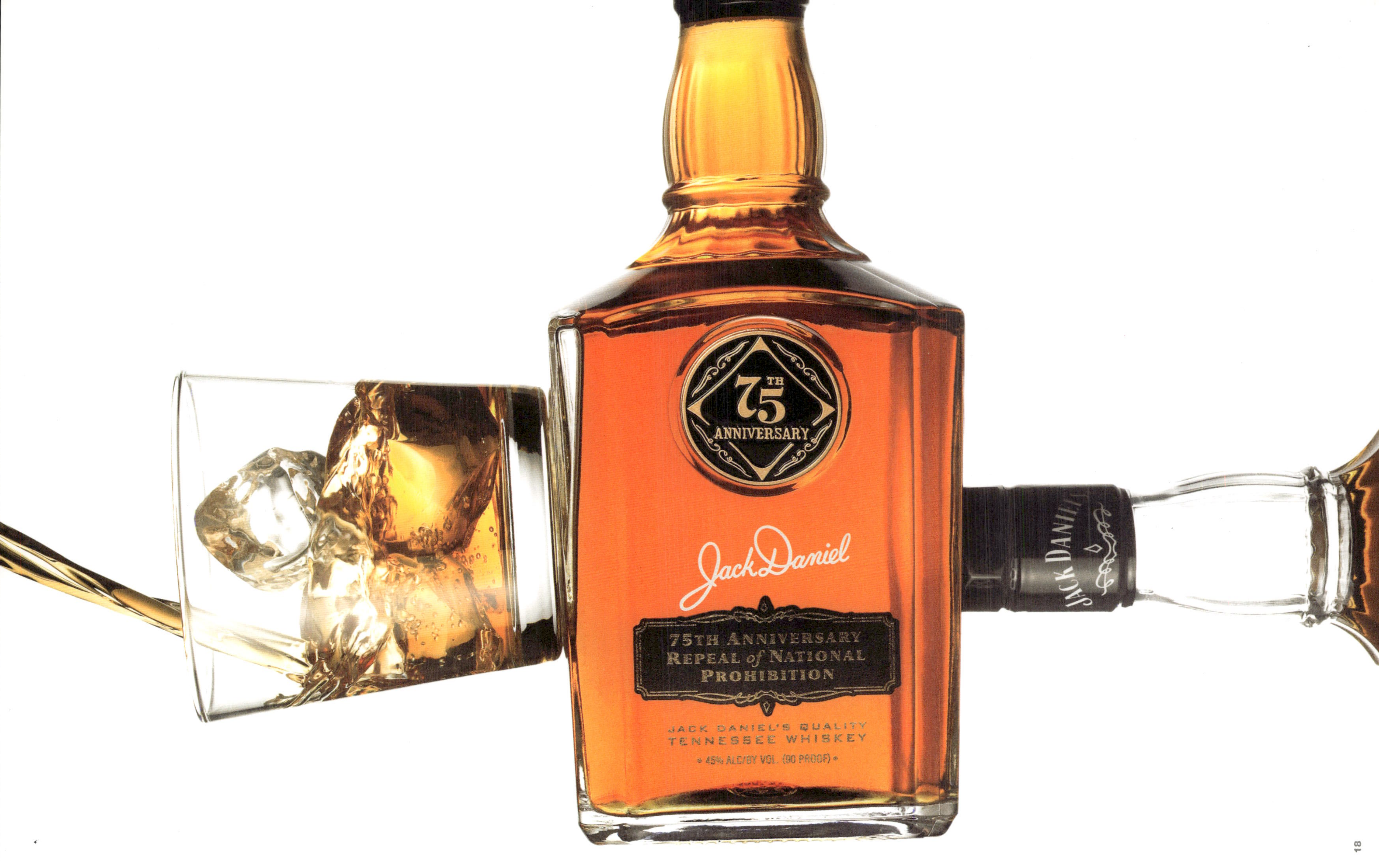

75
TH
ANNIVERSARY
Jack Daniel
75TH ANNIVERSARY
REPEAL of NATIONAL
PROHIBITION
JACK DANIEL'S QUALITY
TENNESSEE WHISKEY
45% ALC/BY VOL. (90 PROOF)
JACK DANIEL'S

What was one of your favorite projects?

One would definitely be designing stamps for the U.S. Postal Service. It had been a dream of mine for a long, long time. One day many years ago, I received a phone call from Ethel Kessler, one of the art directors for the Postal Service, who asked if I would like to design a LOVE stamp- and I just about fainted...seriously! It was an almost surreal event and opportunity that just kind of floated down from heaven and landed in my office. Stamps are an important part of our country's history and it's a true honor to design a stamp. Plus, I love getting mail with my stamps on it! I designed a dozen or so stamps over the years, and I wish I saved every single piece of correspondence that I've received with one of my stamps on it. One time I received a form letter from Sara Palin with my 2007 Presorted Standard American Flag stamp on it applied in a very haphazard crooked manner. This one I saved.

What satisfies you most in your work?

What made me happiest-especially toward the end of my career, was doing meaningful work, work that had a chance to make a difference, whether it was a product on the shelf, or a logo for a non-profit organization. I wanted to work with great clients who trusted me, and clients I could trust. I'd bend over backwards for a client that would let us do our job. I truly believe you cannot produce great work without a great client. When I was young, all I wanted to do was design, design, design all day, all night, and win as many awards as possible. That's cool, but now the satisfaction comes from a very different place.

Tell me about the hard times you've had in gaining your success.

Boy, this could be a long answer. First there are the economic hard times. I started my company in 1981 and as we all know, the economy ebbs and flows, has ups and downs, and does what it's going to do based on myriad factors. Riding the economic roller coaster while trying to run a business and remain dedicated to your clients and employees is very difficult. I never worked with freelance designers—I always had full-time designers who were like family. They were my first priority, and during tough economic times it's sometimes hard to sleep. For me, hanging in there during these times was the toughest part of running an employee-based company. Thankfully though, I have a very strong work ethic which was drilled into me from the day I was born. Head down, and burrow your way out. Stop whining and get something done. Another difficulty is maintaining balance in your life and not being chewed up by this business, which is a matter of experience. A teacher once told me, "Excellent juggling comes from experience; experience comes from horrible juggling."

What would be your dream assignment?

One of my goals was to do more work for non-profit organizations. I started my own 501(c) (3) non-profit, Joey's Corner, in 2005 (joeyscorner.org), named after my son Joseph Michael Osborne (1980-2004). There was one full-time designer and usually an intern or two. We worked for non-profit groups serving children, healthcare, and social issues on an ongoing, full-time basis. In our first year, we completed 50 individual projects! I was asked to speak about Joey's Corner all over the country for many years. I spoke for dozens of AIGA chapters, as well as many, many local art directors' clubs, and university design programs. They usually requested that I speak not only about the kind of work we do, but how we go about working for non-profit organizations. It's really quite phenomenal meeting people in these organizations who are doing the most important work on the planet—work that's desperately needed in the world now more than ever. I'm finding today's young designers are very, very interested in this "do-good" work and in giving back. As a designer, having the ability and power to give back is a blessing, and at one point in my career a large part of my work was dedicated to it.

Who do you admire in the profession in the past or present?

Some of my design heroes are the forefathers of graphic design, before the term even existed. Bradbury Thompson is at the top of my list. I have read much about him and have spoken with people who knew and worked with him. He was a gentleman with a gentle spirit, an intelligent designer and master typographer. I wrote a book about him as part of my MFA thesis many years ago (I went back to school and got a Masters degree 30 years after my BFA from ArtCenter!), called "Bradbury Thompson & Howard Paine." Brad was an art director for the Postal Service, and designed 100 or so U.S. postage stamps; Howard Paine was also a Postal Service art director who designed hundreds of stamps over almost a 30-year span. I was also always influenced by and admired Primo Angeli for many reasons. I wanted to do the kind of work his firm did (think Henry Weinhard and Boudin logos and packaging), and his design firm was here in San Francisco for 35 years, a feat unto itself! And every designer in school or practicing should have Milton Glaser as a hero. In high school, before I even heard the term "graphic design," I had his Bob Dylan poster hanging in my bedroom. I loved it but didn't know exactly why. Now I know.

What about your mentors?

I received my undergraduate degree at ArtCenter College of Design in 1978. I had three particular teachers who had an enormous impact on me. Hal Frazier was my packaging teacher and was well known in the industry. He possessed more taste and style in his little pinky than most designers will have in their entire lifetime. In the same category is Paul Hauge, Hal's former business partner, who taught my print classes. Doyald Young taught me how to "see" in his amazing lettering classes. Doyald also taught me where the terms "labor intensive" and "labor of love" come from! Your mentors are people you want to be like when you grow up. Over the years we became friends and could get together, have lunch and talk about design on a common level. It just blows me away, but I always continued to learn from them. I'd drive back to the office from lunch and think, "Oh my god, I just had lunch with Kit Hinrichs!" (another of my heros).

What is your greatest insecurity?

[Laughs] In any creative endeavor it's pretty easy to feel insecure about taking risks and trying things you're not sure are going to work. You really have to be brave and somehow get over the insecurities of trying something that you've never tried before, or have no idea if it's going to work, and put your ass on the line and find out. One teacher told me, if you're not just a little bit worried, or afraid that what you're doing is not going to work, then you're probably not doing it right. You just have to lay it out there once in a while.

(Opposite page) Jack Daniel's special edition label and bottle structure. Client: Brown Forman; Design: Michael Osborne/Cody Dingle; Photo: Terry Heffernan

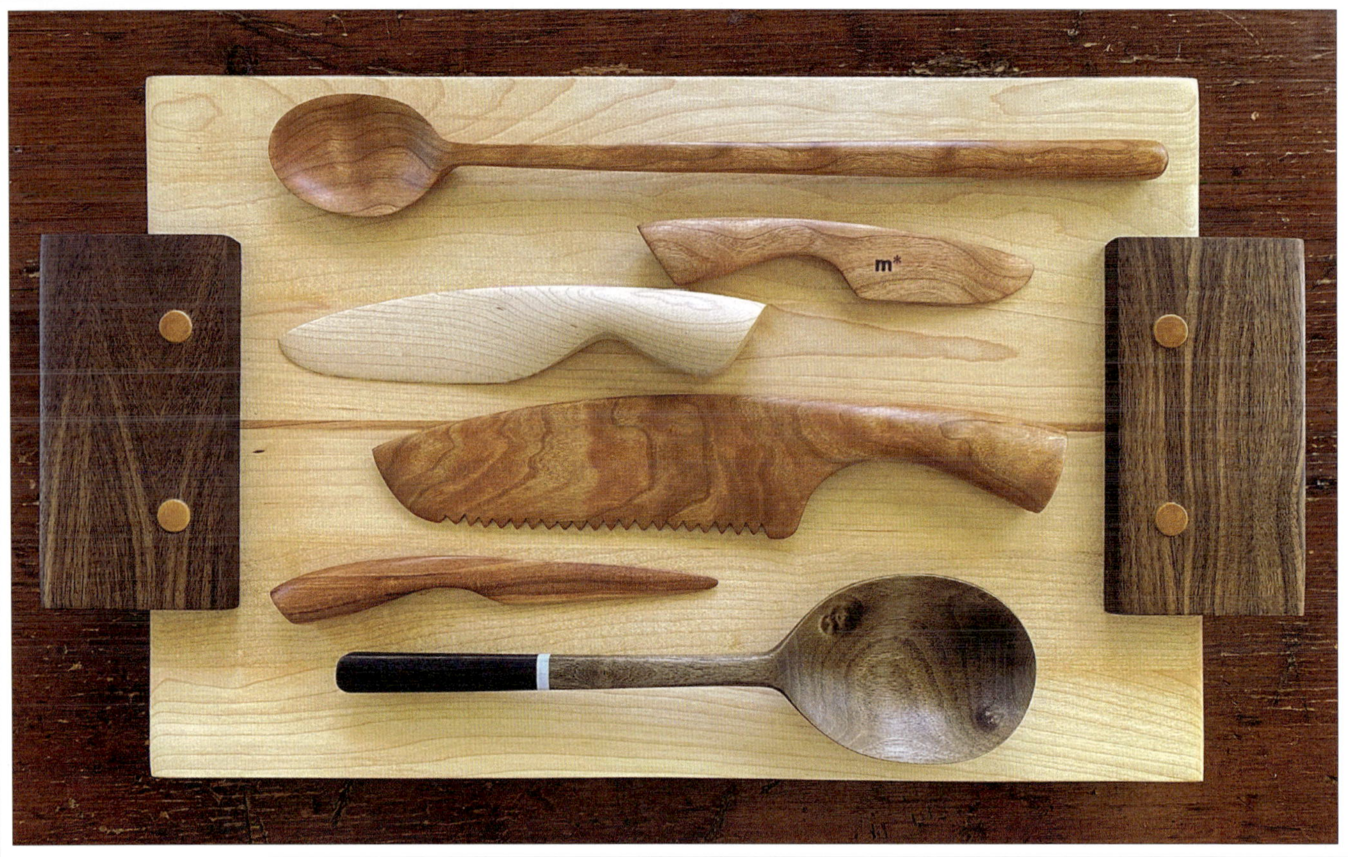

Wood tray and various hand-carved wood kitchen utensils. Design and production: Michael Osborne

*After 36 years in business you retired and closed
your office- what have you been up to since?*
Well, believe it or not, I've gotten into woodworking in a few
different ways. A neighbor talked me into taking a woodworking class with her and it turned out to be a blast. The classes
are held in a huge, beautiful shop at a local high school, and
are taught by some very talented and experienced teachers.
They focus on building furniture, i.e. chairs, tables, stools,
etc., and small projects, all with an eye on the safe operation
of some amazing power tools, which I had never used before.
I've taken 7 or 8 classes now, and I'm most proud of the cherry
wood rocking chair I built before Covid19 hit. I sit and read in
it every morning!

   I've also taught myself how to hand-carve wood objects
such as spoons, butter and cheese knives, and other small
kitchen items. There is an element of design in this work,
much akin to product design, as opposed to the furniture which
is built mostly from plans. I've learned about and have experimented with different species of wood, and thoroughly enjoy
the design aspect of the carving projects. I post (and have sold)

my work on Instagram (@michael0250) and have sold in a
couple of craft shows. Additionally, I have experimented with
and even sold a few wood sculptures, which I plan to continue...talk about fun!

Do people ever ask you if retirement is boring?
They do, and I can't understand it for the life of me! How can
a designer ever be bored? There's so much to do, so much to
learn, there's never enough time! It's on the same level as a
question I used to get from students all the time, "What do
you do when you run out of ideas?" What? Really? How in the
world can you run out of ideas? In regards to design, ideas and
solutions are based on the problem at hand, the answer lays
inside the question. Look deeper or from a different angle into
what you already know, and there it is...an idea, and even a
mediocre idea can lead to a brilliant idea if you keep at it. Head
down, and burrow your way out

Michael Osborne Design *www.modsf.com*
See his Graphis Master Portfolio on graphis.com.

AS A DESIGNER, HAVING THE ABILITY AND POWER TO GIVE BACK IS A BLESSING, AND AT ONE POINT IN MY CAREER A LARGE PART OF MY WORK WAS DEDICATED TO IT.

Michael Osborne, *Former President and Creative Director, Michael Osborne Design*

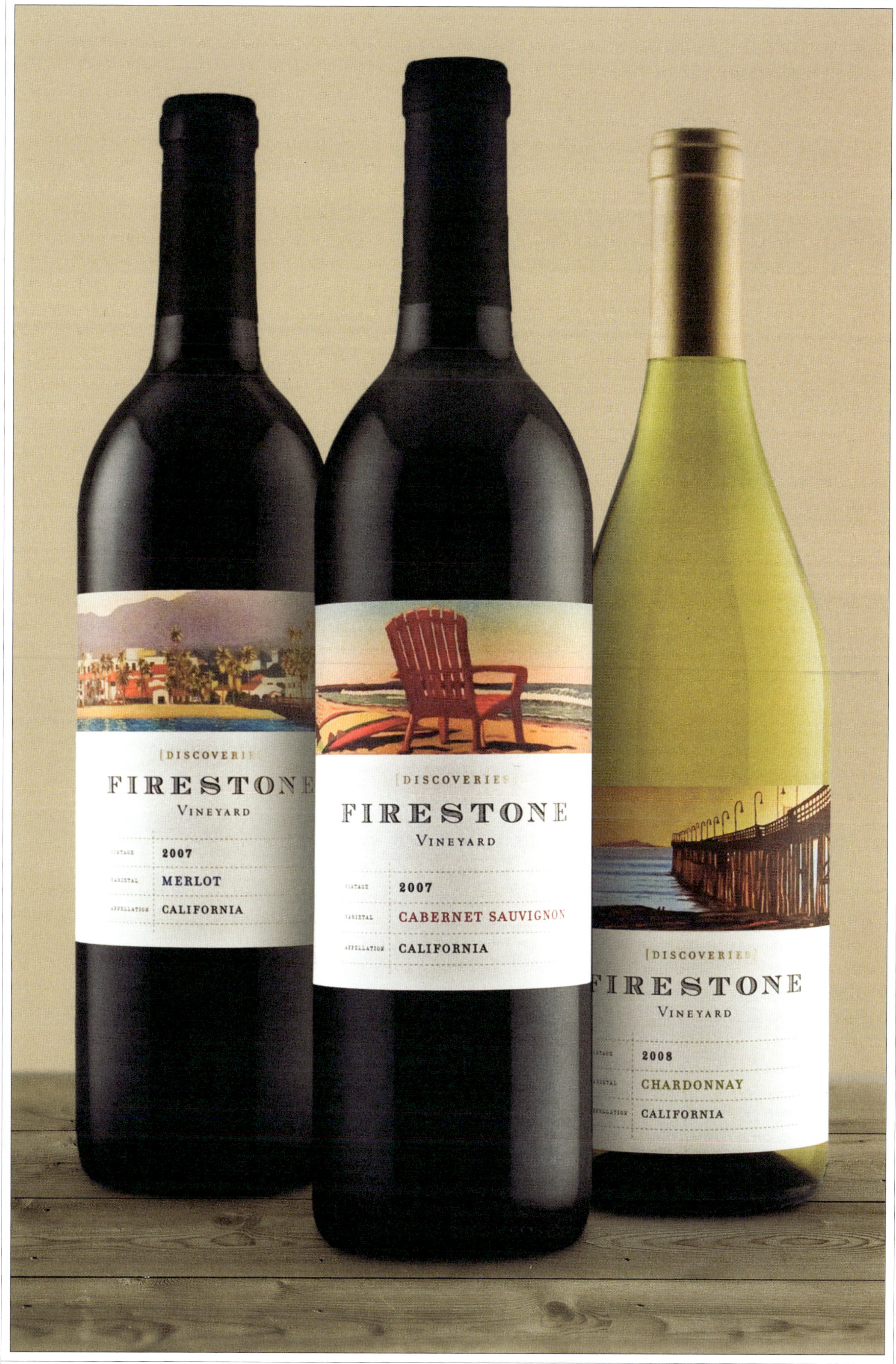

Discoveries wine label series. Client: Firestone Vineyard; Design: Michael Osborne/Alice Koswara; Illustrations: Steve Cook

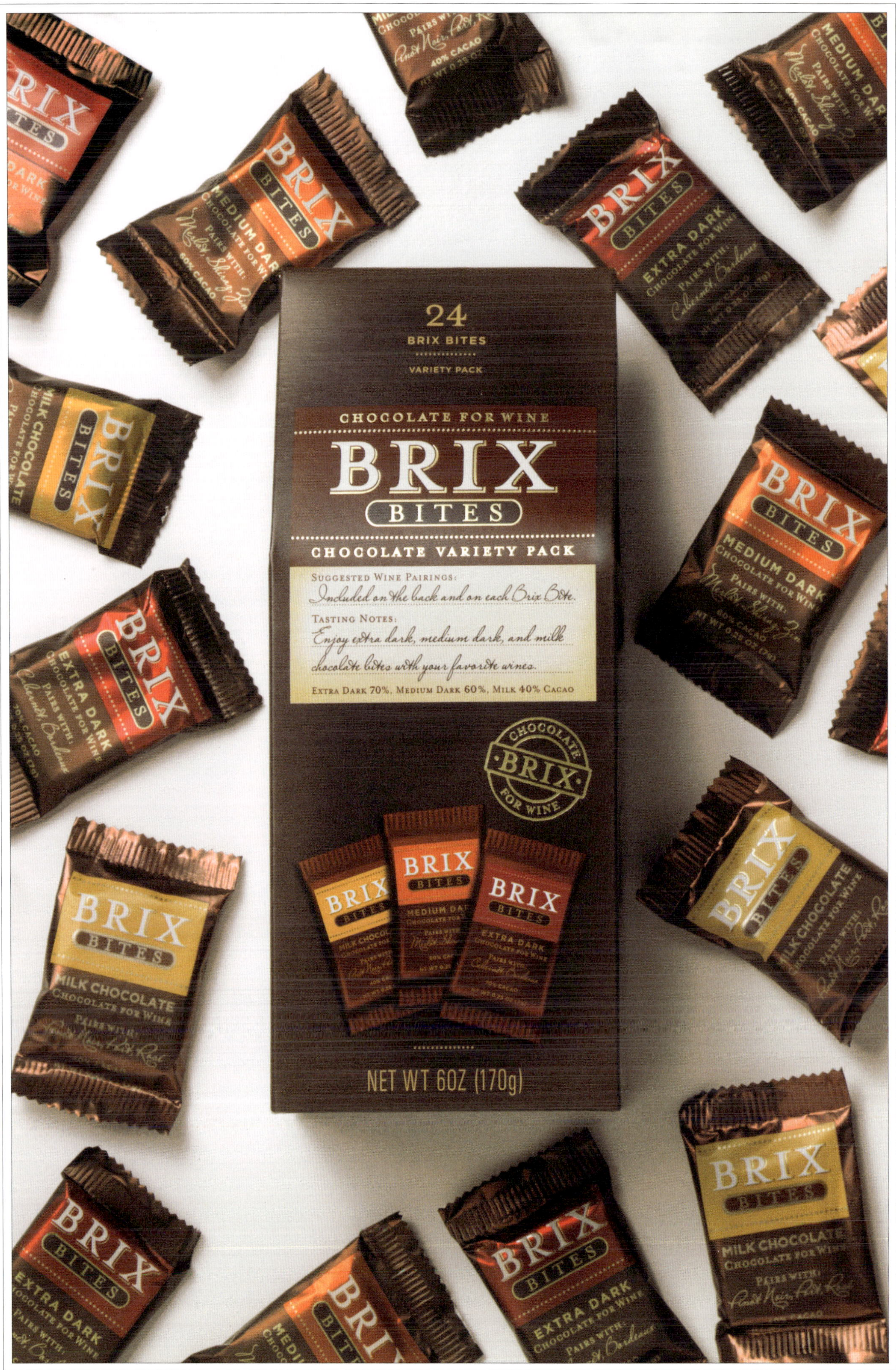

Chocolate packaging. Client: BRIX; Design: Michael Osborne/Jane Anderson

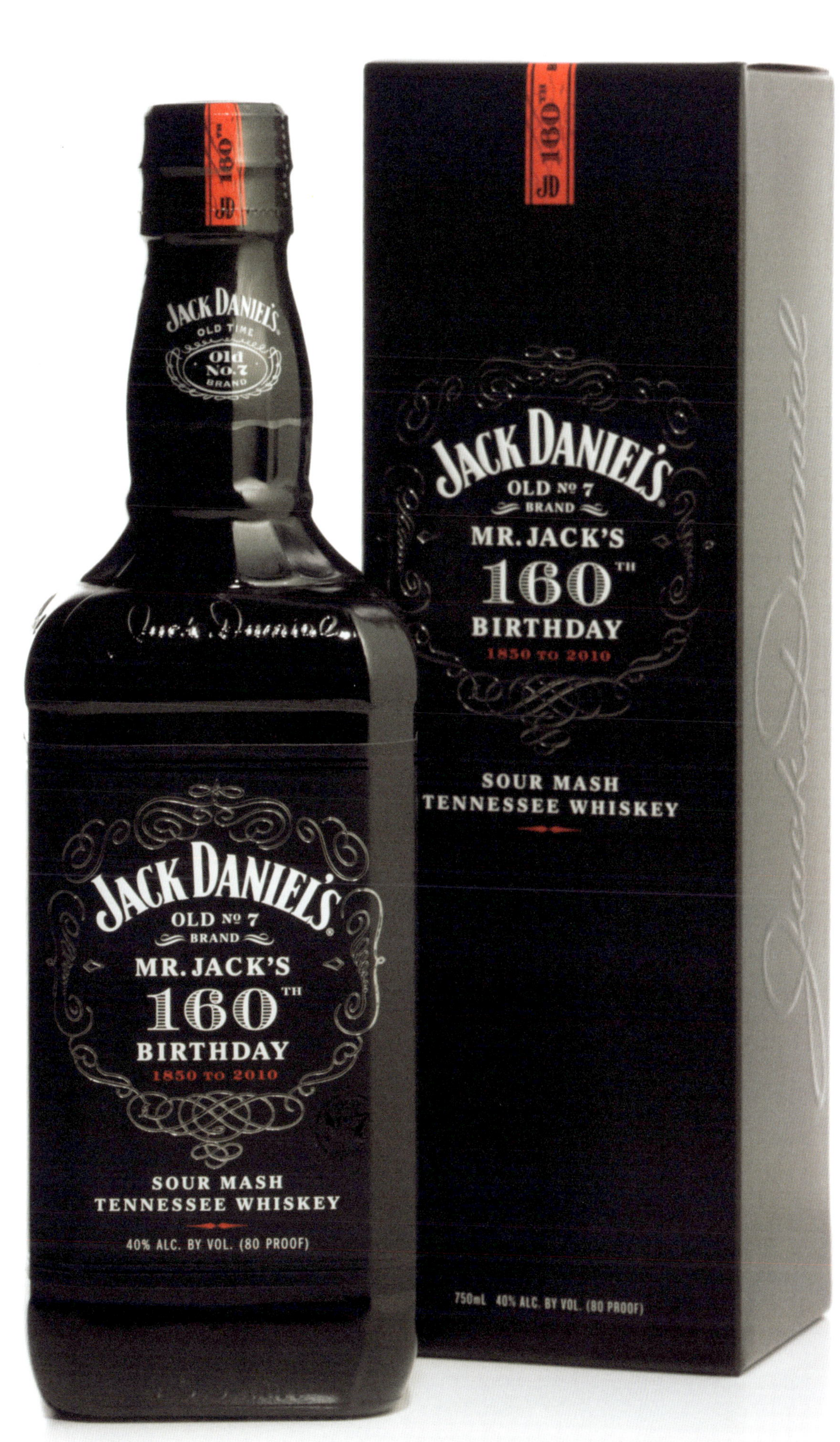

Jack Daniel's 160th Birthday edition label, black bottle, and gift box. Client: Brown Forman; Design: Michael Osborne/Alice Koswara

CLAIRE AND FIDEL DO EXCEPTIONAL WORK WHICH
MAKES COLLABORATING WITH THEM A NO BRAINER.

WHAT TRULY MAKES WORKING WITH THEM A
GREAT EXPERIENCE IS THE ATTENTION TO
DETAIL AND PASSION THEY BRING TO A PROJECT
EACH AND EVERY TIME.

Paul Weeks, *Photographer*

BEFORE WE HIRED THEM, WE HAD GREAT
CONTENT BUT POOR DESIGN. NOW, WE HAVE
GREAT CONTENT THAT LOOKS FABULOUS, AND
AN AWARD-WINNING MAGAZINE.

Léo Charbonneau, *Editor, University Affairs magazine, published by Universities Canada*

UNDERLINE CREATES DESIGN THAT'S SMART,
RESTRAINED, AND BEAUTIFUL. THEY DRAW FROM
HISTORY WITHOUT REPEATING IT. THEY MODERNIZE
WITHOUT SEEMING TRENDY.

THEIR WORK POSSESSES THAT RARE, ENVIABLE
TRAIT OF BEING BOTH TIMELESS AND OF ITS TIME.

Leo Jung, *Creative Director, California Sunday Magazine*

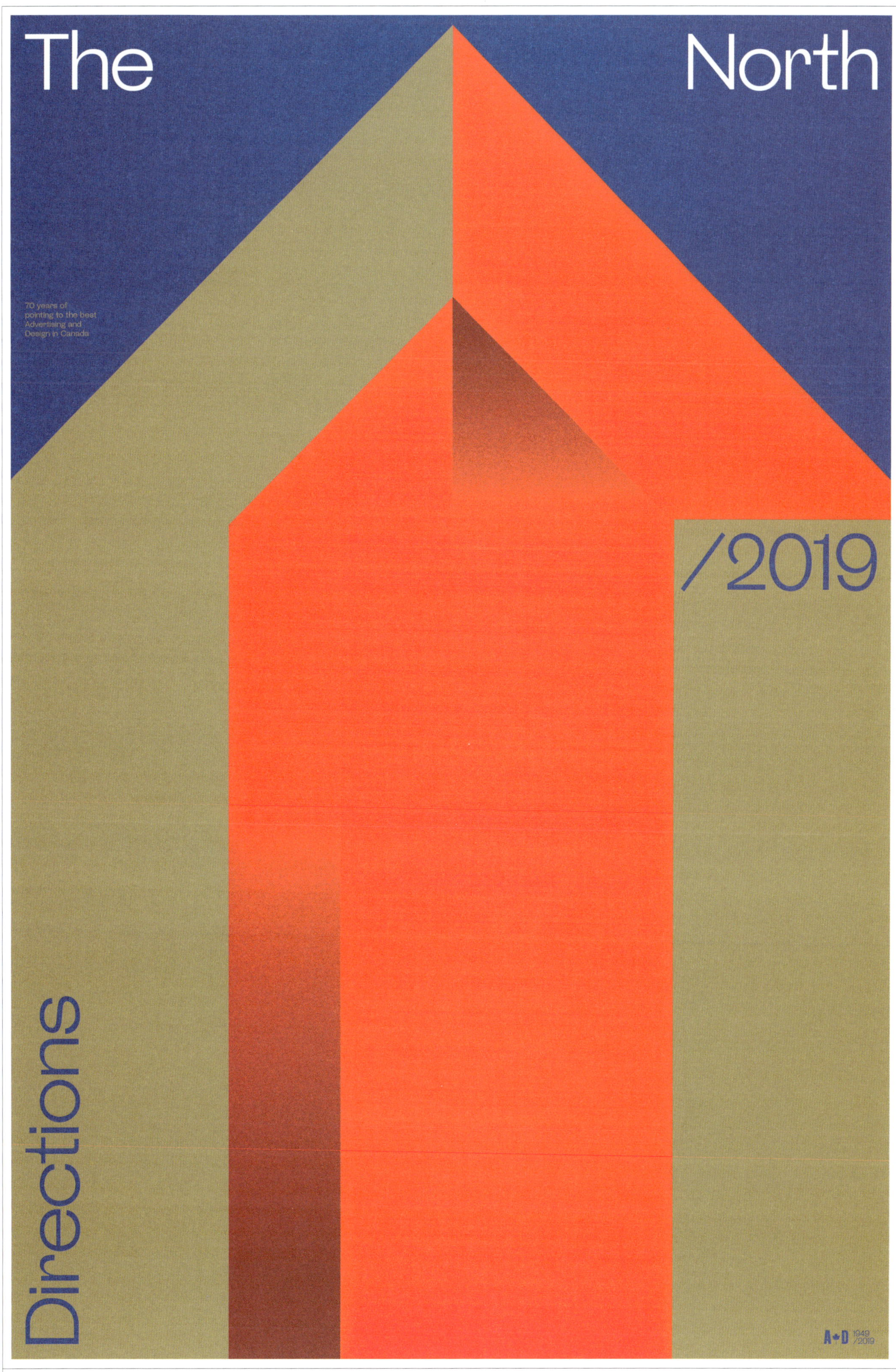

Advertising & Design Club of Canada, Call for entries poster, 2019, Underline Studio

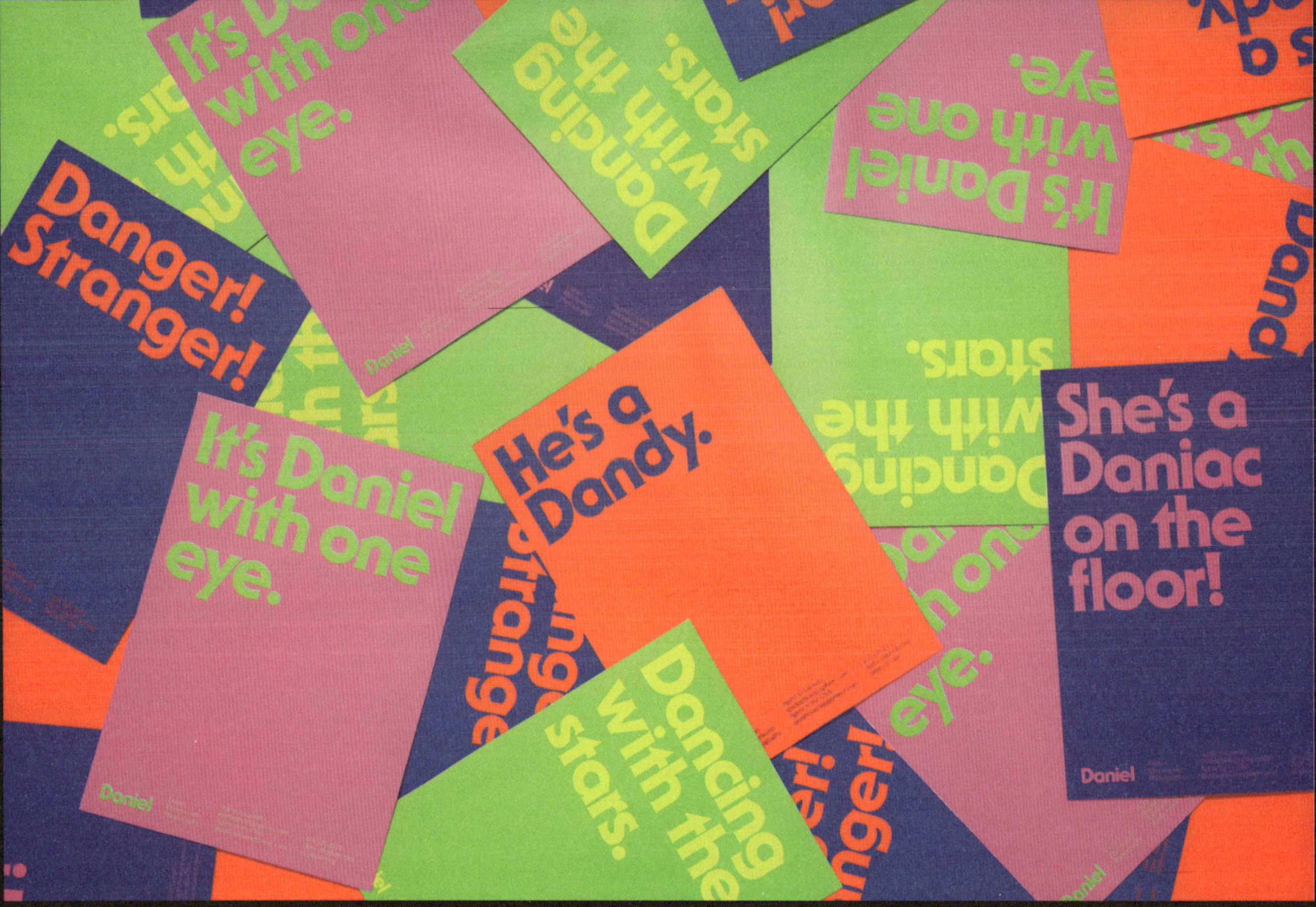

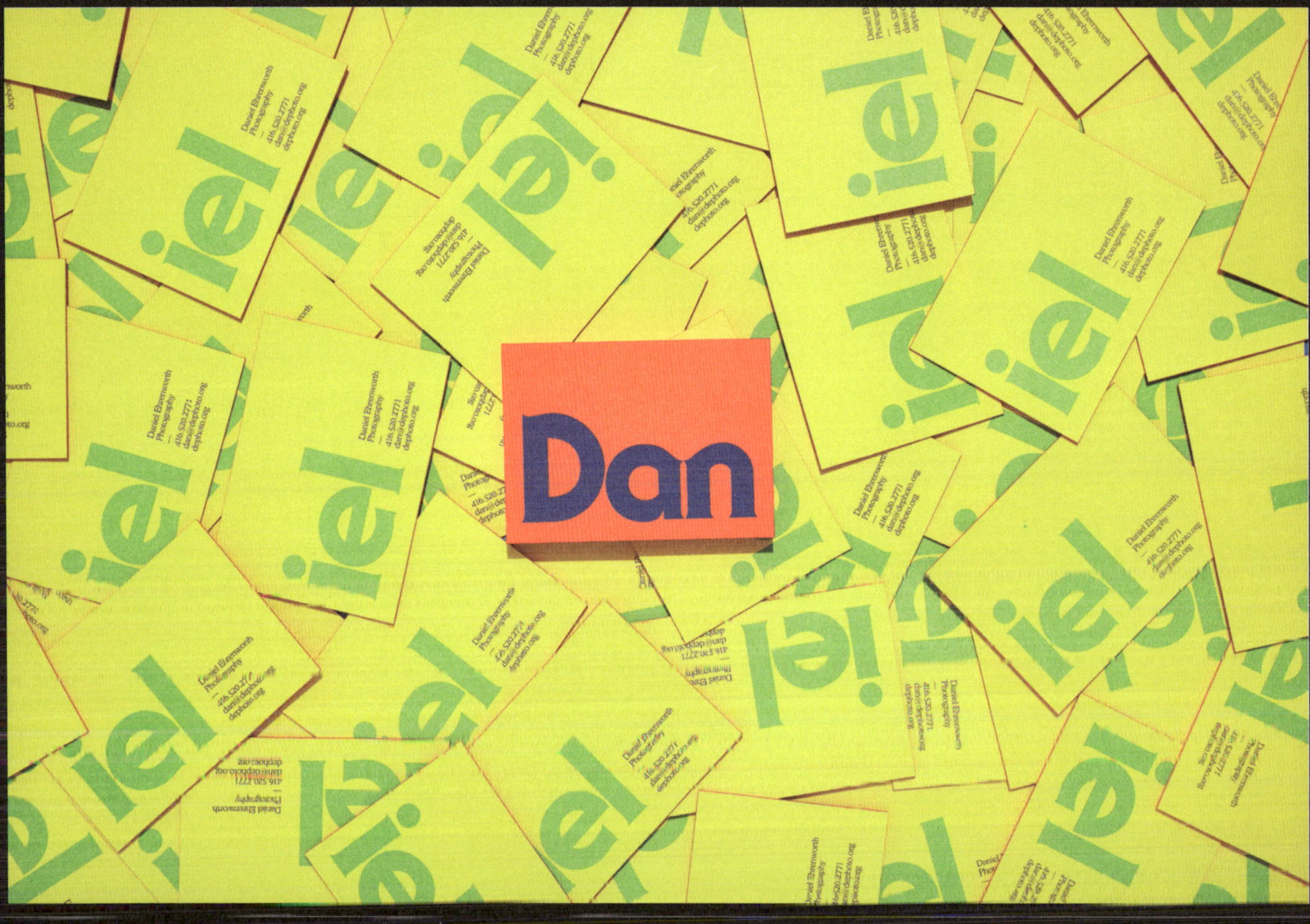

Daniel Ehrenworth Photography Brand Identity, 2017–2020, Underline Studio

What makes Underline Studio great doesn't require a lot of explanation. You just need to look at the work. But maybe I can add a few words to connect the dots. I've had the good luck to collaborate with Claire and Fidel, Underline's founders, as both thinkers and creators — and their ability to balance those roles effortlessly is the key to everything. Their work is thoughtful without being self-absorbed. Smart but never smartass. Meticulously executed, yet never precious. And while the studio has a distinctive style, it's not imposed on clients but rather leveraged to their advantage. ■ Like all strong designers, Fidel and Claire are ready to fight for what they believe — but always graciously, with diplomacy grounded in firm conviction. Often very firm. I guess that may mean they're not for everyone, though it's hard to imagine any brand or organization that wouldn't benefit from what they have to offer. Except maybe a client that makes vinyl car mats. Or fake crab legs. Or empty populist promises. But for the rest of us, Underline creates the kind of beautifully crafted and impeccably tasteful work that makes us feel proud of our own good taste in embracing it.

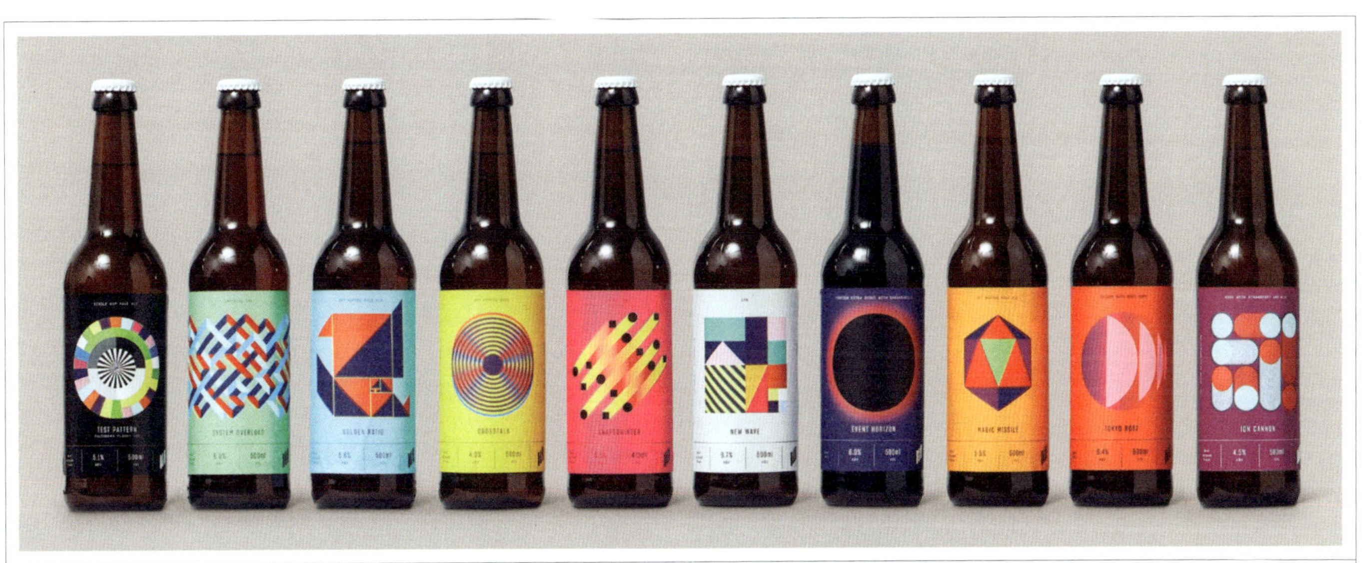

Halo Brewery, Packaging, 2016-2020, Underline Studio

YOU HAVE TO CARE ABOUT THE PEOPLE YOU'RE DOING THE WORK FOR. HAVE AN UNDERSTANDING AND RESPECT FOR WHAT THEY ARE STRIVING TO ACHIEVE. **Claire Dawson,** *Creative Director and Partner, Underline Studio*

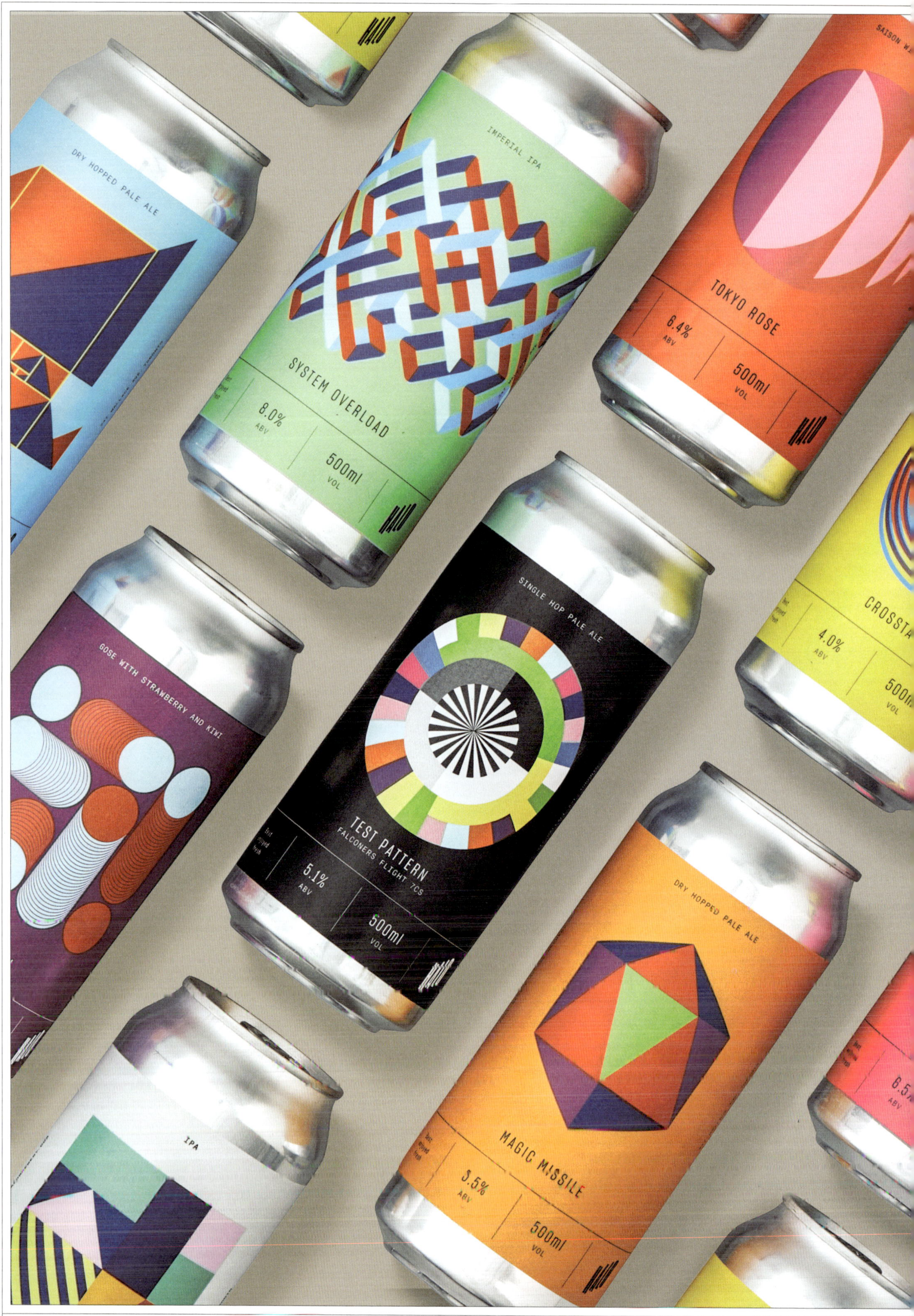

DRY HOPPED PALE ALE
IMPERIAL IPA
SYSTEM OVERLOAD
8.0%
ABV
500ml
VOL
HALO
TOKYO ROSE
6.4%
ABV
500ml
VOL
HALO
GOSE WITH STRAWBERRY AND KIWI
SINGLE HOP PALE ALE
TEST PATTERN
FALCONERS FLIGHT 7CS
5.1%
ABV
500ml
VOL
CROSSTA
4.0%
ABV
500ml
VOL
DRY HOPPED PALE ALE
IPA
MAGIC MISSILE
5.5%
ABV
500ml
VOL
HALO
6.5%
ABV

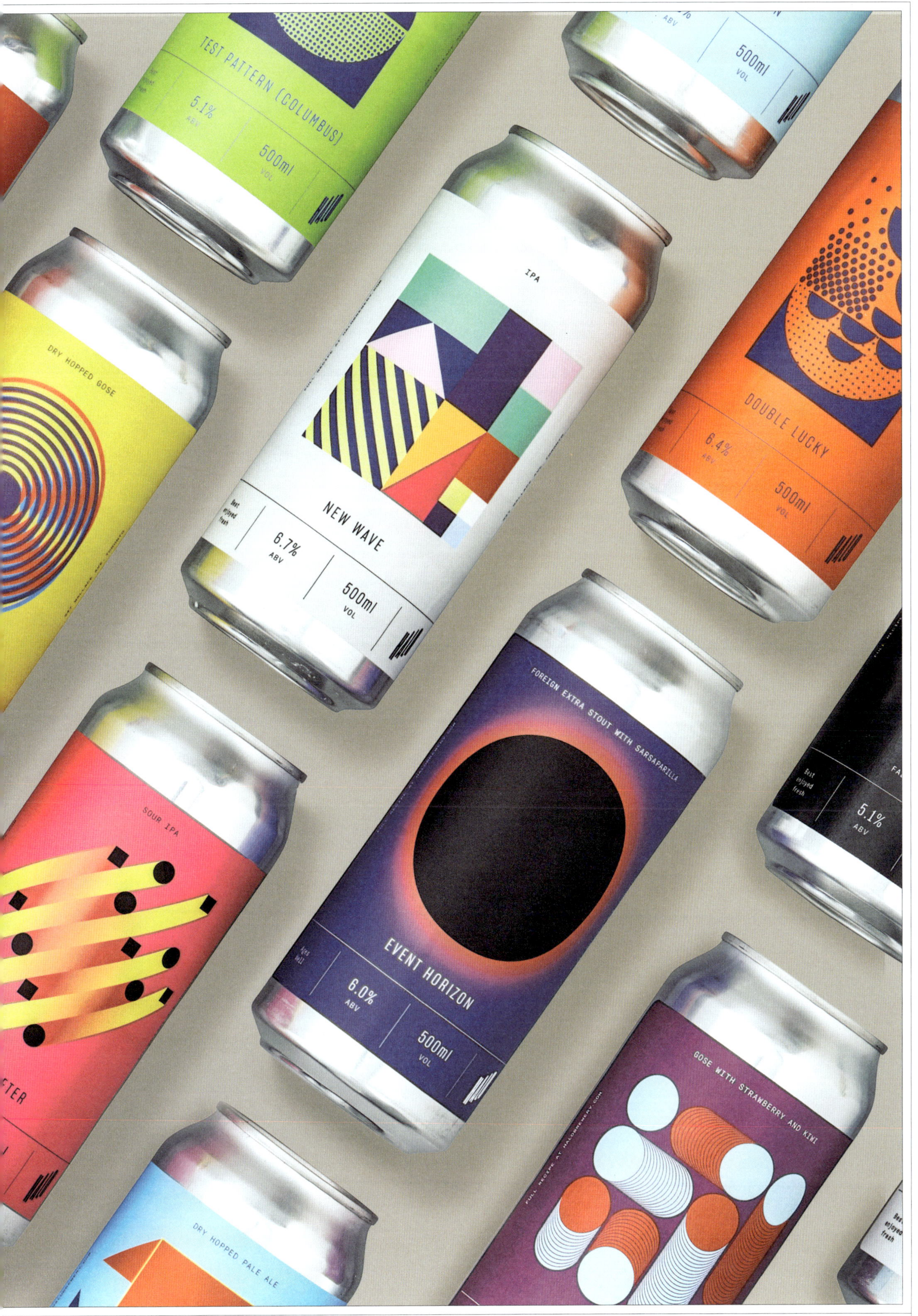

Halo Brewery, Packaging, 2016-2020, Underline Studio

What is your work philosophy?
Claire Dawson: It's not a philosophy per se, but there are some tenets we follow: Work hard. Be thoughtful. Have fun.

Who is or was your greatest mentor?
Fidel Peña: My stepfather, Augusto Crespín, an artist who showed me that you can make a living making art, and who also introduced me to other great artists, writers, and poets from El Salvador. Other influential people in my life have been my previous bosses Diti Katona and John Pylypczak from Concrete Design, Fernando Gutiérrez from Pentagram, and my College professors Roger Hathaway and Giles Morin. Finally, Tibor Kalman who proved to my younger self that graphic design does not need to serve commercial interests only.

Who were some of your greatest influences?
CD: At the beginning of my career really my biggest influences were books (remember those?). It was where I learned about all the usual suspects: Tibor Kalman, Zuzana Licko, Paul Rand, etc. I would spend hours in the university library pouring over them. Of course, my influences also include my first bosses Diti Katona and John Pylypczak from Concrete Design, and from school my professors David Scadding, Wojtek Janczak, Don Newgren, and Jimmy Peng. As well as the many people that have worked with us at Underline, we work very closely together and I've been influenced by them all.

Who among your contemporaries today do you most admire?
FP: There are many designers doing incredibly beautiful work today, perhaps more than at any other time. But I gravitate towards designers and artists who question our way of seeing the world such as Ruby Broobie (broobs), Experimental Jetset, Ronal Rael, Johanna Toruño, and Uğur Gallenkuş

What are the most important ingredients you require from a client to do successful work?
FP: Complete trust that we can deliver what they need to succeed in their field, and an understanding of how design can help them communicate and amplify their message.
CD: It may sound a bit cliché, but I think you also have to care about the people you're doing the work for. I'm not talking about developing great friendships necessarily, but having an understanding and respect for what they are striving to achieve.

What advice would you have for students starting out today?
FP: Work hard, be kind and be authentic. If you haven't figured out who you are, don't worry there's plenty of time for

that, but once you find out, be yourself, even if you feel that by doing so you may be deviating from others' expectations of your work.
CD: To learn to really listen, because it never stops being an important part of your work. You need to have a conversation with clients, question and dig down to find the root of the problem that needs to be solved. It will make your design so much better and more successful.

What are some things you wish you knew about the industry when you first started?
FP: That there is little room in design for non-European narratives, and that due to a general lack of awareness, these narratives need to be constantly reinvented and communicated. I've learned that success in design has a lot to do with privilege (my own included) and luck, as well as talent and hard work.

What do you value most?
Doing beautiful work that conveys challenging or important questions at the same time. Also, family and community.

How do you define success?
FP: Doing what you love while being able to be awed by being alive in this world.

What part of your work do you find most interesting?
CD: That things are always changing and you are constantly challenged with new problems, new clients from new fields, new things to learn. And that you can bring to this work so many influences and draw from many diverse fields. A piece of music might inspire how we design a book, or a book can help influence a brand.

What makes Underline Studio stand out among your contemporaries?
Better answered by someone other than us!

What is your greatest professional achievement?
It would be founding Underline and navigating its ups and downs for over 15 years.

What is it about Design that you are most passionate about?
CD: Simply put - making things. Researching and understanding a problem and then shaping and crafting a beautiful solution.

Underline Studio underlinestudio.com

WORK HARD, BE KIND, AND BE AUTHENTIC,
BE YOURSELF EVEN IF YOU DEVIATE FROM
OTHERS' EXPECTATIONS.

Fidel Peña, *Creative Director and Partner, Underline Studio*

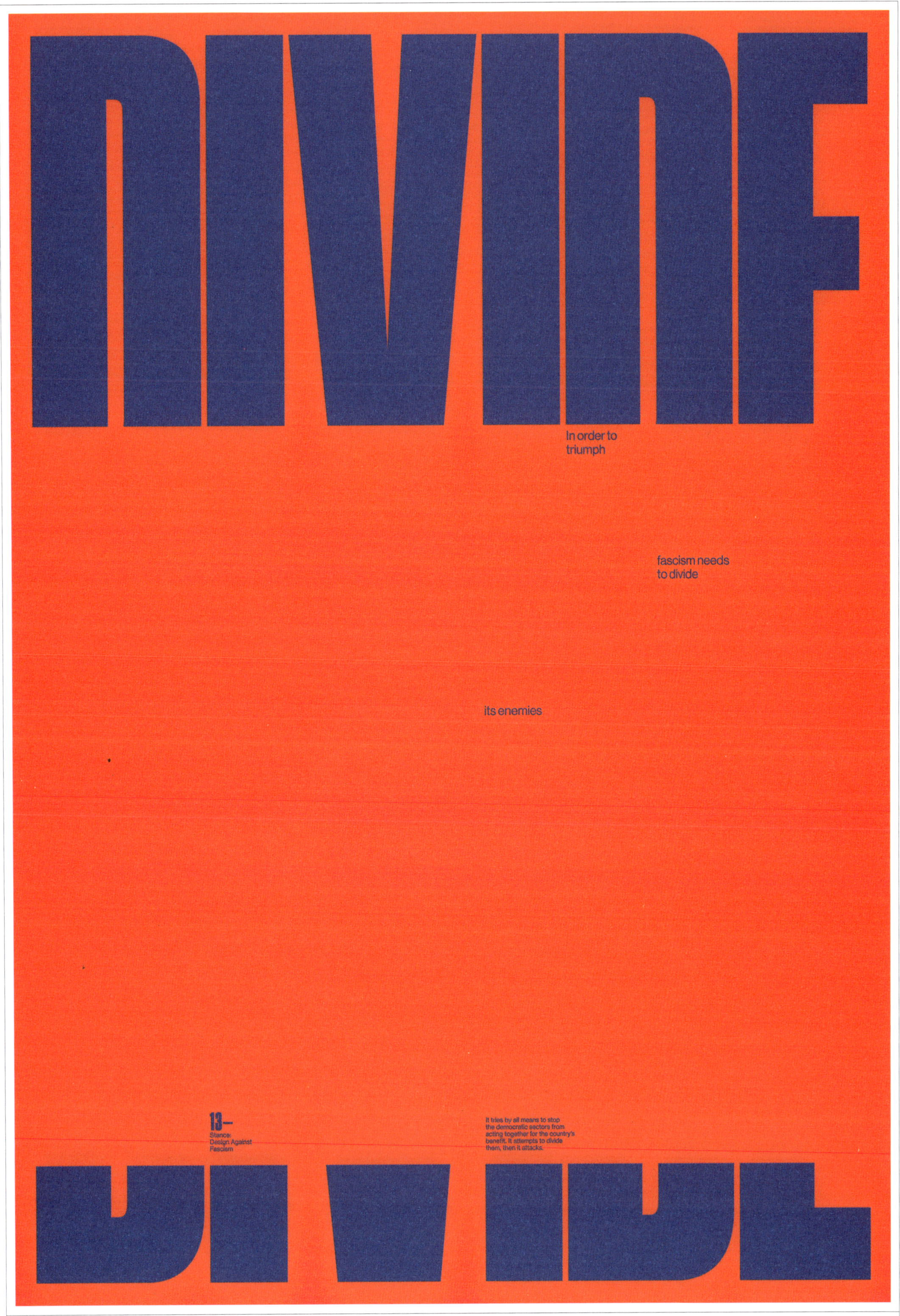

Sur Gallery, Stance: Design Against Fascism, Poster, 2018, Underline Studio

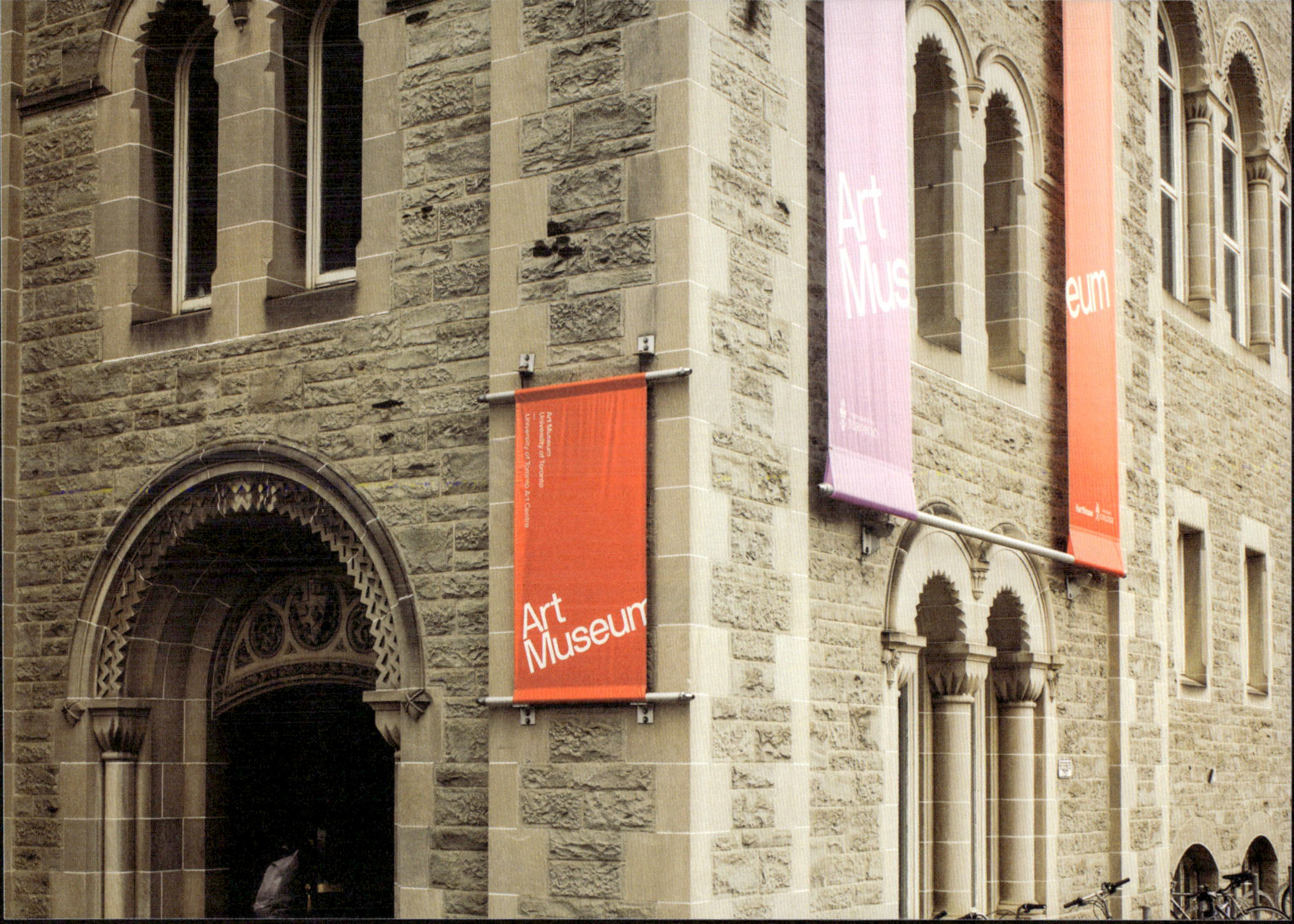

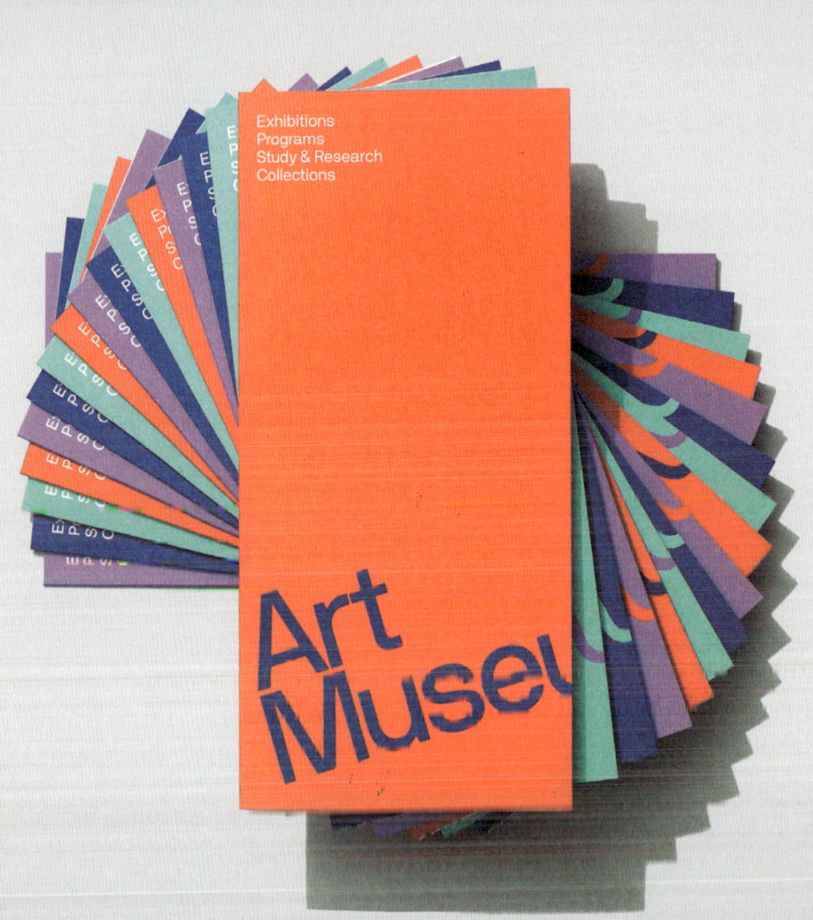

The Art Museum at University of Toronto, Brand Identity, 2016, Underline Studio

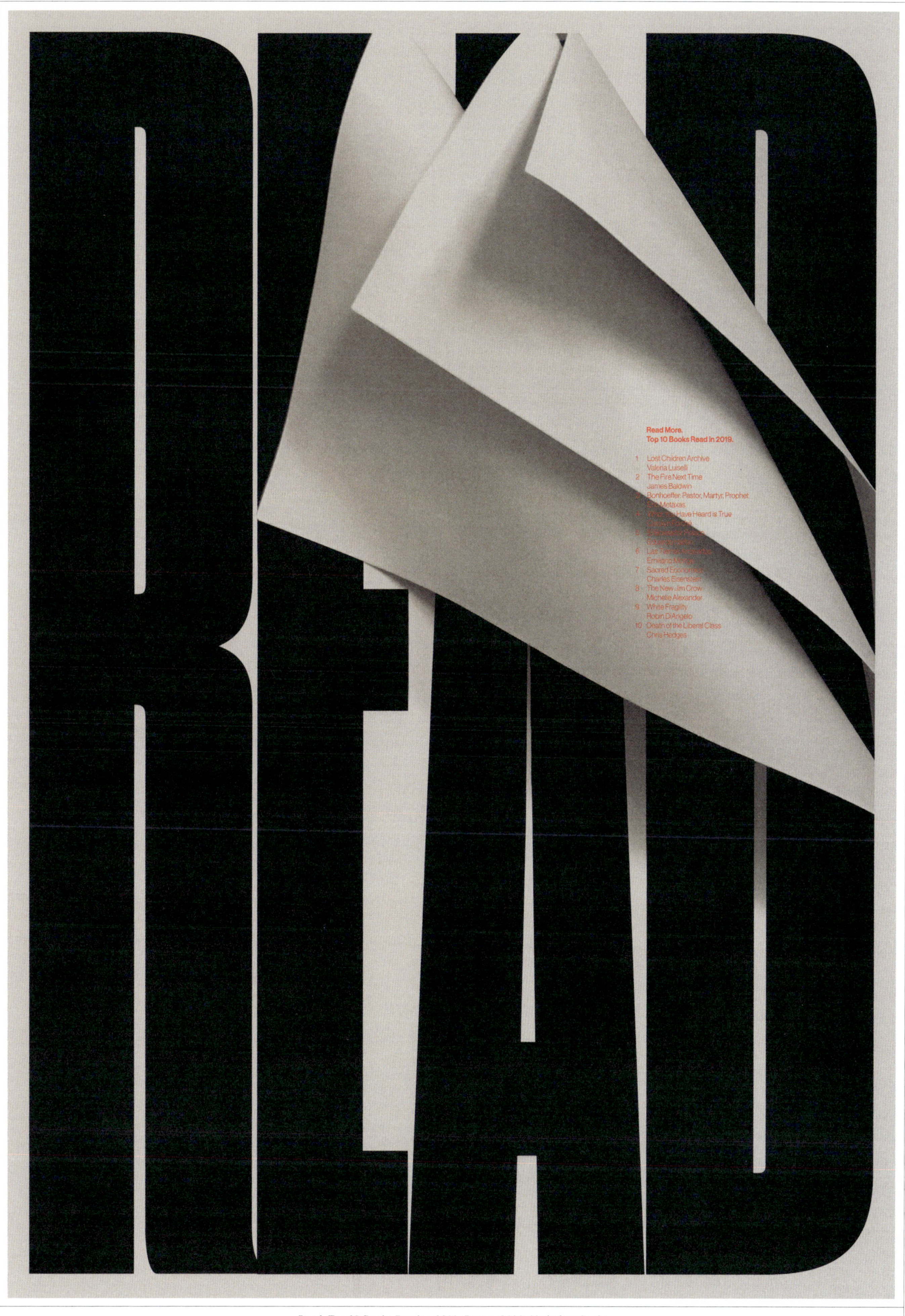

Read, Top 10 Books Read in 2019, Poster, 2020, Underline Studio

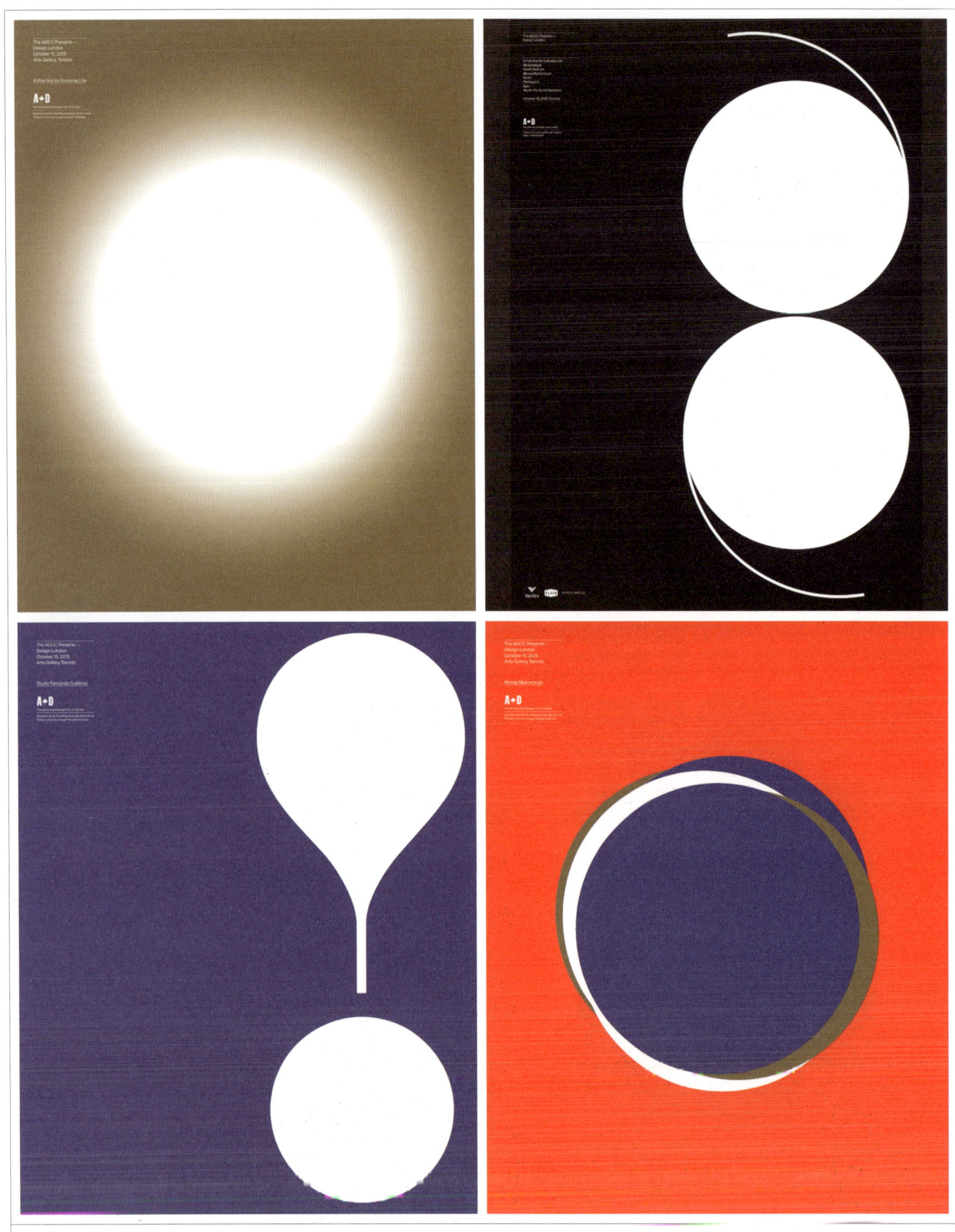

Advertising & Design Club of Canada, Design London Posters, 2016, Underline Studio

GRAPHIC DESIGN DOES NOT NEED TO SERVE COMMERCIAL INTERESTS ONLY.

Fidel Peña, *Creative Director and Partner, Underline Studio*

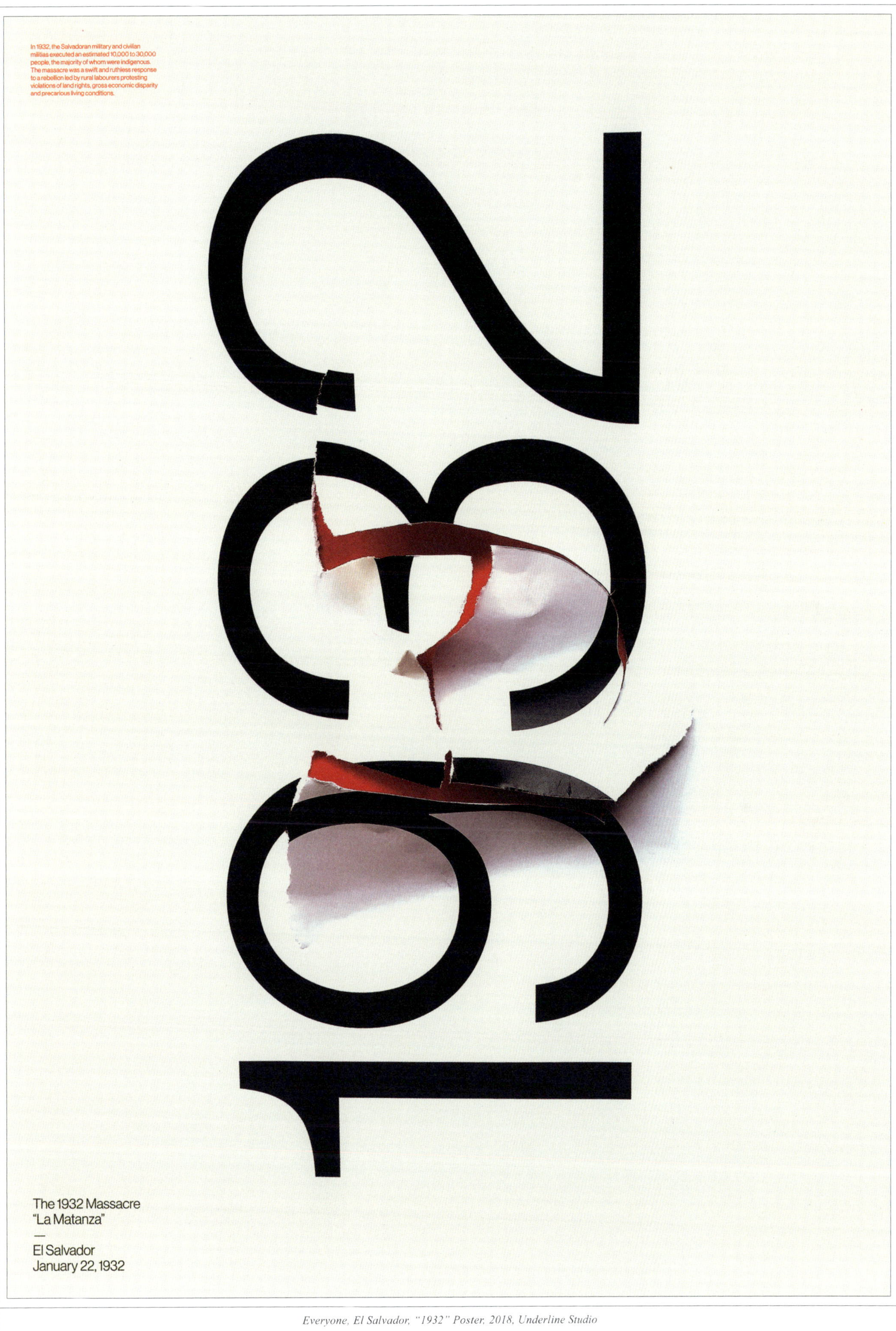

Everyone, El Salvador, "1932" Poster, 2018, Underline Studio

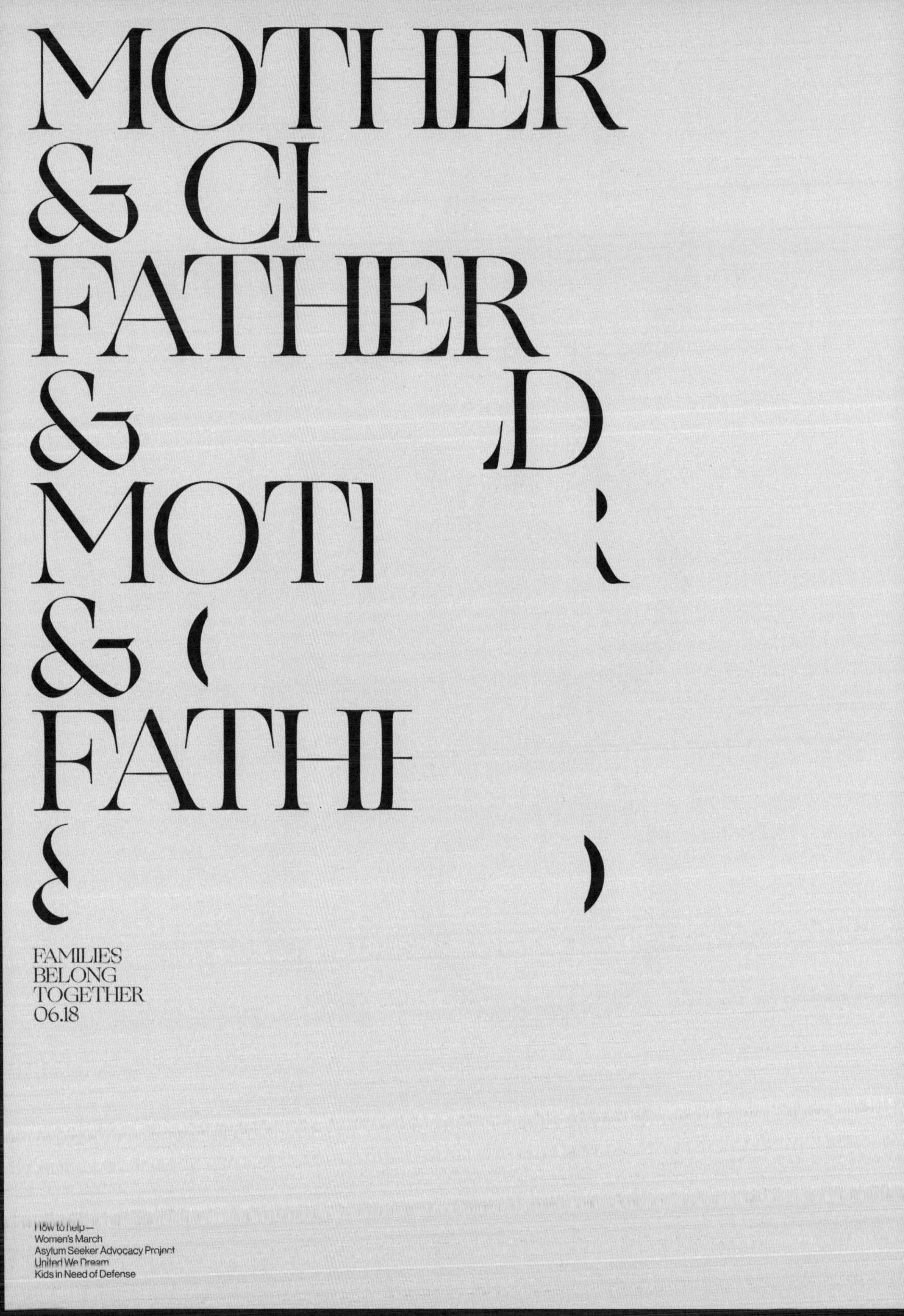

MOTHER
& CF
FATHER
& D
MOTI   R
& (
FATHE
&   )

FAMILIES
BELONG
TOGETHER
06.18

How to help—
Women's March
Asylum Seeker Advocacy Project
United We Dream
Kids in Need of Defense

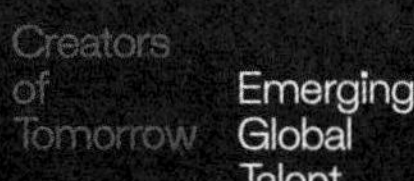

Native Magazine: Creators of Tomorrow, Poster, 2019, Underline Studio

HE IS ONE OF THE WORLD'S MOST EMINENT POSTER DESIGNERS. HE HAS A UNIQUE ABILITY TO REVEAL POLITICAL AND HISTORICAL MESSAGES.

Finn Nygaard, *Danish Graphic Designer & AGI Member*

HE IS ONE OF A KIND! UWE YOU ARE WONDERFUL! STRAIGHT, FUNNY, AND AN EXTREMELY TALENTED DESIGNER. ALWAYS GOOD FOR A SURPRISE.

Fritz Gottschalk, *Swiss-Canadian Graphic Designer, Gottschalk+Ash Int'l & AGI Member*

I HAVE KNOWN UWE SINCE THE '80S WHEN I WAS ATTRACTED BY HIS VISIONARY POSTERS. HIS TEXT AND IMAGE MELT INTO ONE AND RESULT IN SOMETHING SPECIAL.

Gunter Rambow, *German Graphic Designer, Photographer & AGI Member*

HE IS AN EXCELLENT COMMUNICATOR AND AN INTELLIGENT, CULTIVATED PERSON. HIS POSTERS ALWAYS HAVE A STRONG MESSAGE.

Melchior Imboden, *Swiss Graphic Designer and Photographer & AGI Member*

HE IS THE FIRST GERMAN GRAPHIC ARTIST TO MAKE THE BOUNDARIES BETWEEN ART AND DESIGN, BETWEEN POLITICS AND COMEDY, AND MAYBE EVEN BETWEEN RIGHT AND LEFT DISAPPEAR.

Fons Hickmann, *Graphic Designer & AGI Member, Fons Hickmann m23*

EVERY POSTER IS AN EXPERIENCE. AS IF HIS POINT OF VIEW WERE IN ANOTHER DIMENSION. THERE IS ALWAYS HUMOR AND UNEXPECTED RESULTS.

Catherine Zask, *French Graphic Designer & AGI Member*

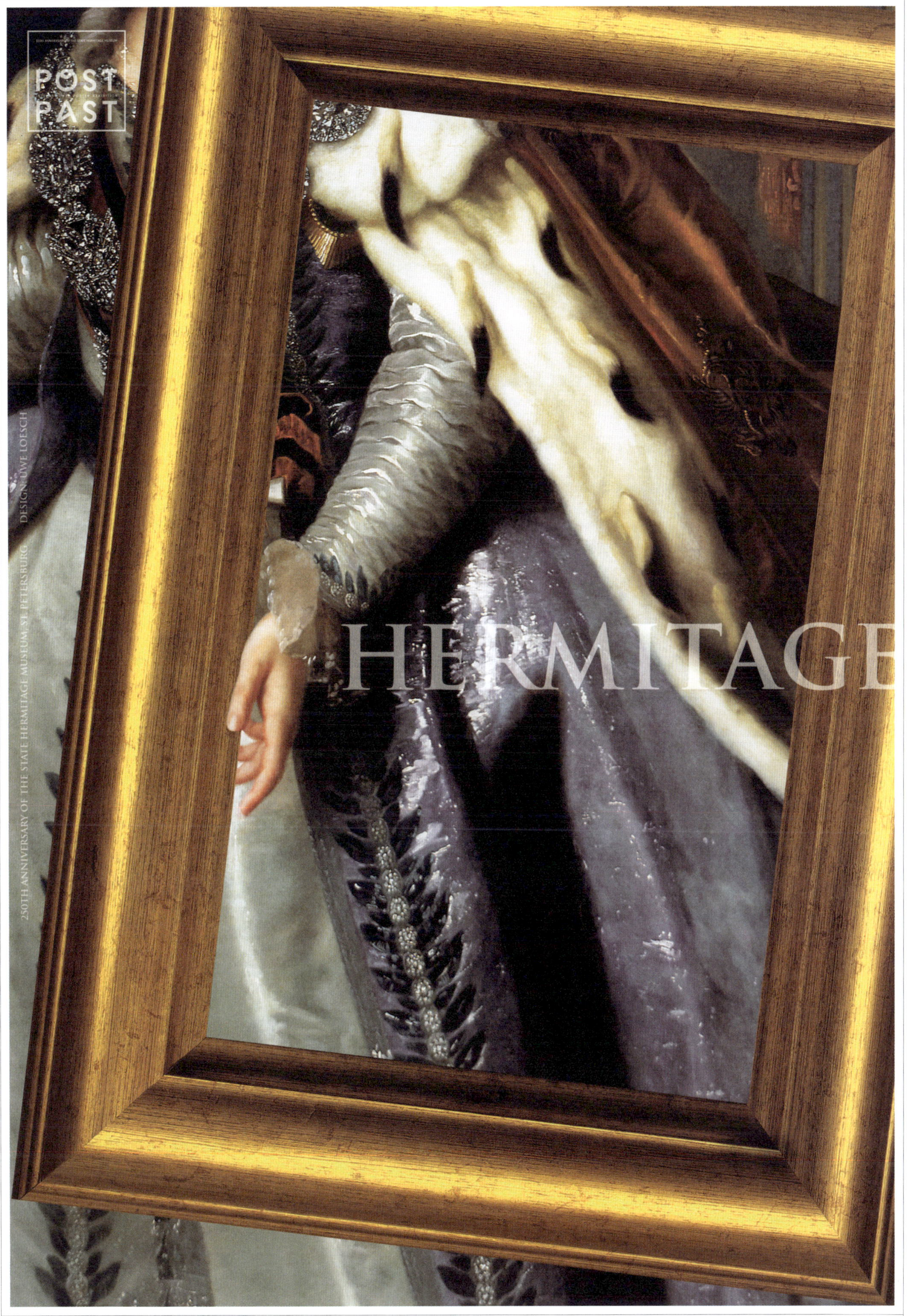

Hermitage. 250th anniversary of the State Hermitage Museum St. Petersburg. 2013

Introduction by Alain le Quernec *French Designer, Poster Artist & AGI Member*

Uwe Loesch appeared in the little world of poster design at a time when the German poster style was based on a narrative photo montage, or photo collage in a more or less surrealistic atmosphere. From the beginning, his work was a radical change. Uwe developed the same design language we know today. His disconnection with a trend or a fashion may be the reason why this language remains timeless and authentic. His style is unique and any attempts to use his codes would immediately appear as plagiarism. All his works respect the minimalistic dogma of what a poster should be, "a telegram" as said by Cassandre. That means that the eye must see and read the content in half a second. All his posters are constructed in that way where text and image occupy and structure the space of the paper, with order and discipline. We get the feeling that nothing could be moved, not even one millimeter. Nevertheless it happens many times that it takes a while before you catch and understand the depth of the message, giving at first glance the feeling that Uwe missed the aim, that his arrow missed the target. But if you study the poster a little more, you'll be surprised to see the target moving towards the arrow. With this metaphor, I try to signify that Uwe brings something new, something unexpected, a new dimension to the demand. Uwe's work is not an illustration of something already defined as most poster designers do with their talent. It's rather an interpretation, an open door for a deeper point of view. ▪ Uwe belongs to the few designers who privilege the poster media in graphic design, who demonstrate that graphic design, and especially poster design, is something more than a decorative art, or a pretty fashionable envelope that vanishes in a few days like a poster in the street. That, for me, makes the difference between Uwe and most of the over-talented graphic designers.

UWE LOESCH KNOWS THE DIFFERENCE BETWEEN STOPPING AND THE "I-PUNKT," WHICH HIGHLIGHTS. IT HINTS AT AN OFFER OF FURTHER FANTASY AND FURTHER ENJOYMENT.

Dr. Stefan Soltek, *Director of the Klingspor Museum Offenbach*

UWE IS A PRIVILEGED ARTIST, PHILOSOPHER, AND INDEPENDENT THINKER WHO DOESN'T RENOUNCE HIS ORIGINS. HE EXPRESSES HIMSELF WITH RIGOROUS, MINIMALIST, CONCEPTUAL GRAPHISM.

Mariusz Knorowski, *Chief Curator of the Poster Museum at Wilanow*

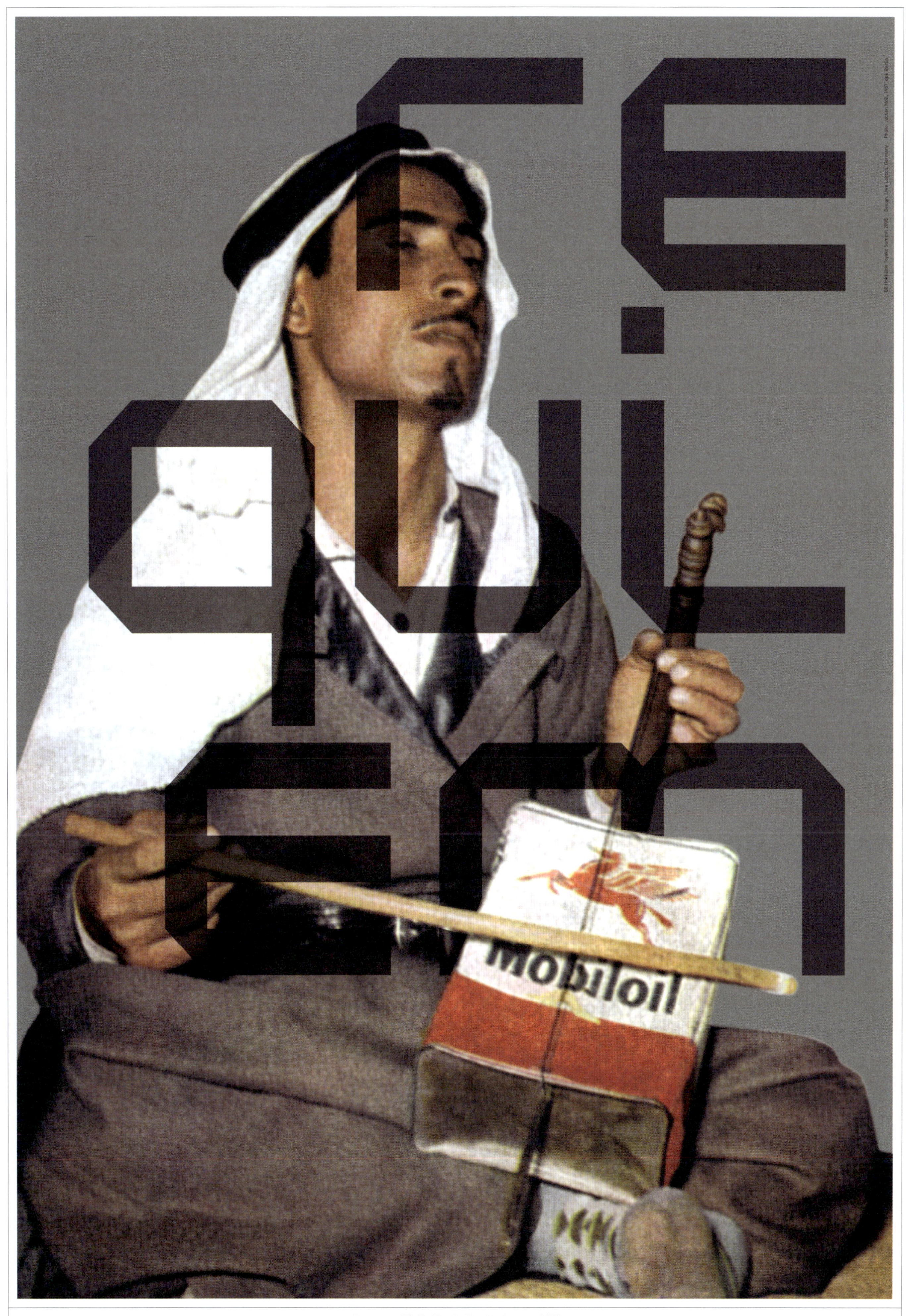

Requiem, G8 Hokkaido Toyako Summit 2008

What inspired or motivated you into your career?
The Unbearable Lightness of Being.

What is your work philosophy?
I see more or less, nevertheless.

Who is or was your greatest mentor?
Art and kitsch, facts and fiction. In the Odyssey, Mentor was the son of Alcimus.

What has been your most memorable project?
Punktum. - a beauty spot only. And www.scheisse.de. (www.shit.de) the shaved Hitler as a skinhead.

What is the most difficult challenge you've had to overcome?
I crossed the Sahara several times in the 1980s. On the first trip, I discovered after a day that "the end is where we start from." We were driving eight hours in a big circle unintentionally. It was a special experience of anticipation or even squaring the circle.

Has there ever been a project or client that has surprised you in any way?
In 1990, I installed green posters without any text or images on over 250 trees in Frankfurt. This non-verbal communication was nevertheless very successful.

Who were some of your greatest past influences?
Man Ray: "From now on I will do the things that I shouldn't do."

Who among your contemporaries today do you most admire?
My two-year-old granddaughter Yuna. She is very charming, intelligent, sophisticated, and downright clever. Hopefully she won't become haughty some day.

What would be your dream assignment?
It would be to cross the Atlantic in a sugar bag one day.

What are the most important ingredients you require from a client to do successful work?
The belief in art to fail.

Who have been some of your favorite people or clients you have worked with?
After more than fifty years of working and doing nothing, I remember many loyal allies with whom I could steal horses. So I don't want to let anyone ride ahead.

What is your proudest professional achievement?
Many of my students have become very successful. 16 have been appointed to a professorship worldwide.

What is the greatest satisfaction you get from your work?
The upright walk.

What part of your work do you find most demanding?
The unsuccessful attempt to improve the Japanese flag.

What professional goals do you still have for yourself?
Stay calm, keep cool.

What is something you wish you had known when you first started out?
Eggheads also boil only with water.

What advice would you have for students starting out today?
My advice would be: Be yourself. Help yourself. Please yourself. Trust yourself. Do it yourself!

What interests do you have outside of your work?
The gradual formulation of thoughts while walking.

What do you value most?
The patience of my cat, my wife, my daughters.

What would you change if you had to do it all over again?
Oh, that's hard to answer. "Never change a winning team." Everything was as easy and peaceful as in a "terribly happy family." But maybe we were lonely as a team?

Where do you seek inspiration?
Language itself is a terrific source of inspiration. And an empty glass of wine.

How do you define success?
Success closes the gap between luck and intellect or the perfect mark-to-space ratio.

Where do you see yourself in the future?
Waiting for the sunrise.

Uwe Loesch www.uweloesch.de
See his Graphis Master Portfolio on graphis.com.

UWE HAS BEEN EXCEEDINGLY LUCKY TO HAVE BEEN MARRIED TO YOUNG SOOK, A STUNNINGLY BEAUTIFUL AND SMART YOUNG KOREAN LADY WHO HAS CLEARLY INSPIRED HIM TO EXTREME ECCENTRICITIES RESULTING IN UNPREDICTABLE BRILLIANT WORK. **B. Martin Pedersen,** *Designer*

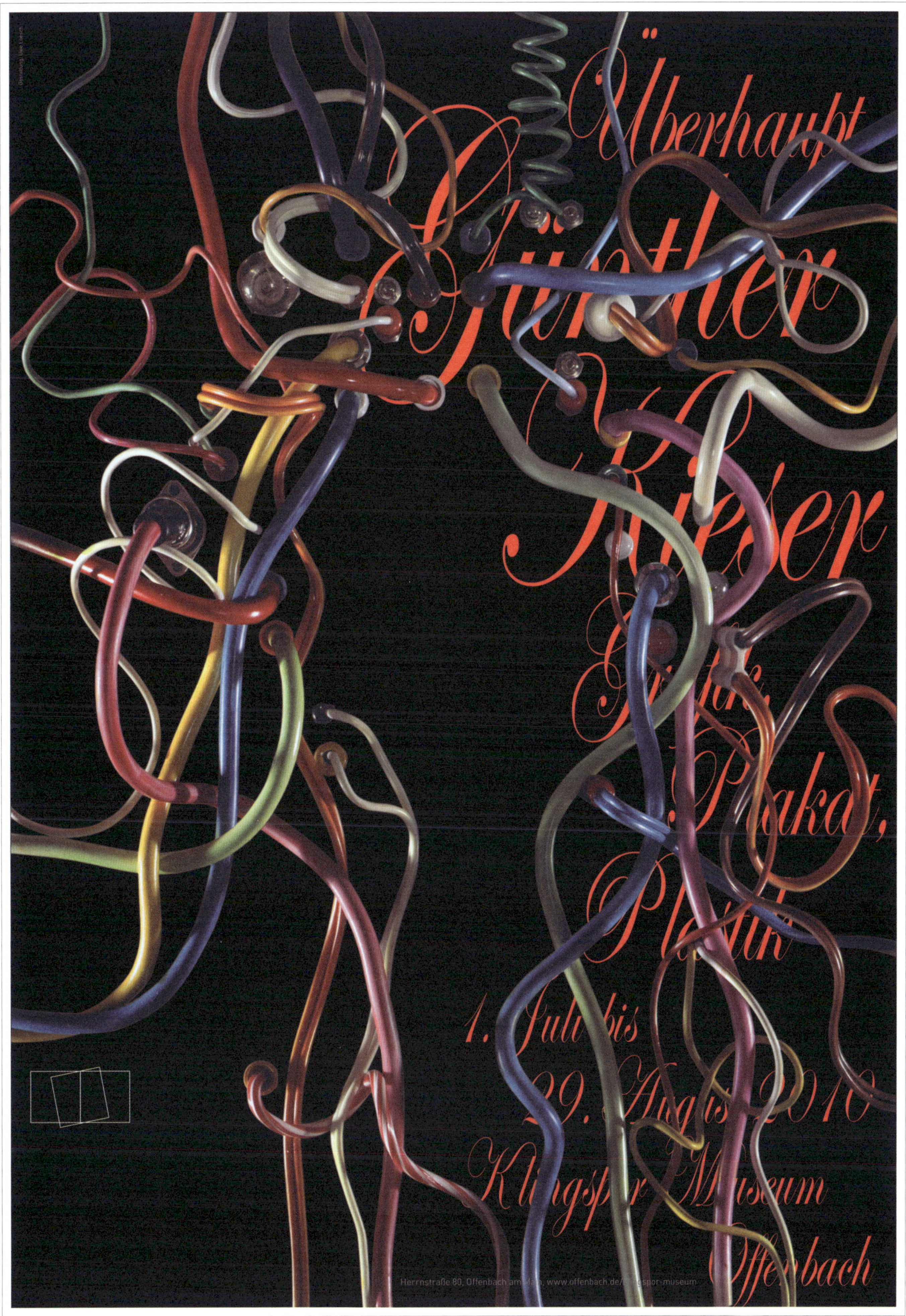

Ahead. Günther Kieser, Klingspor Museum Offenbach, 2010

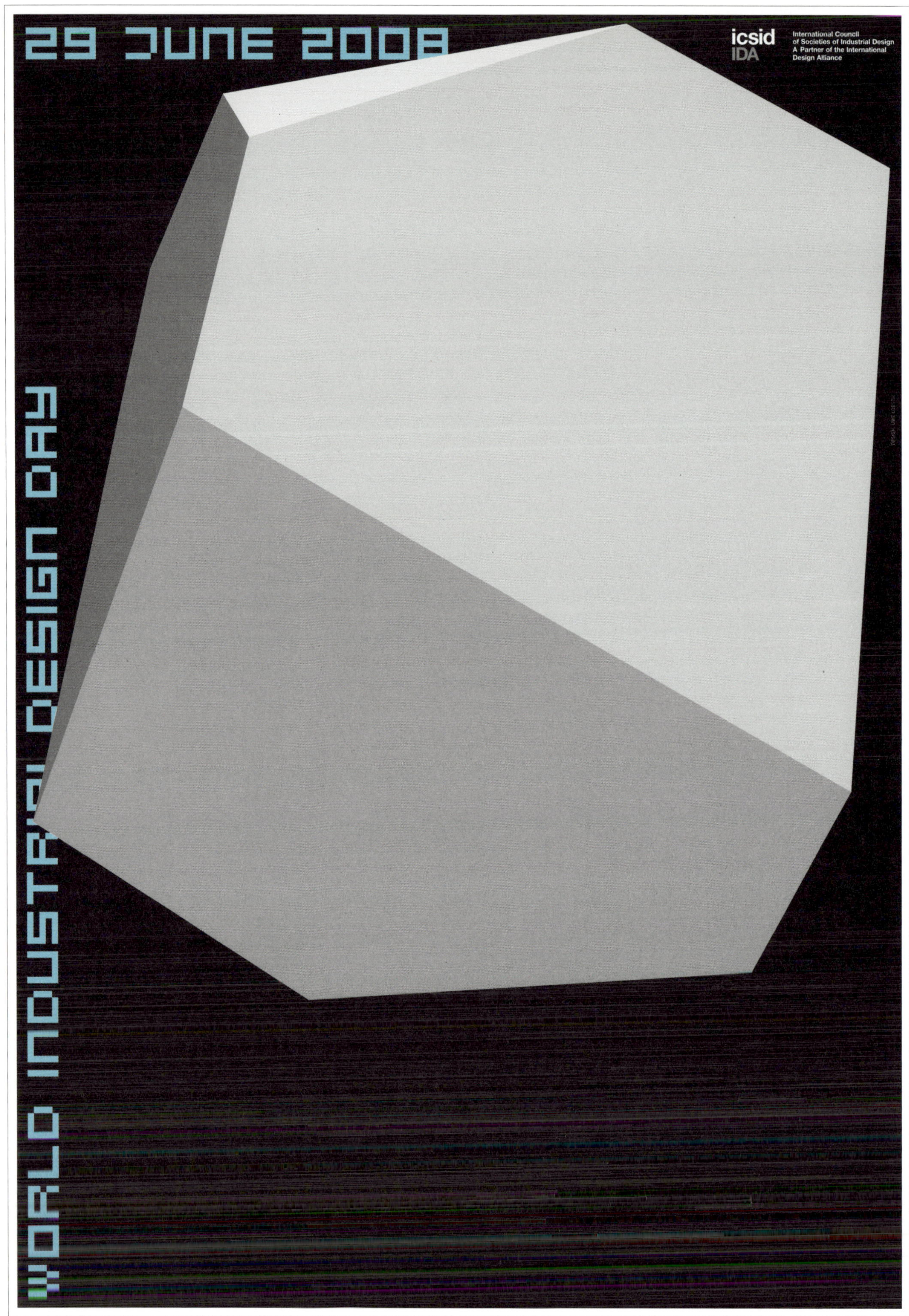

World Industrial Design Day 2008, icsid International Council of Societies of Industrial Design, 2008

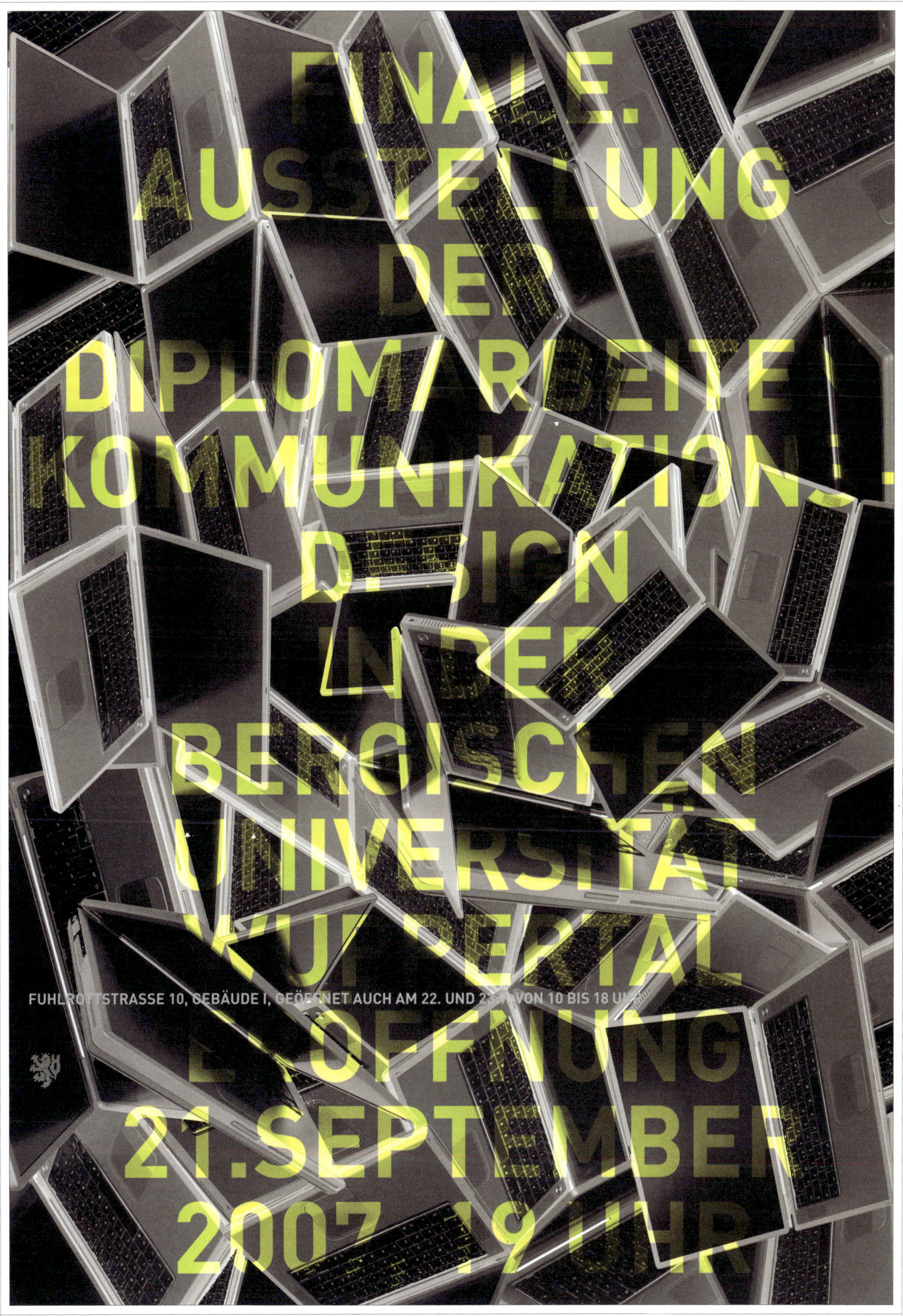

Finale. Diploma works of the department Communication Design at the University of Wuppertal, 2007

Die 68er.
Kurzer Sommer – lange Wirkung
Historisches Museum
Frankfurt am Main
1. Mai bis 31. August 2008
Gestaltung: Uwe Loesch
Generation 68. Short Summer - Long Lasting Ideas. Historical Museum Frankfurt am Main, 2008

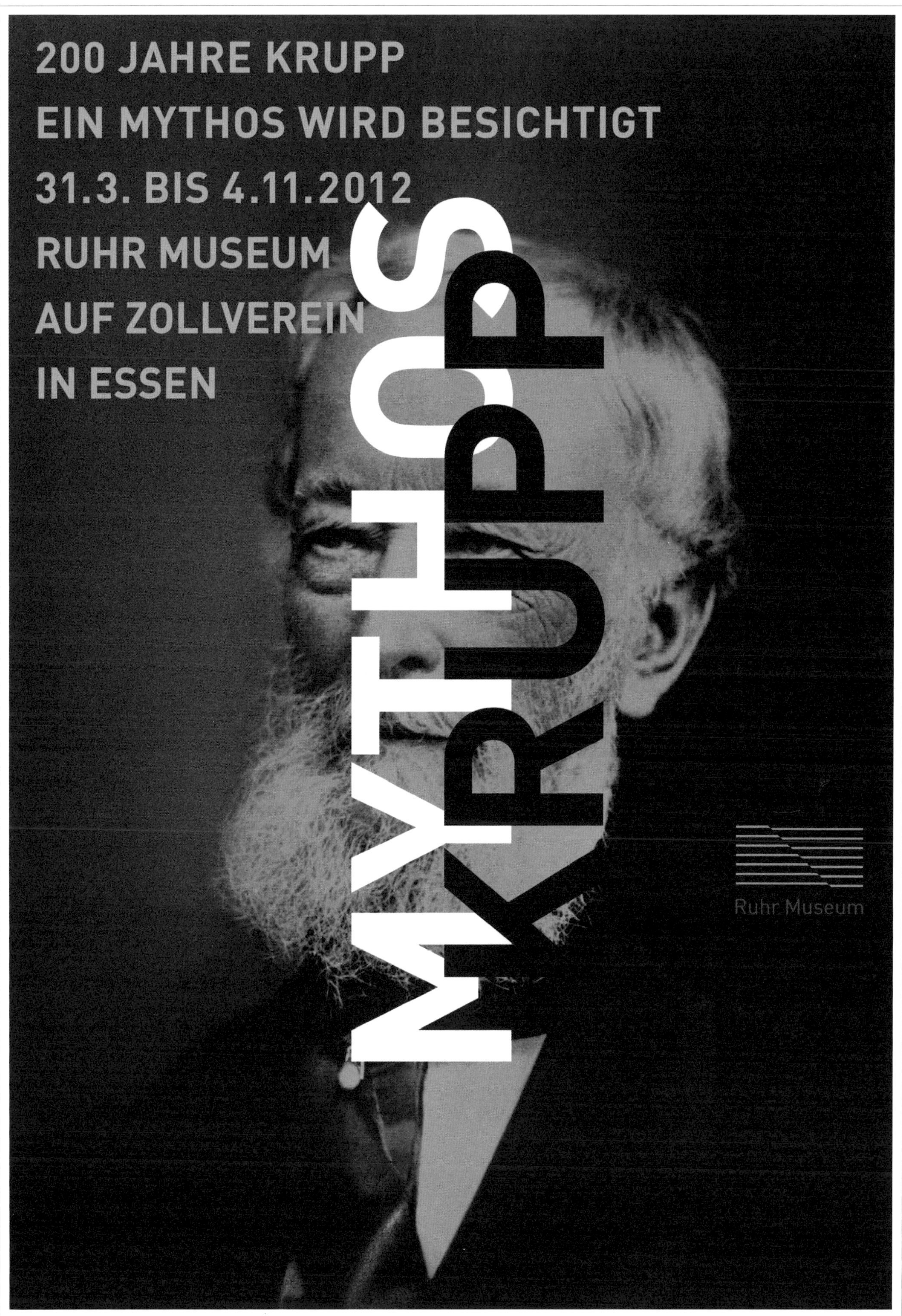

200 Years Krupp. A Myth Is Surveyed, Ruhr Museum Essen, 2012

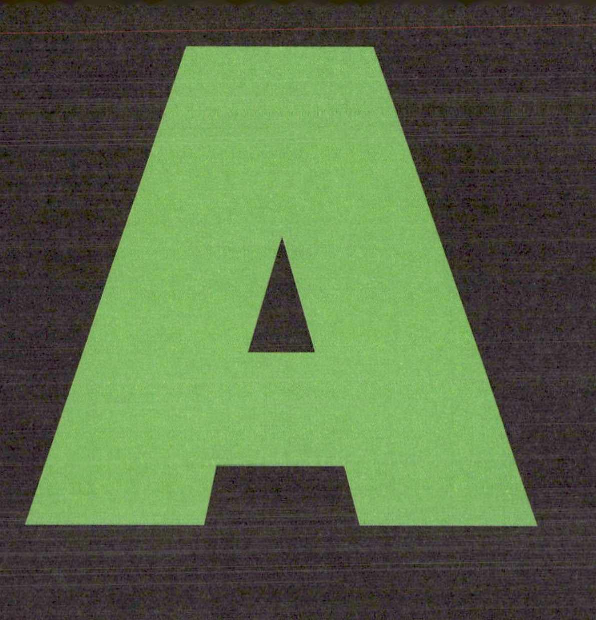

A

50 JOHN FAIRLEY, CURIOUS PRODUCTIONS / UK

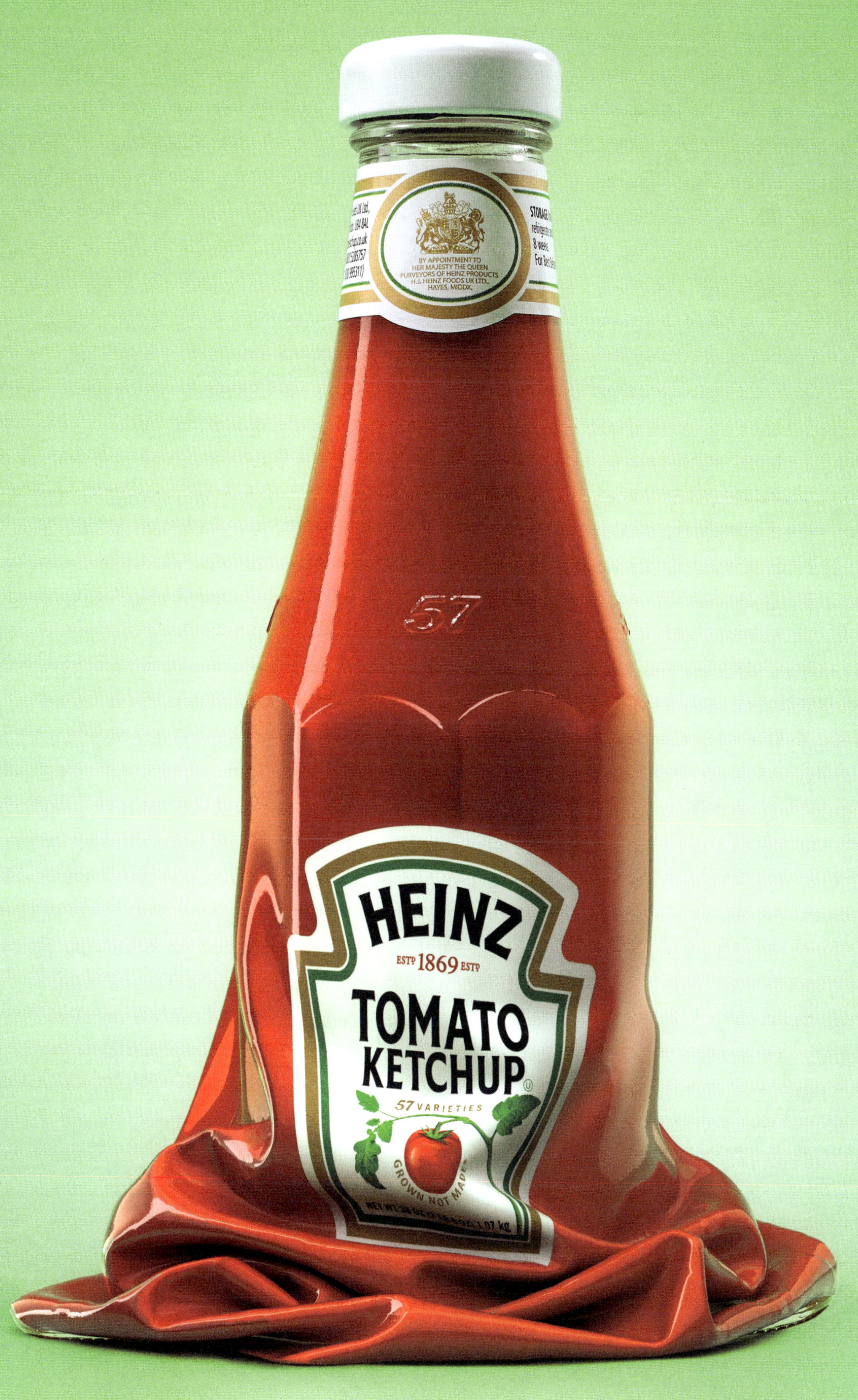

BY APPOINTMENT TO
HER MAJESTY THE QUEEN
PURVEYORS OF HEINZ PRODUCTS
H.J. HEINZ FOODS UK LTD,
HAYES, MIDDX.
57
HEINZ
ESTD 1869 ESTD
TOMATO
KETCHUP
57 VARIETIES
GROWN NOT MADE
NET WT 38 OZ (2 LBS 6 OZ) 1.07 kg

FEW KNOW A WORKMAN FROM A WERKMAN.
THE DIFFERENCE BETWEEN JOHN BROWN AND
BROWNJOHN. SOME EVEN CONFUSE RAND PAUL
WITH PAUL RAND. NOT JOHN. HE KNOWS STUFF.

Dave Dye, *CCO and Founder of Love or Fear*

I HAVE BEEN LUCKY TO WORK WITH JOHN ON
MANY PROJECTS. HIS DEEP UNDERSTANDING OF
THE PHOTOGRAPHIC PROCESS, CLEAR THINKING,
AND THOROUGH PREPARATION ALWAYS HELP
US PRODUCE A GREAT CREATIVE RESULT.

Jonathan Knowles, *Photographer, Graphis Master*

I'M A BIG ADMIRER OF JOHN'S GRAPHIC DESIGN.
EVERYTHING HE TOUCHES IS ALWAYS
IMPECCABLE WITH BEAUTIFUL, WELL-CONSIDERED
TYPOGRAPHY AND ART DIRECTION.

Mark Denton, *Art Director, Coy! Communications*

(Page 49) "Ketchup;" Photographer: Dan Humphreys; CGI & Retouching Artist: Curious Studio / (Opposite page) Portrait of John Fairley; Photographer: Darren Filkins

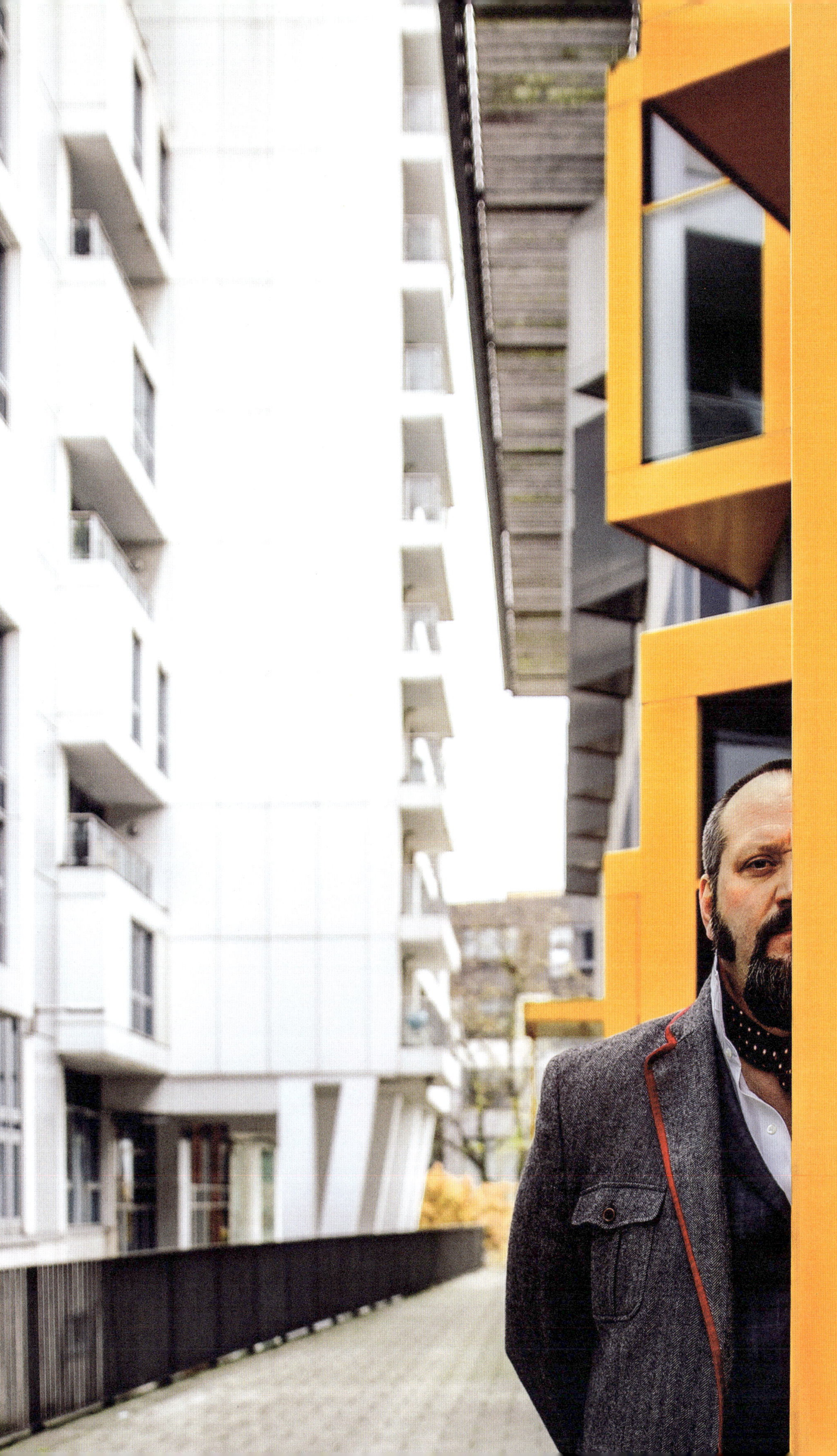

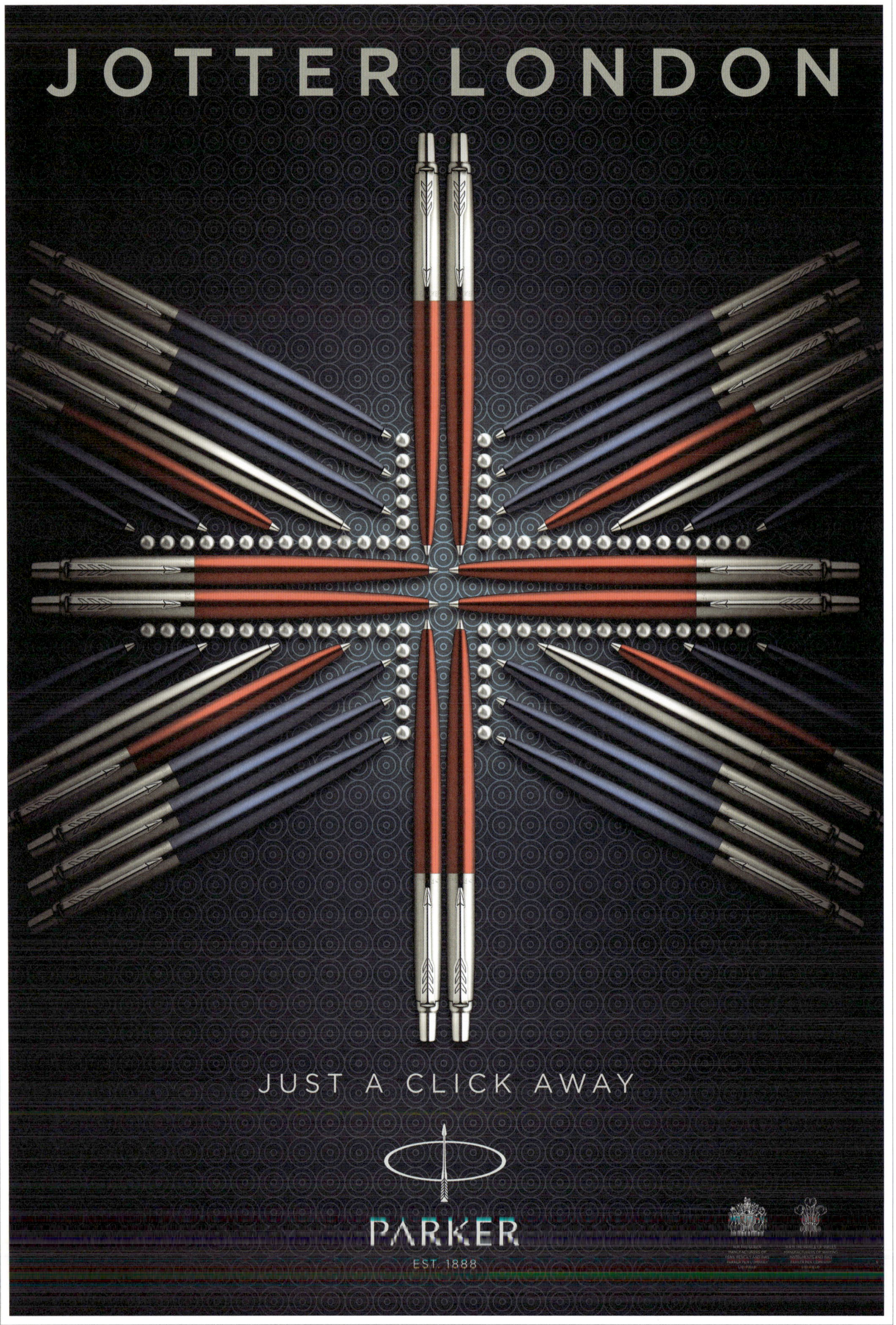

"Parker Union Jack;" Client: Luxor; Agency: Curious Productions; Photographer: Dan Humphreys; Shoot Production: Curious Shoot Team; Retouching Artist: Curious Studio

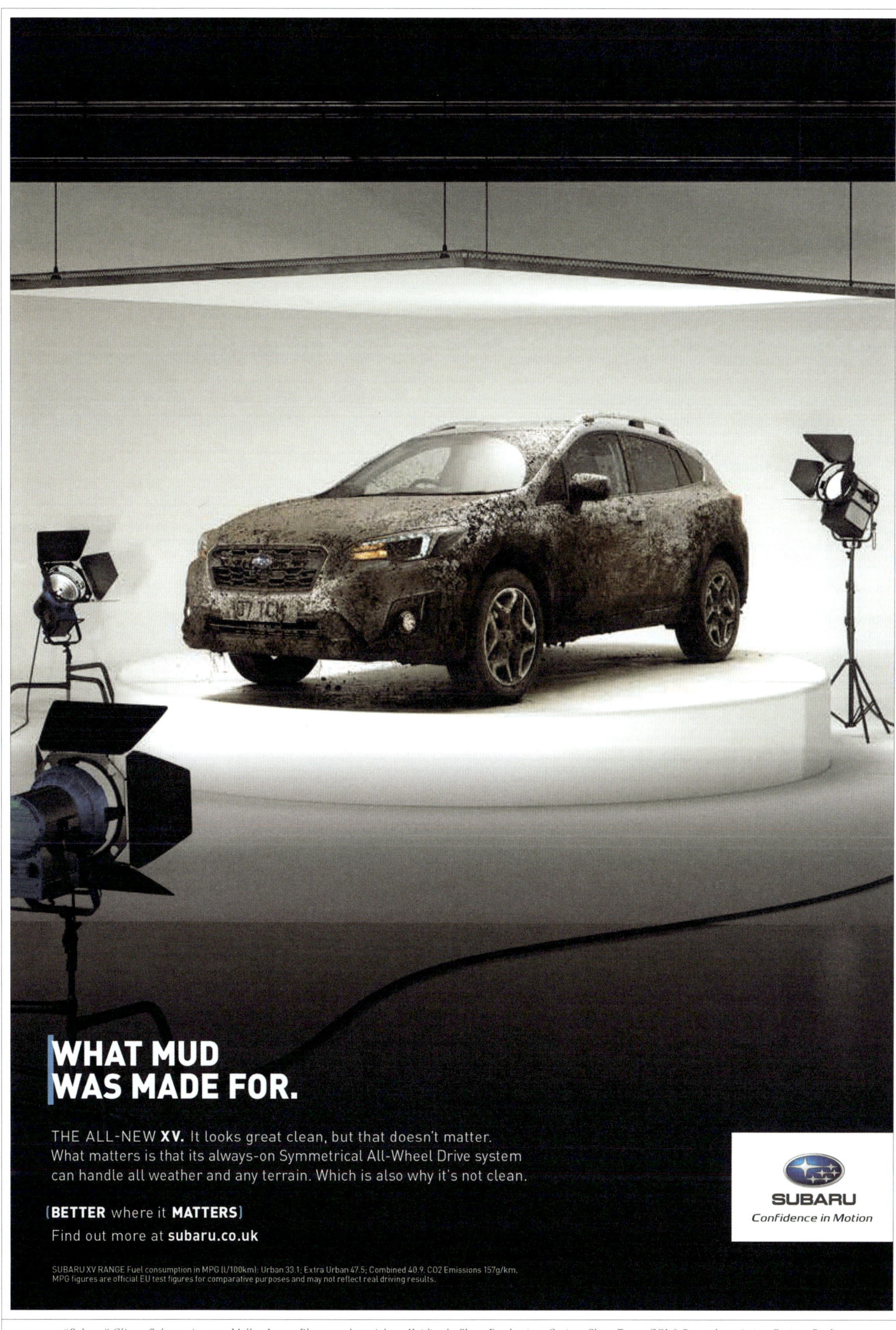

"Subaru" Client: Subaru; Agency: Mullen Lowe; Photographer: Ashton Keiditsch; Shoot Production: Curious Shoot Team; CGI & Retouching Artist: Curious Studio

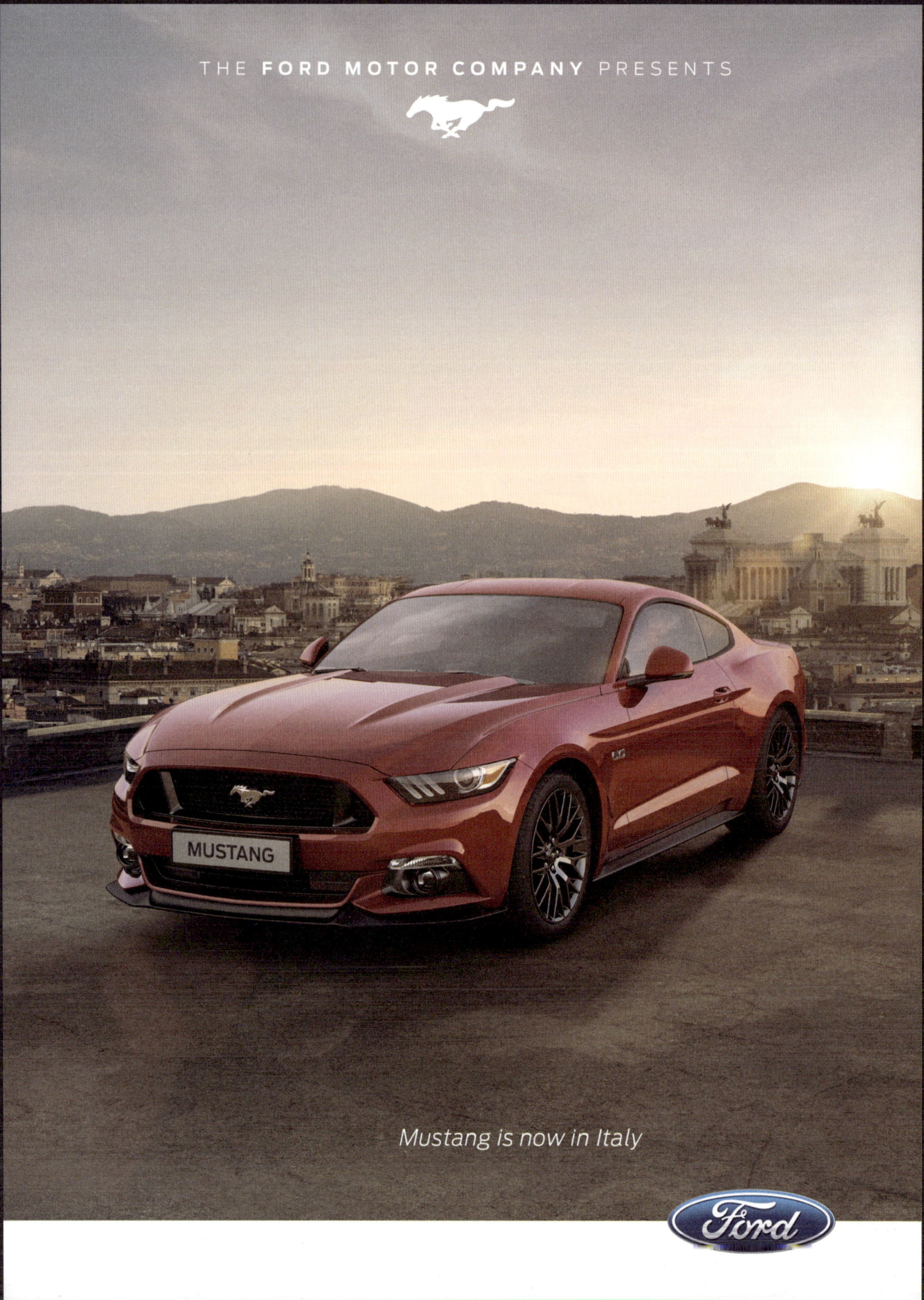

John created and led the design of Creed Fragrances & Aramis rebranding and brand imagery. It was a true pleasure working with John and to see how he skillfully led the creative and design teams through the creative process: from ideation through to the final brand advertising imagery and brand copy. John delivered a sophisticated and unique advertising campaign and brand identity which is still now being used globally. ■ I felt that John was like no other Creative Director I've met, he is immersed in his craft and creates outstanding advertising campaigns, delivering above and beyond the briefs he has been given. John is truly a unique and very talented Creative Director.

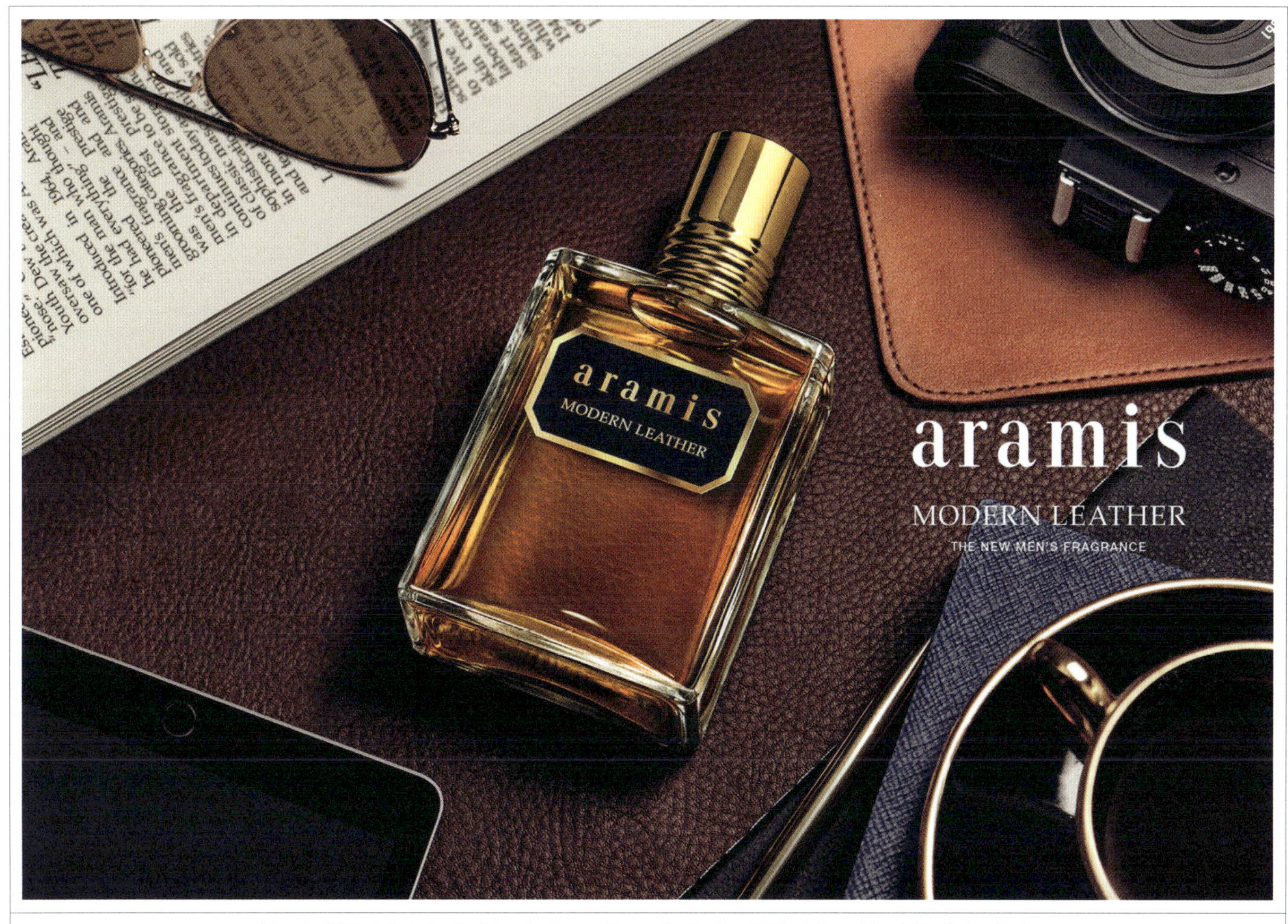

"Aramis;" Client: Estée Lauder / Aramis; Agency: Curious Productions; Studio & Retouching Artist: Curious Studio

MY INTERNAL 'BULLSHIT' DETECTOR IS NOW
SO FINELY TUNED THAT IT OFTEN KNOWS THAT
AN EIGHTY-PAGE POWERPOINT PRESENTATION
COULD HAVE BEEN NAILED IN EIGHT.

John Fairley, *Design Director, Curious Productions*

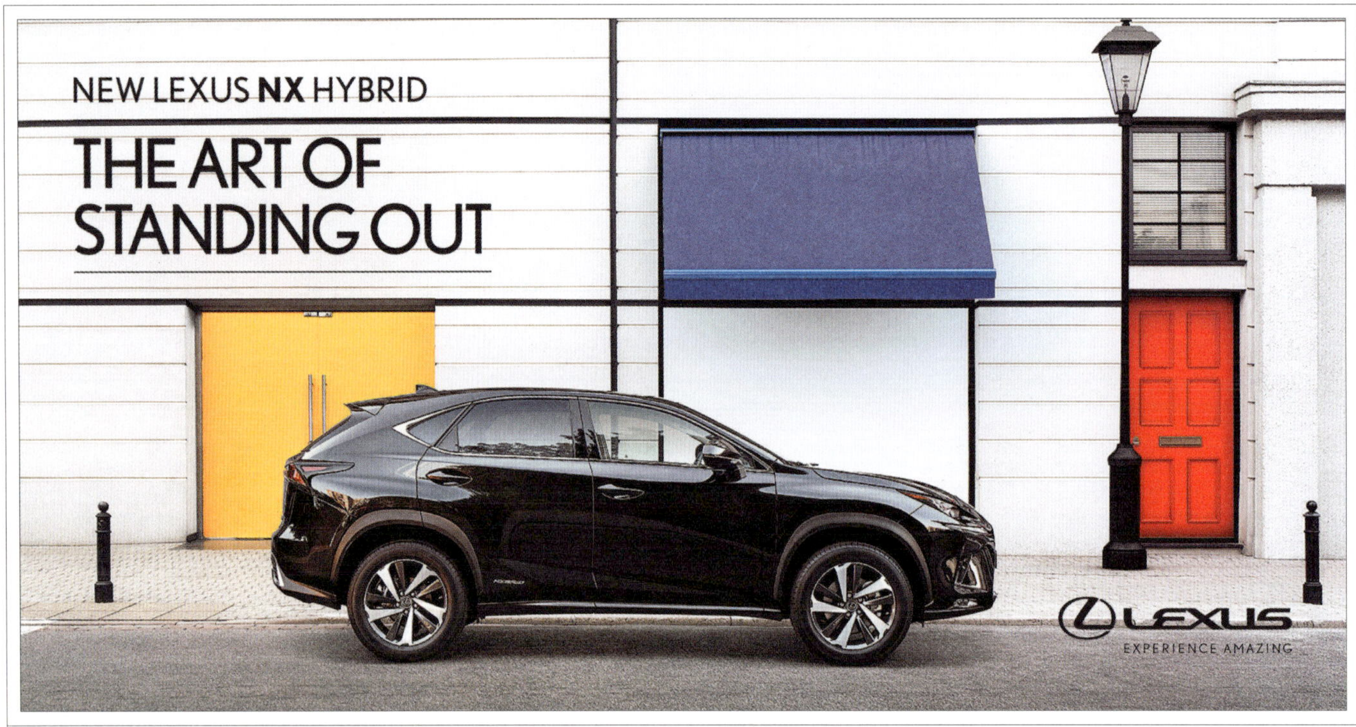

"Lexus;" Client: Lexus; Agency: The & Partnership; Photographer: Calle Stoltz; CGI & Retouching Artist: Curious Studio

What inspired or motivated you into your career?
When I was 13, I chanced upon two books sitting on the bookshelves in the art department at school. These were 'Milton Glaser Graphic Design' and 'Roger Dean – Views'. I loved these books and wanted to emulate the work within them. It was at this point I knew I wanted to be a designer.

What is your work philosophy?
It's very simple. Make brave, bold, creative work by collaborating with the very best people and be genuine and kind in the process.

Who is or was your greatest mentor?
I was fortunate enough to spend time with the late, great Alan Fletcher early in my career. He was an inspiration both on a personal level and in helping me define the sort of work I wanted to do.

What is it about advertising that you are most passionate about?
Other than the cast of colorful characters I've met and the fun I've had along the way, the sort of advertising that resonates with me has the ability to entertain, persuade, and change people's perceptions and opinions. Above all, I passionately believe that advertising has to be memorable.

What is the most difficult challenge you've had to overcome?
Admitting to myself that I can't do everything.

What would be your dream assignment?
Designing and art directing the Pirelli Calendar.

Who were some of your greatest past influences?
Milton Glaser and Roger Dean were the earliest influences, but I have always greatly admired the design work of Paul Rand, Massimo Vignelli, Herb Lubalin, Saul Bass and, of course, Alan Fletcher. My passion for advertising has been stoked by George Lois, Helmut Krone, Robert Brownjohn, Armando Testa, and David Abbott.

Who among your contemporaries today do you most admire?
At Curious, I'm fortunate to be surrounded by a rich diversity of talent but outside those walls I'm a big fan of Pentagram, Lippincott, and Superunion. From the world of advertising art direction it's Mark Denton, Dave Dye, and Alexandra Taylor. My favourite copywriter is Paul Burke and my favourite photographers are Nick Knight, Jonathan Knowles, and Giles Revell. In typography it's the powerful work of Neville Brody, Alan Kitching, and Jonathan Hoefler. From film, Ridley Scott, Quentin Tarantino, and Peter Greenaway and finally I love the illustrations of Mat Maitland, Maria Rivens and Sir Peter Blake.

What are the most important ingredients you require from a client to do successful work?
Creative people work best with clients when there is openness and integrity from the get-go. It's vital that you like and understand the client and vice-versa. I also believe that the best relationships flourish once the meeting is over and you all decide to carry on chatting further over a big glass of red

What is your proudest professional achievement?
Waking up every day happy in the knowledge that I make my living from doing what I really love. That's a rare privilege.

Has there ever been a client or a project that surprised you?
I devised and produced a very successful piece of communication for Parker Pens when I was working at another agency. I then left that agency and joined Curious. About 18 months later, I got an email out of the blue from a company in India saying that they'd loved my work for Parker and would I be interested in talking to them about future advertising work. I was then on a plane to Mumbai to meet the clients and we've been working with them ever since. Yes, we all have to find work but now and again, work finds you.

What is the greatest satisfaction you get from your work?
The thrill of seeing work in which I've been involved appear

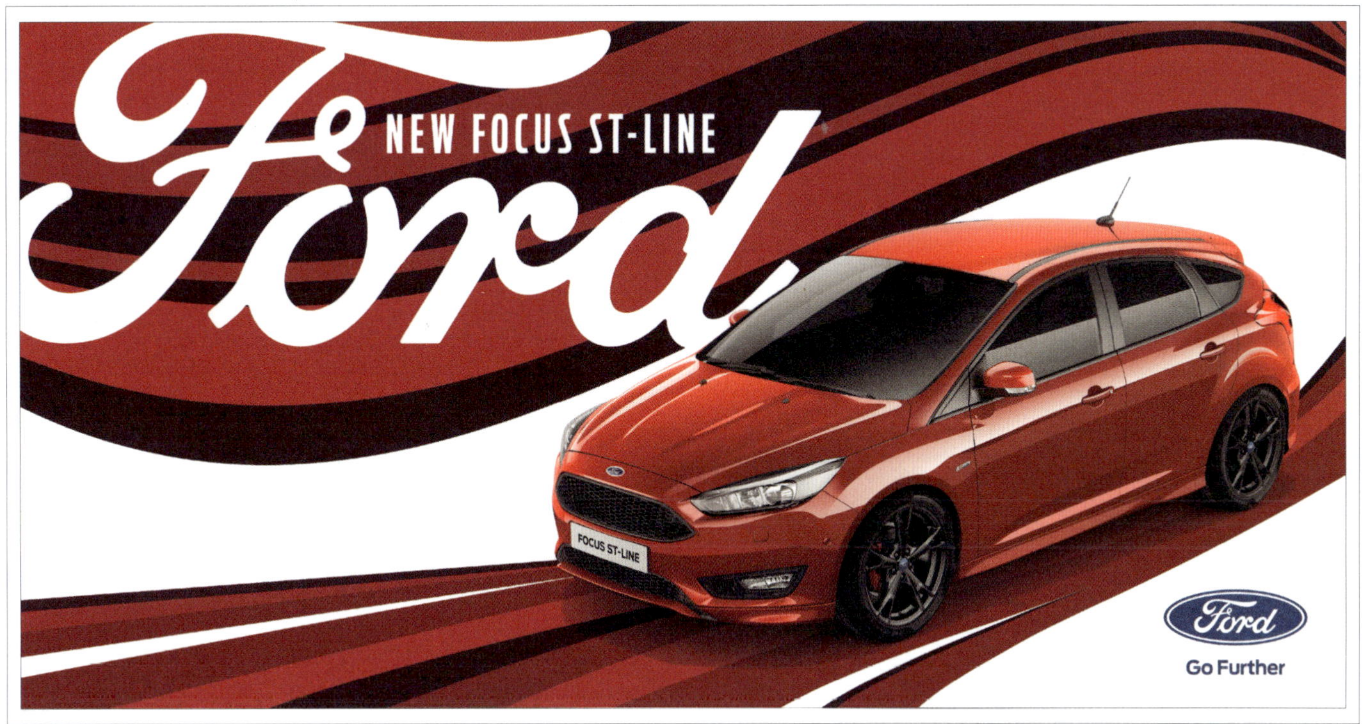

"Ford Focus;" Client: Ford; Agency: GTB; CGI & Retouching Artist: Curious Studio

out there in real life. It gets me every time. Contributing to the world's visual culture is endlessly gratifying.

What part of your work do you find most demanding?
It's often very demanding working via Zoom or email. Wherever possible, I prefer to talk directly or meet face-to-face — this is not always possible, especially when a project is in production. I find this part of my job challenging, particularly when unplanned amendments ping into your inbox. Across the ether, things can often get lost in translation between client, agency and creative. Also, my internal 'bullshit' detector is now so finely tuned that it often knows that an eighty-page PowerPoint presentation could have been nailed in eight.

What is something you wish you had known when you first started out?
Get everything down in writing and know when to walk away.

What advice would you have for students starting out today?
Understand that it's okay to make mistakes and always focus on the idea before the execution.

What do you value most?
I cherish my wife, my son and my daughter above all else. The happy times we share keep me grounded and remind me just how precious life is. For me, love and laughter are the keys to happiness and I'm blessed to have three people who provide those things every day. Other than my family, my most treasured possession is my imagination. Without it, I could never have enjoyed such an interesting and rewarding career.

What would you change if you had to do it all over again?
Very little. I've been extremely fortunate in the choices I've made. To a certain extent, I believe you make your own luck, so when I've realised things aren't making me happy I've always moved in a different direction.

Where do you seek inspiration?
Other than my family, friends and colleagues, I have a huge collection of books on art, advertising, film and design. I love nothing more than sinking into a comfy chair and losing myself in their pages, soaking up the words and images like a sponge.

How do you define success?
Quite simply knowing that my contributions to both my home and working lives have made a positive difference. With work, if something I have done changes behavior or challenges convention then that's a great outcome. My health and financial stability are obviously important, but I really love what I do and this is what defines me. Add in a little luck and that should yield success.

Where do you see yourself in the future?
Apart from continuing to nurture my family and watch my children grow, I hope to continue to make things. I have the good fortune to work at Curious, creating, producing, and delivering work that resonates with other people. I feel fortunate to have a career that, if it weren't my job it would be my hobby. Long may it continue.

Curious Productions www.curious-productions.co.uk

CONTRIBUTING TO THE WORLD'S VISUAL CULTURE IS ENDLESSLY GRATIFYING.

John Fairley, *Design Director, Curious Productions*

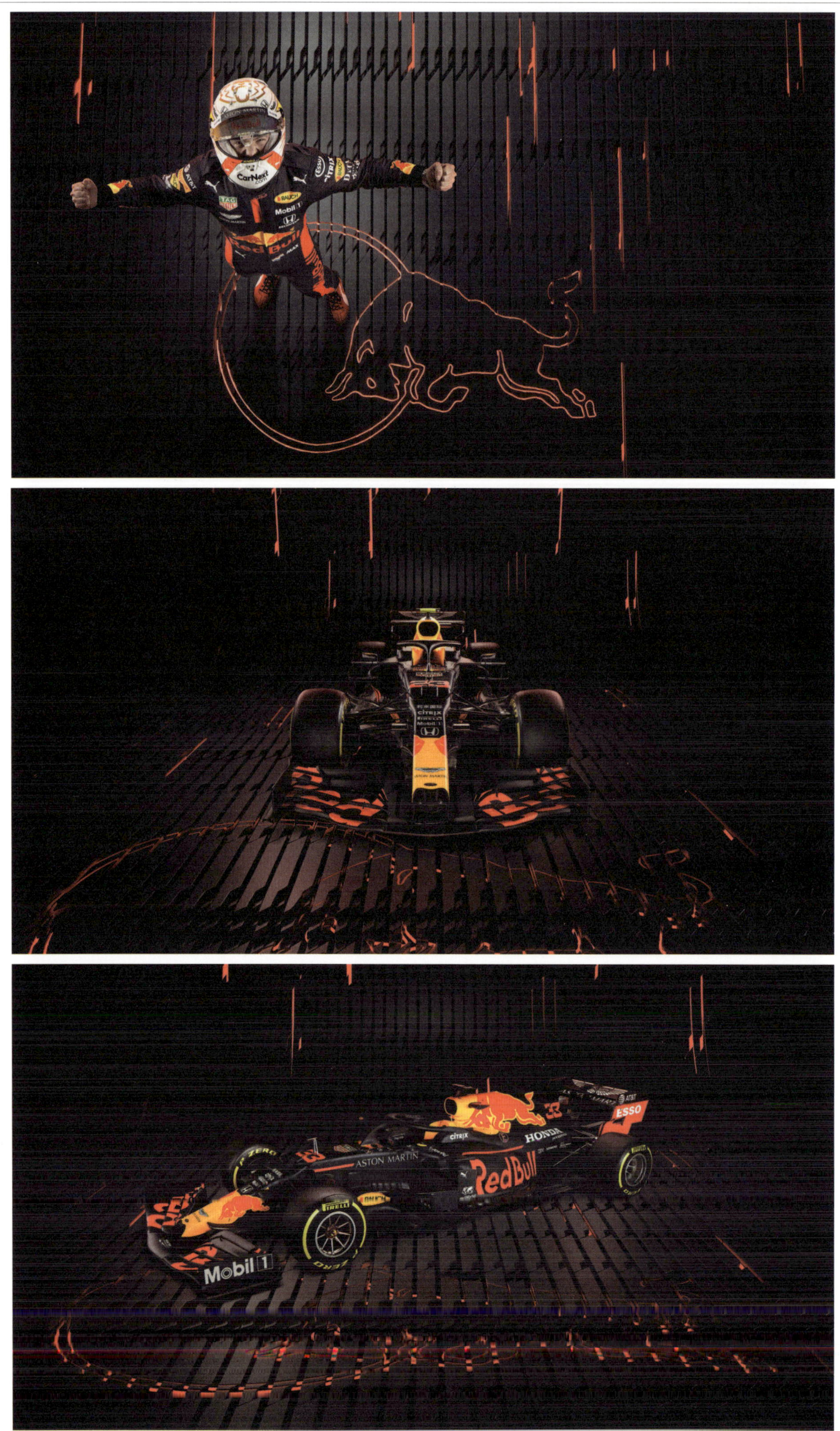

Red Bull; Client: Red Bull; Photographer (Drivers): Dustin Snipes; Photographer (Cars): Thomas Butler; CGI & Retouching Artist: Curious Studio

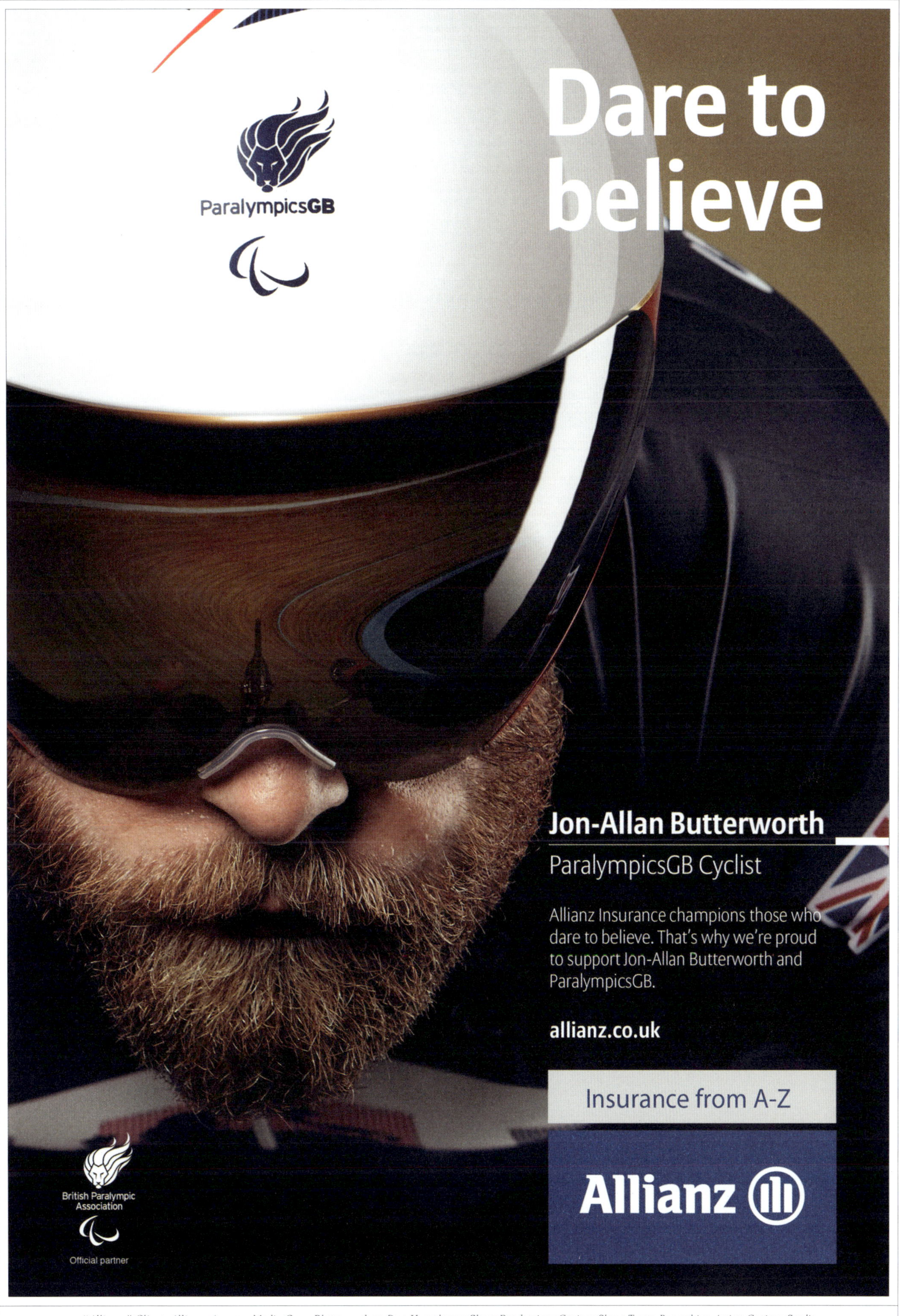

"Allianz;" Client: Allianz; Agency: Media Com; Photographer: Dan Humphreys; Shoot Production: Curious Shoot Team; Retouching Artist: Curious Studio

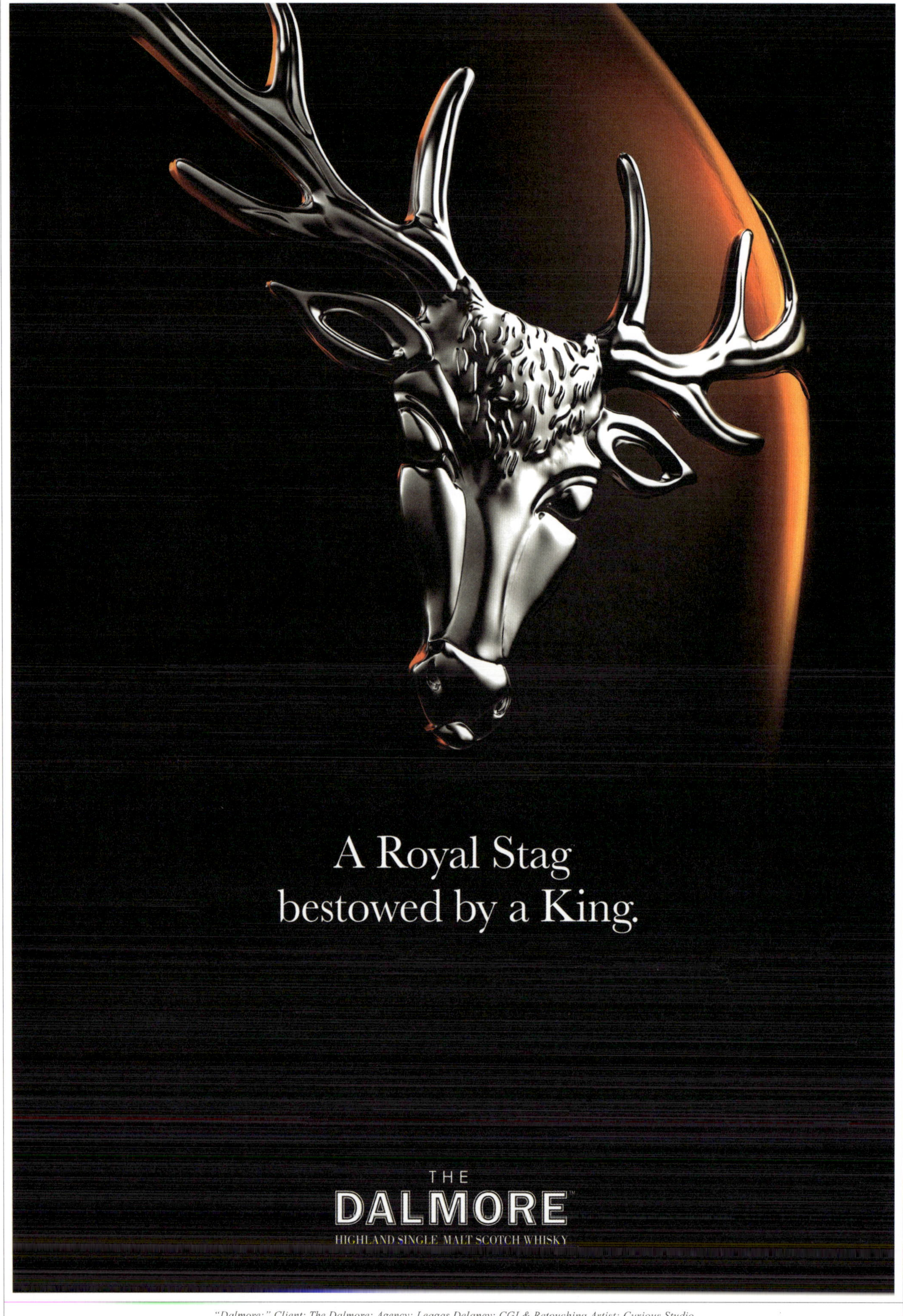

"Dalmore;" Client: The Dalmore; Agency: Leagas Delaney; CGI & Retouching Artist: Curious Studio

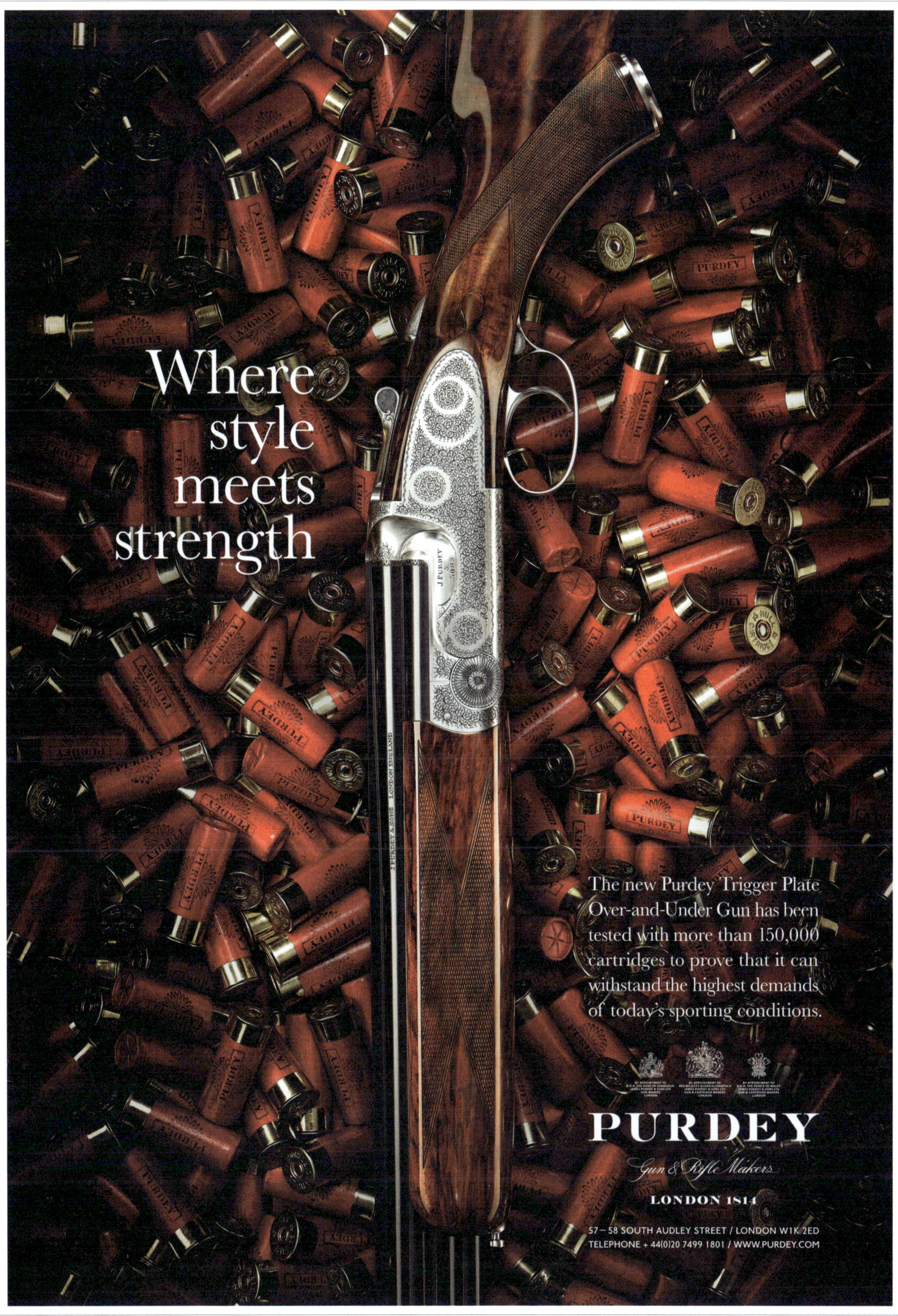

Client: James Purdey & Sons; Creative Director: John Fairley; Photographer: Dan Humphreys; Shoot Production: Curious Shoot Team; Retouching Artist: Curious Studio

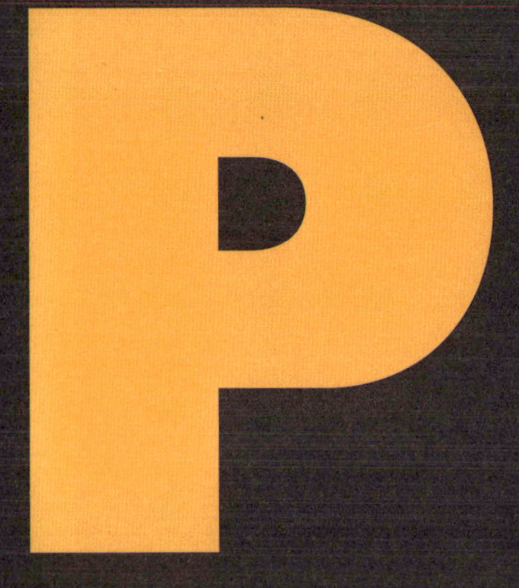

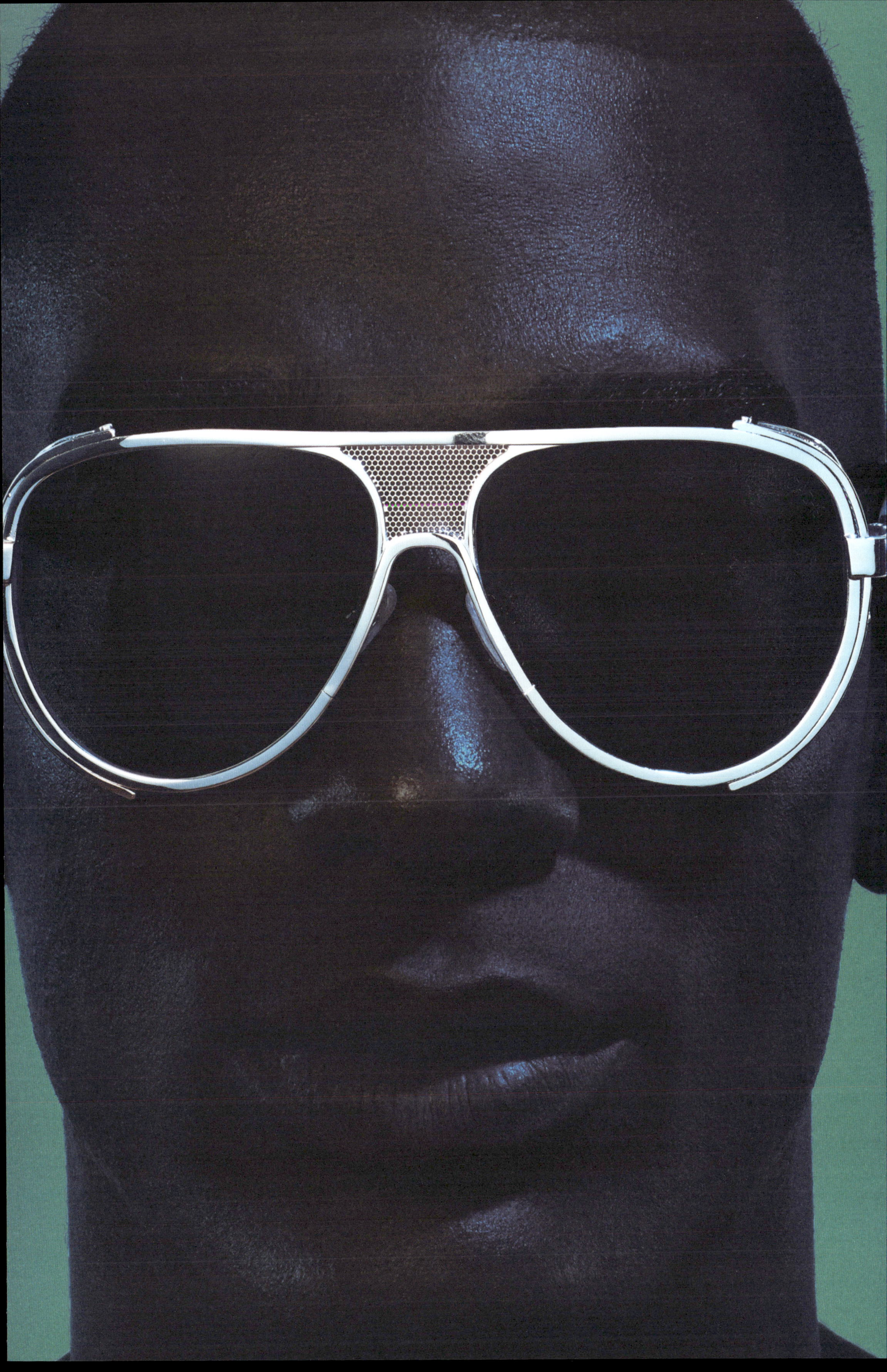

ATHENA ALWAYS HAS ELECTRIC ENERGY
AND BOUNDLESS IDEAS FOR HER PROJECTS.
I AM ALWAYS ASTONISHED BY HER UNIQUE,
POETIC, AND POWERFUL CREATIONS.

Robert Stevens, *Former Int'l Photo Editor, Time Magazine; Former Editor, Life Picture Collection*

ATHENA BRINGS A WONDERFUL ENERGY TO SET. SHE
HAS A CLEAR VISION OF WHAT SHE WANTS
BUT ISN'T AFRAID TO EXPERIMENT IN THE
CREATIVE PROCESS. A RARE COMBINATION!

Aurelie Jezequel, *Executive Producer, Ajproductionsny, inc.*

SHE IS ONE OF MY FAVORITE PHOTOGRAPHERS
TO WORK WITH. SHE UNDERSTANDS LIGHT,
COMPOSITION AND HAS THE ABILITY TO CAPTURE
THE EMOTIONS OF SUBJECTS BETTER THAN
ANY PHOTOGRAPHER I'VE EVER KNOWN.

Sandy Armeni, *Fashion Director, Harper's Bazaar Greece*

HFR WORK IS VISUALLY ARRESTING AND BEAUTIFUL!
FROM THE FIRST DAY I SAW IT I WONDERED WHO
WAS THE PHOTOGRAPHER THAT DID THIS. BRILLIANT!

B. Martin Pedersen, *Designer*

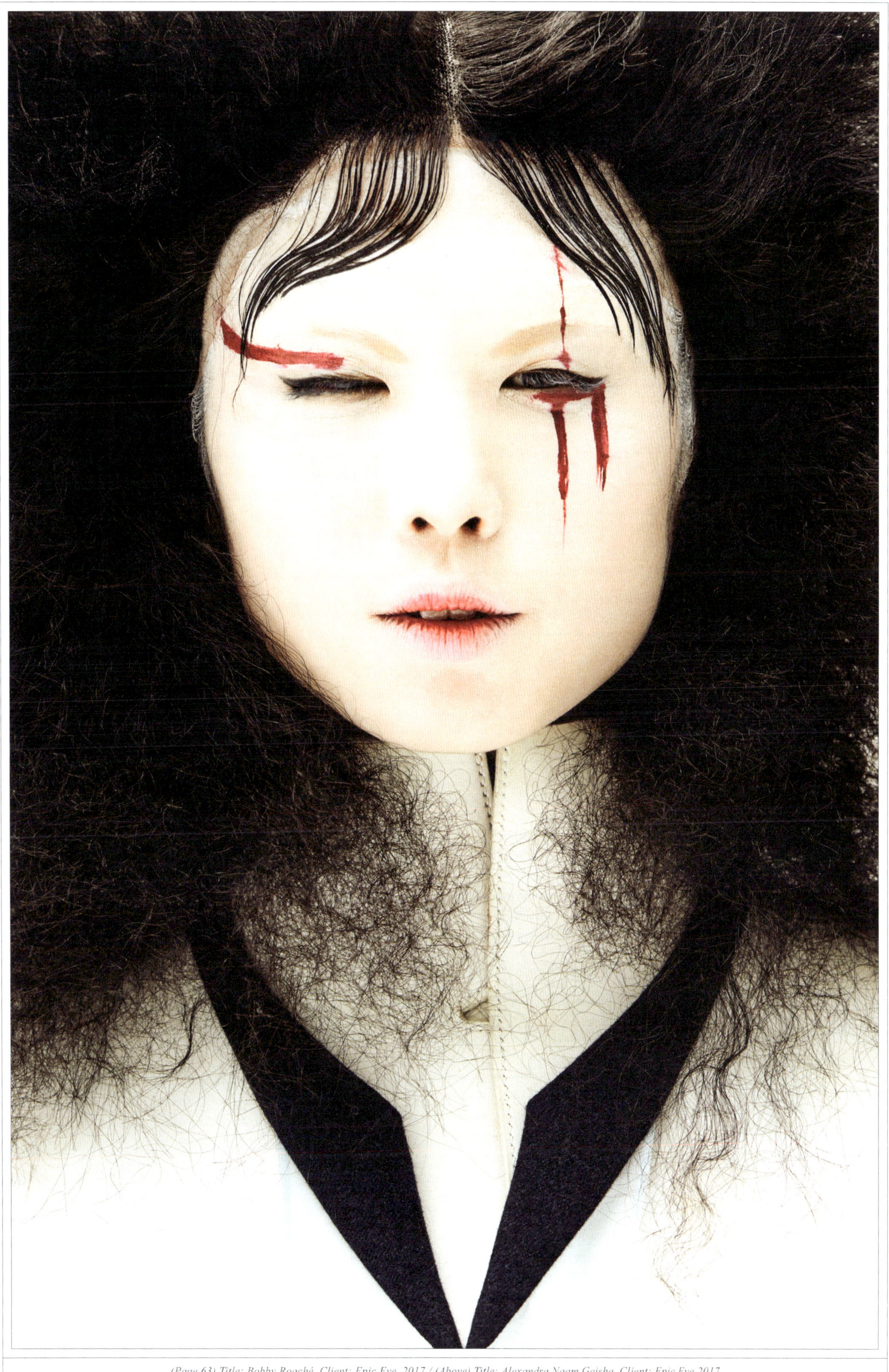

(Page 63) Title: Bobby Roaché, Client: Epic Eye, 2017 / (Above) Title: Alexandra Naam Geisha, Client: Epic Eye 2017

Introduction by **Toshiaki & Hisa Ide,** *Founder/Partner/Exec. Creative Director, & Design Director, IF Studio*

We have worked together with Athena for 7 years now. She is a great talent in the creative field. Design today is all about collaboration and, unlike the 90's or early 2000's, you can't rely on craftmanship only. One needs to be flexible and collaborative. The overall look and feel is critical. We collaborate and work together to make something great. ▪ Athena brings in charisma and positive energy once she steps into the room. We may not always agree, but the creative collaboration is easy—a conversation explored from many perspectives. Influenced by her work in theater, film, and photojournalism, Athena's photography stands out in that she dives into storytelling and expresses the theatricality of a moment in a single frame. ▪ Her work goes deeper than the 2-dimensional photographic print. She facilitates and expresses the entire design process at IF Studio as the Associate Creative Director. She develops the design concept, understands the product, and incorporates the marketing and advertising goals while balancing the budget and communicating with the creative and client teams—which is quite unique. Her strength is this multifaceted approach while still expressing a sense of relationship and an emotional connection to design.

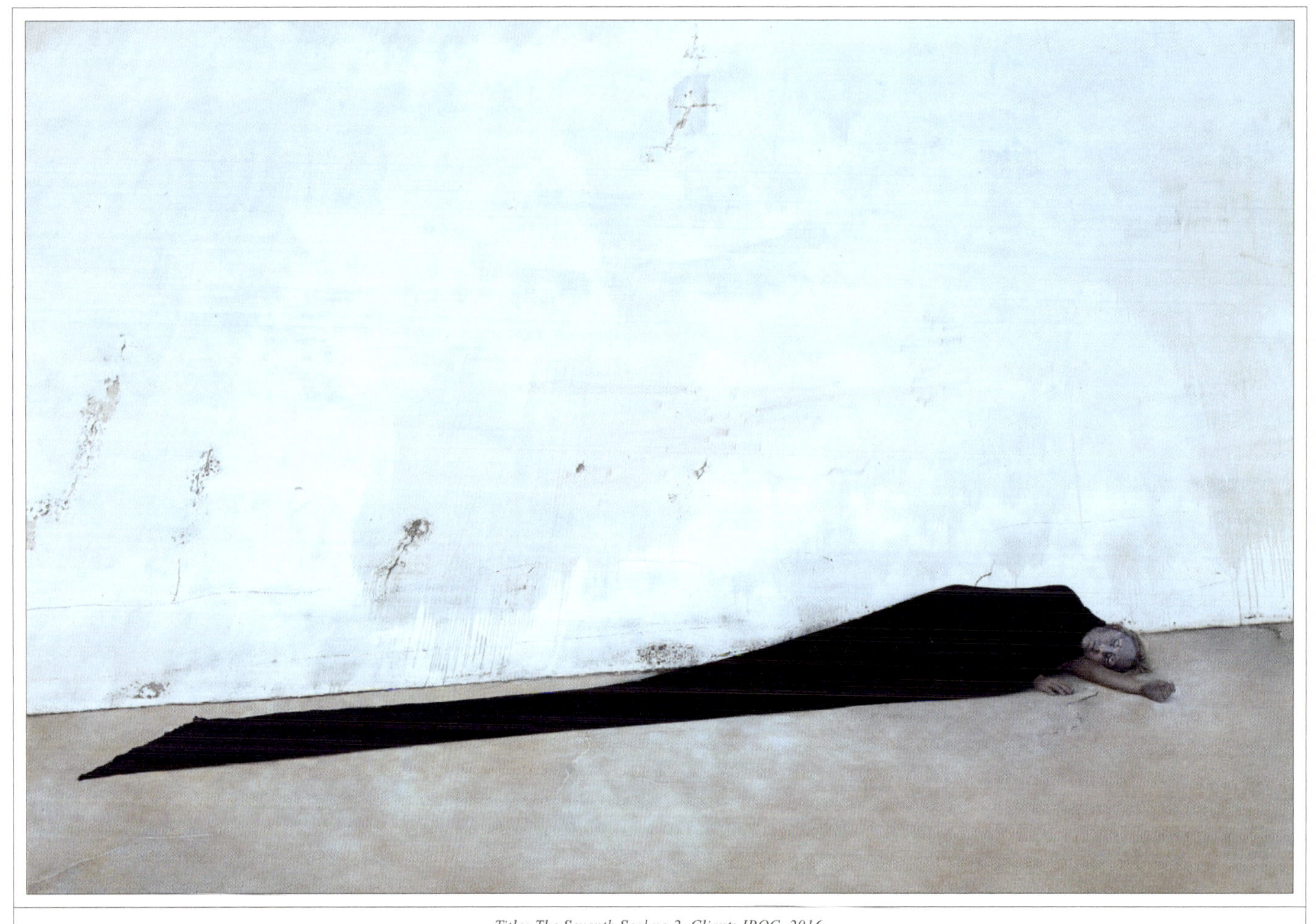

Title: The Seventh Seal no.2, Client: IBOC, 2016

IF YOU FIND YOURSELF SAYING "BUT" OR "IF" OR "I'M TRYING", NO MORE EXCUSES! GET CREATIVE!

Athena Azevedo, *Photographer & Associate Creative Director, IF Studio*

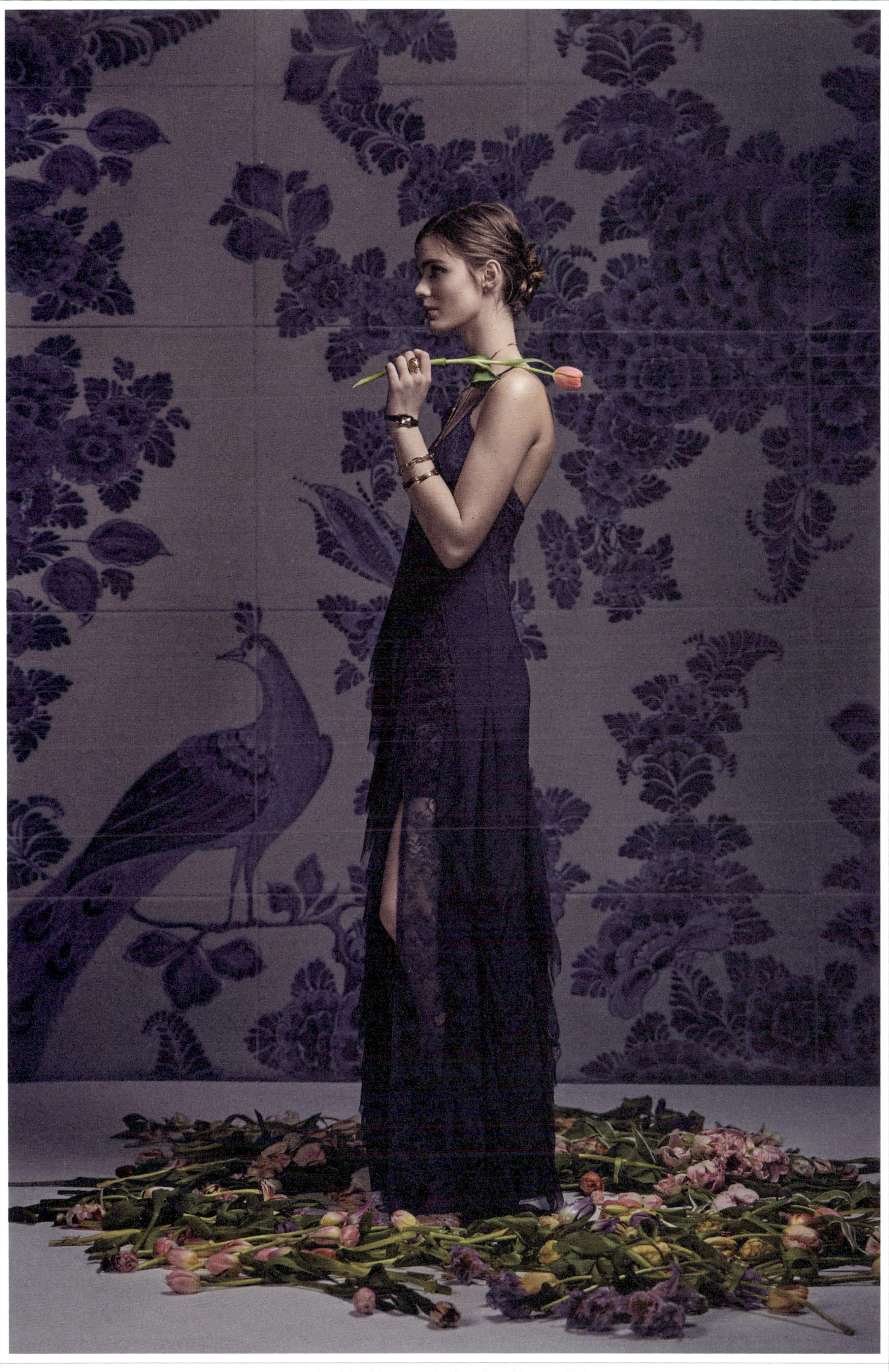

Title: 19 Dutch Portrait no.1, Client: Carmel Partners, 2018

What inspired or motivated you into your career?
For as long as I can remember I was an artist. I loved to draw and paint; it became a big part of my identity. As a child, after visiting the NYC museums, a big goal of mine was to exhibit in art museums. I did a biographical report in the fifth grade on Georgia O'Keeffe and it was then that I learned that a female artist could have such an elegant life and impactful career. That was an important seed of motivation.

At age 8 I took my first photograph with my grandmother's camera and fell in love with the magic of the medium. When I was 18 my Uncle gave me his old T101 Minolta with a broken light meter. I loved taking photographs. That camera accompanied me everywhere for years. Then I got a job at a print development shop, I worked as a photojournalist for the university newspaper, and I consistently photographed marketing material for a non-profit performing arts center.

Later in NYC, I met Bruce Davidson in a difficult moment. He was one of my photography heroes. That encounter resulted in a sweet friendship. He looked out for me and encouraged me. I'll always remember him saying to me, "Hang in there, kid"

What is your work philosophy?
Within the creative department at the studio, we quote the Andy Warhol phrase: "Don't think about making art, just get it done. Let everyone else decide if it's good or bad, whether they love it or hate it." If you want to produce and ultimately grow then you can't afford to get hung up on yourself. Other important work mantras: Know yourself. Stay flexible and present to the situation. Take action and keep listening. Take ownership and trust your collaborators.

Who is or was your greatest mentor?
My parents taught me to celebrate creativity as an exercise in integrating one's spiritual, intellectual, and physical aspects. They encouraged curiosity and empowerment through community engagement and communication. They also demonstrated that a career path could be an act of creation – it doesn't have to be "standard" or "expected." A pointed vision coupled with an open mind, persistence, and patience can yield adventuresome results. Other mentors lasted for a short moment but made a big impact, like Bruce Davidson. Dave Martin, Louisa Etter, Karen Lovass, Janet Delaney, and Ken Light were teachers that gave me the tools for the craft and a greater knowledge of communication and art practice.

Amy Frankel, the managing partner at IF Studio, has been an important mentor for the business and marketing side of the industry. My greatest creative professional mentor is the genius designer Toshiaki Ide. (I am lucky Hisa Ide shares him with me!) We've worked together now for 7 years. Sometimes he gives me a hard time, he pushes me beyond my comfort zone.

The first projects we conceptualized were some social justice posters, and the first Brazilian Opera poster for the non-profit I run. He helped me take my photography to the next level through choosing the strongest image in the edit. Selecting the most graphic image taught me how to photograph with the needs of the product and ad campaign in mind. He has advocated for my growth by consistently assigning projects to me.

What is it about photography that you are most passionate about?
The best photographs are taken with a forgotten question. They become answers to it. As a photographer, you and your team are the conduits for what needs to be communicated. There is something zen about photographing because you have to balance the conscious goal, and at the same time, leave your subconscious to find and capture the image that has the most

impact. Photography is about all the elements coming together in one moment of harmony. It's the ultimate collaboration between opposites: light and shadow, subject and photographer, motion and stillness, teamwork and individualism. It's the articulated space between things. I find photography to be very profound and exciting.

What has been your most memorable project?
There have been many memorable projects. I remember "15 Renwick Penthouse." It was the first high-stake project that I was awarded at IF Studio, on the shoulders of the extremely successful campaign with the photographer Henry Leutwyler – who is also a Graphis Master. We had a fantastic team and there was a lot of pressure there. The final images still bring me joy.

However, the most memorable project for me was the photography for "The Seventh Seal" opera posters. It was a minimal team: the model, the make-up artist, all natural sunlight and myself in front of the National Museum in Brasilia. The focus and integrity necessary in a project like that still fills me with pride. This project also took my work to the Museum of Modern Art in Stockholm (Moderna).

What is the most difficult challenge you've had to overcome?
Starting up my career in NYC was very challenging and it took years to feel some sense of substance and accomplishment from it. The 12-year journey was laced with difficult periods for different reasons. At the moment of this interview, I'm currently experiencing the collectively difficult challenge of the Covid-19 pandemic. It's absolutely nerve-wracking.

How does working as an in-house photographer affect you creatively?
The main way that it affects me creatively is that I have to be flexible, and as a result I have a stylistically varied portfolio. For example, one project may require natural light, a soft focus and shutter drag while another job will require a hyper-stylized execution in order to naturally integrate computer illustrations. This certainly keeps me on my toes and I'd like to think that, as a result, my signature is seen in the way that I approach storytelling rather than in one given technique.

I work in an environment where I have deep relationships and constant communication not only with my creative teams but also with the account team. We are always working together and responding directly to the client needs. Sometimes it is very obvious that we are operating as "one brain." The boundaries blur. We've developed the concept. By the time the shoot day comes, I know the ins and outs of the product. The whole creative process is very integrated and I think this helps a lot in communicating the brand even down to the details.

Who were some of your greatest past influences?
As mentioned before, Georgia O'Keefe, her husband Alfred Stieglitz, and the movement of artists they built around them. Henri Cartier-Bresson was a phenomenon – as a photojournalist, he could capture the essence of the story simultaneously with a highly graphic image full of movement. Richard Avedon inspires me to bring out the personality of the models with a balance between calculated image and spontaneity. I love how dynamic his images are – like dance, there is a lot of "performance" in his photographs – even when they are portraits.

Irving Penn for his poetry and composition, and the way that he could elevate all his subjects to something mysterious and iconic. Pierre Verger, who was French but made Brazil his home and documented the people with a deep strength and respect. He approached photography like an anthropologist.

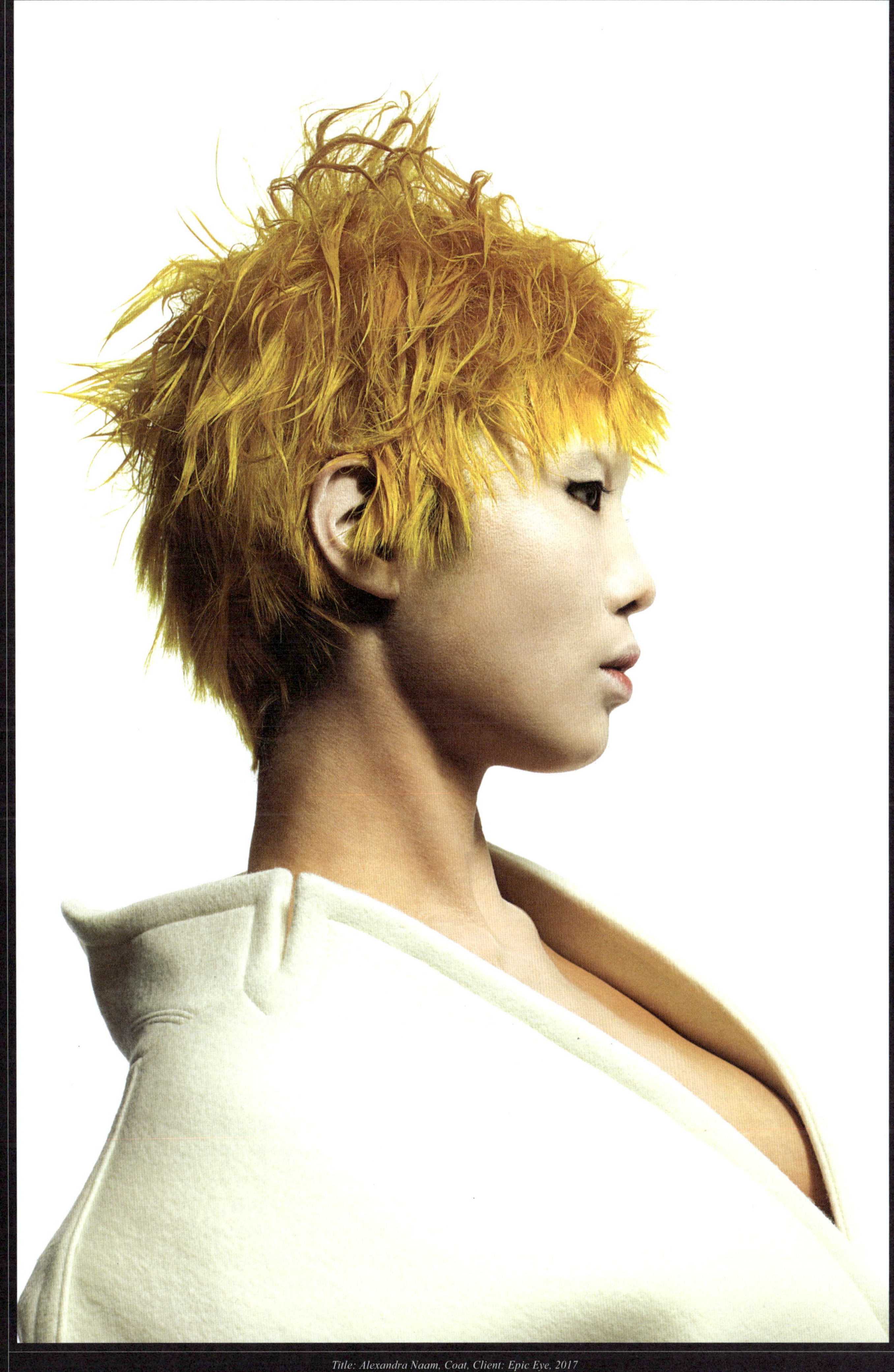

Title: Alexandra Naam, Coat, Client: Epic Eye, 2017

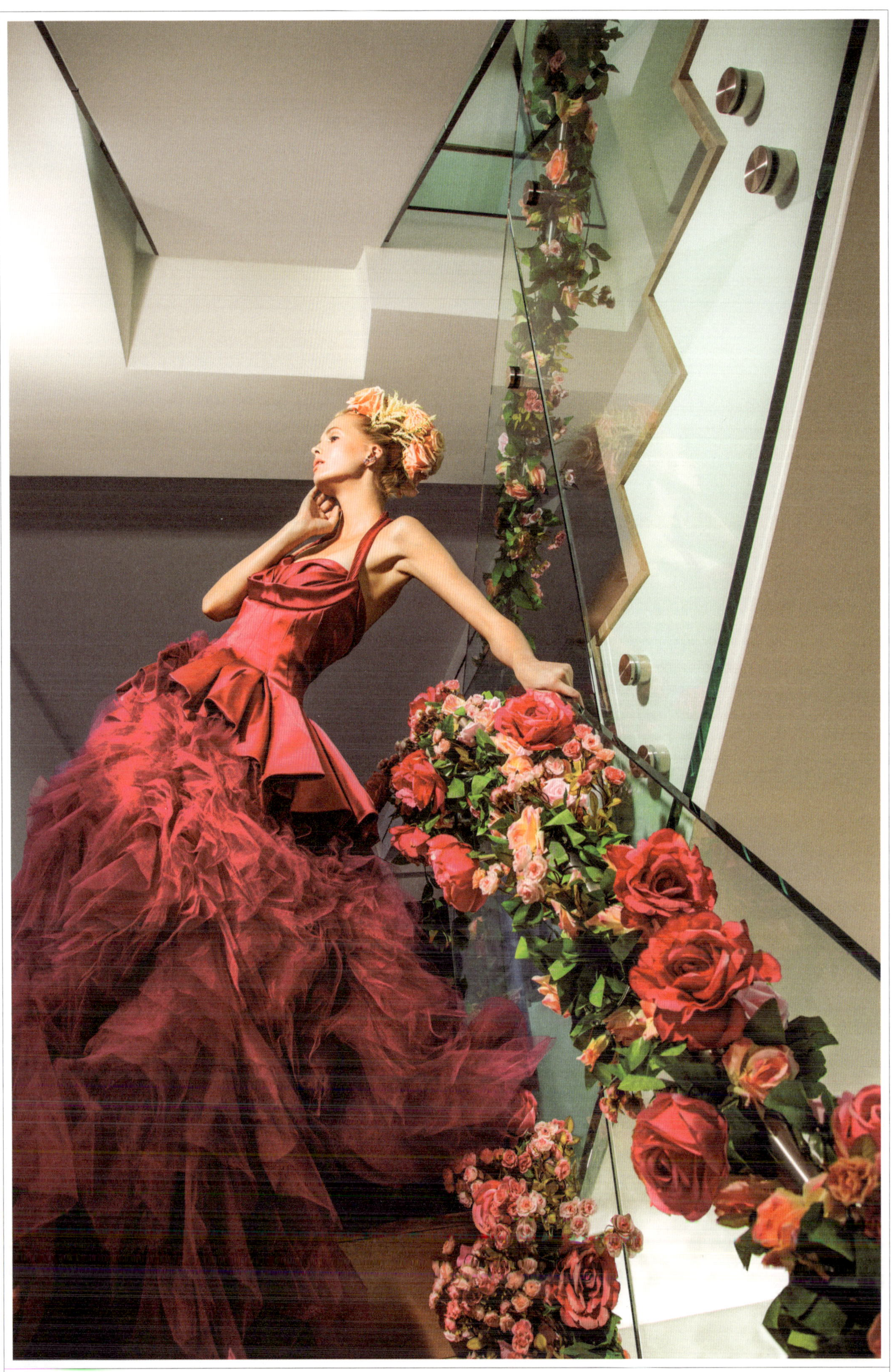

Title: 15 Renwick Staircase, Client: IGI US, 2016

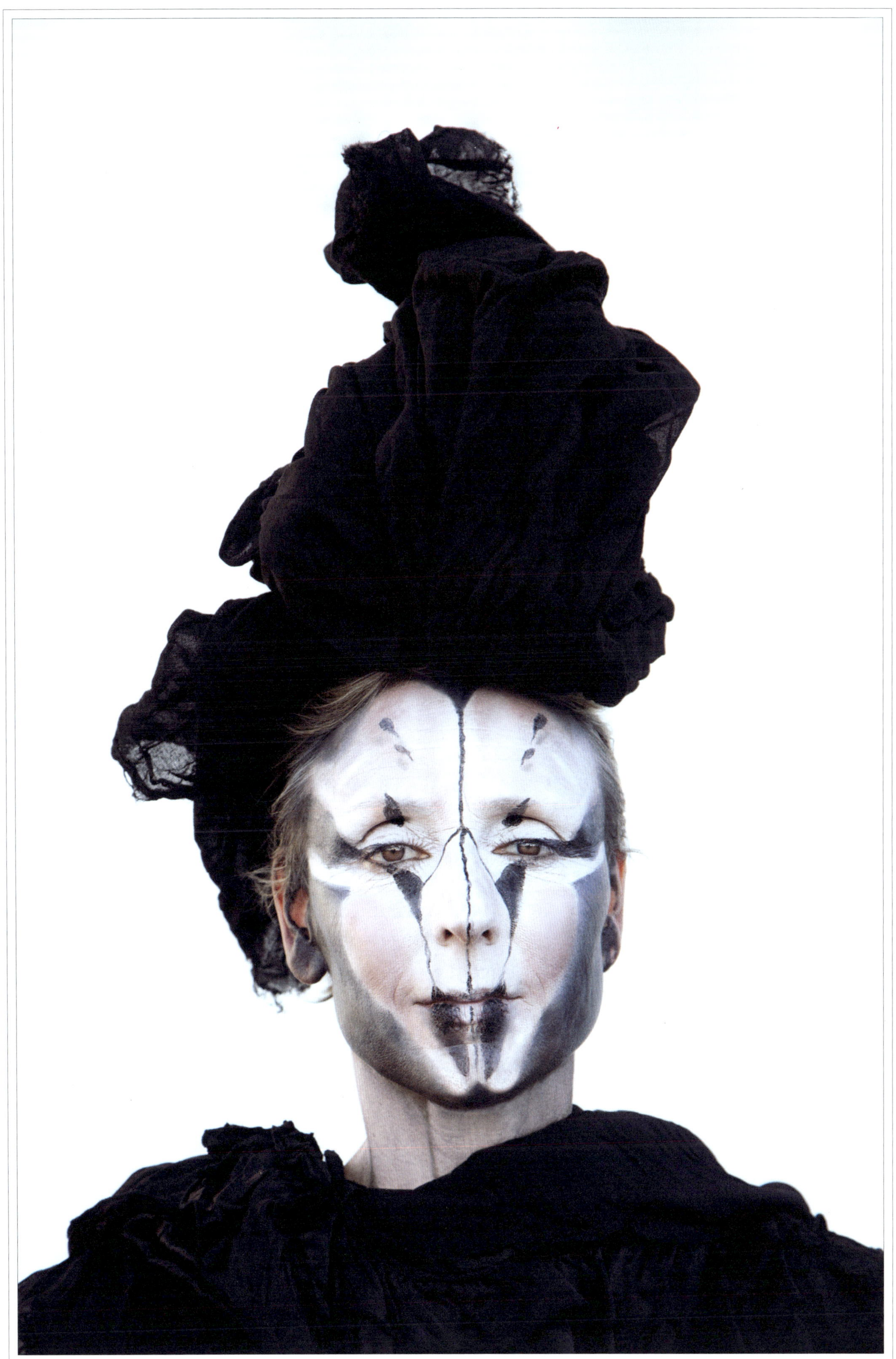

Title: The Seventh Seal no.1. Client: IBOC, 2016

I love Herb Ritz for his strong graphic images and dramatic natural light.

Who among your contemporaries today do you most admire?
This is a difficult question. The Magnum photographer, David Alan Harvey, who created Burn Magazine (ten years ago he was throwing epic photography parties at his loft in Williamsburg), Bess Greenburg who ran a four year standing pop-up gallery called 25CPW, and Alan Chin who is a co-founder of Red Hook Editions. I admire them as photographers who built a community around them and have given opportunities to others despite the extremely competitive environment. They hold a higher value of humanism. In commercial and fashion work, there is the Polish photographer Dominik Tarabanksi. He is always working to achieve poetry with his images and has a distinct and refined style.

There is the Chinese photographer Chen Man. Her work is exquisite and I love how she represents women as powerful and sexy. I admire her for being a fearless female with a distinguished creative voice. For similar reasons I admire Laurie Frankel, Donna Ferrato, Dominique Isserman, Annie Leibovitz and Ellen von Unwerth. We also happen to be alive at a time when photography is still relatively new so there are still many major influencers of the field that are alive, some are even in their 80s or 90s. I almost feel embarrassed to say they are my contemporaries since they have careers that are double my lifetime under their belts. To name a few that I admire: Hiro, Nick Knight, Tim Walker, Sebastião Salgado. Then there is Steven Meisel - who both synthesizes influences from the greats and created his own unique voice that isn't afraid to make statements about his politics and beliefs. Such is similar with David LaChapelle – who I've grown to appreciate as a true artist.

What would be your dream assignment?
As a career milestone, I'd love to do a series of cover and feature stories with Vanity Fair, Vogue, or one of the top fashion magazines. It means a lot to me when I can find ways to make the worlds I love merge. It would be a dream to have one of our operas produced at a major opera house and then be tasked to creative direct and execute on the staging and projection art, and then photograph the poster and marketing material. Then the ultimate fulfillment of a childhood dream would be to have a solo exhibition in MOMA or Photographisk. That would mean that I've really built a significant body of work at a consistently high level and have effectively touched and communicated with people.

Who have been some of your favorite people
or clients you have worked with?
The team at IF Studio are certainly some of my favorite people. It's enjoyable to go to work every day and to develop brands and campaigns from start to finish. I'm also really grateful that we work with lovely vendors who have become like old friends and allies in success: my line producers Aurelie Jezequel, Angelika Saint Aignan, and Amy Yu. Then there are the stylists that have become like family: Sandy Armeni and Yui Ishibashi. Client wise, the best are those that know what they want and trust us to fully execute on an idea and to take some risk. They become our champions and advocates and keep us motivated, even when communicating their needs. Carmel Partners, Zeckendorf, Standard Group, and Compass are clients that have worked with us to push the envelope in the marketplace – which is always exciting for the agency. Ryan Serhant, the super broker from HBO's Million Dollar Listing has been a fantastic client. He is always clear on what he is ask-

ing for, trusts the creative and gives precise and simple feedback. The creative is more impactful because it stems from the first creative instinct, which is usually very pure and effective.

What is your proudest professional achievement?
Getting honored with the Graphis Master's designation.

What is the greatest satisfaction you get from your work?
It's a fantastic feeling when both you and the client are excited about the creative process and the results. Those are the moments when the entire team celebrates together. Then there is the day-to-day satisfaction, and the humor and humanity that my colleagues and I share when we interact with one another.

What part of your work do you find most demanding?
I love the action when we are creating; so even though production time is highly intense, the passion to photograph keeps driving me. In contrast, I actually find the more tedious things to be the most demanding. For example, record keeping, receipts, and filing – I really have to "sit myself down" in order to keep organized.

What professional goals do you still have for yourself?
For the first two years at university I was a cinema major. I'd like to loop back to that beginning and conceptualize and direct the moving image for commercials, film, and theater.

What is something you wish you had known
when you first started out?
I would have asked more for what I wanted sooner in order to align my work with my actual talents. I grew up in a single mom household, so I had learned to hold back on expressing some desires so as to not burden the family budget. As a consequence, within the workplace, it took me a while to differentiate unnecessary self-sacrifice from the power of genuine contribution.

What advice would you have for student photographers
starting out today?
As a student, first recognize that you are in a phase that affords you the luxury to experiment and build your base skills and follow your interests, – these will service you as you move forward. Second, learn to draw and paint to sharpen your ability to see. Third, learn to produce – whether that is for you or for others. There is nothing worse than sending your work out to art buyers, editors, and contests and never hearing back – this can leave you feeling distressed and depressed. Waiting for someone to produce for you is a mistake, if you have a great idea, just do it. Make it happen however you can – it's the experience and expanding work that you'll be making that will keep you fresh. Eventually more of those outside opportunities will come. I've produced some of my best work with the conditions of limited resources; so if you find yourself saying "but" or "if" or "I'm trying", no more excuses! Get creative!

You're also the Executive Director of the International Brazilian Opera Company. Can you tell us a little about how and why you became interested in opera?
I never thought that I would be a founder and executive director of an opera company; however, I had a desire from about age 13 to create and run an international art's non profit that would connect people from around the globe. I also grew up in a household that appreciated all types of music. We were encouraged to freely play with the many instruments that we had in the house. Then I met João MacDowell, who would later become my husband, and while we were dating it became

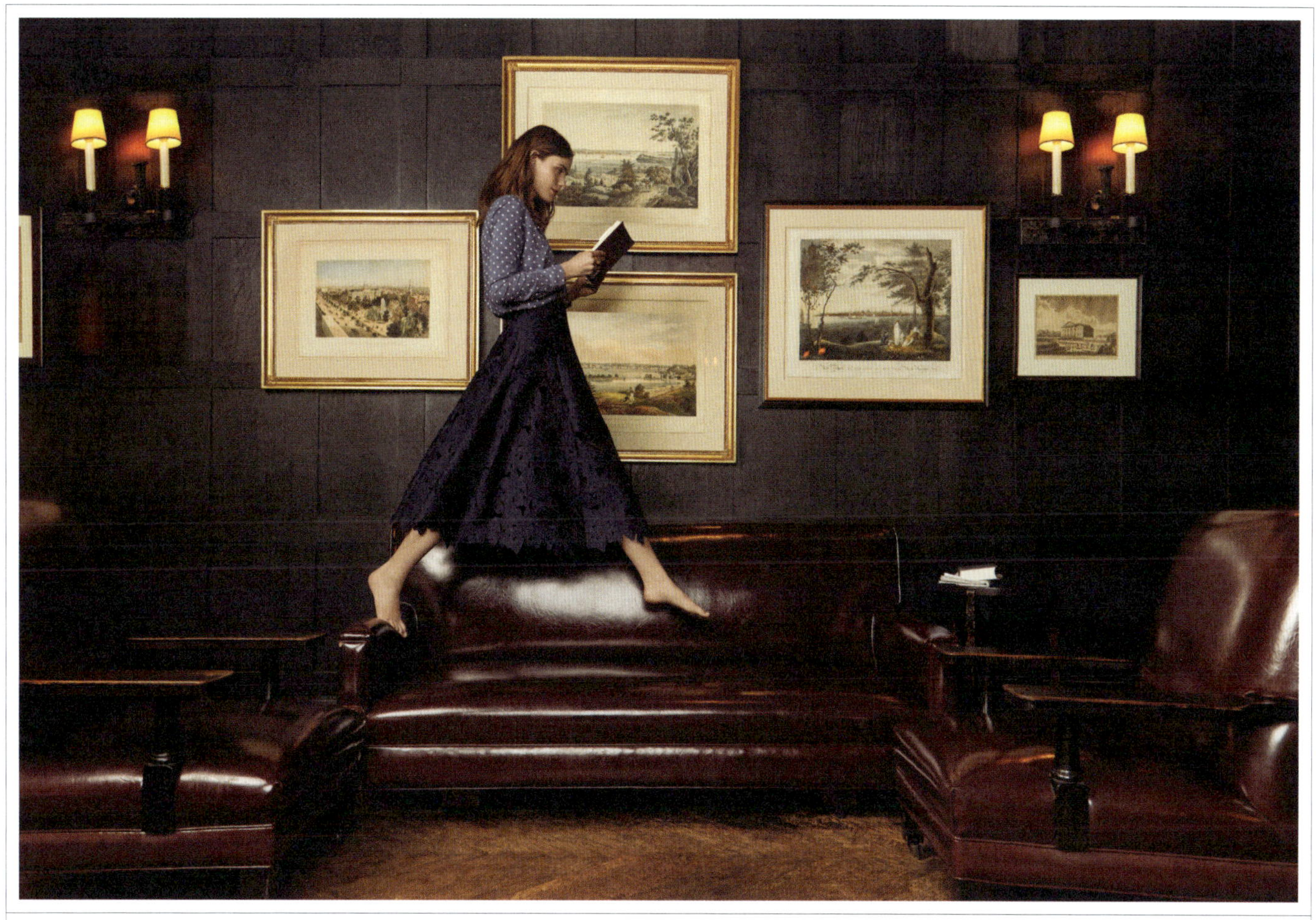

Title: 19 Dutch Book, Client: Carmel Partners, 2018

apparent that he had the ambition to start an opera company; so, I said, "Let's do it!" He already had a really supportive network of creatives; so after the first company concert we were able to put funds down to establish the organization as an official 501c3. It's been a fantastic journey and we've presented in NYC, Stockholm, and São Paulo. For the past 5 years that we've been developing "The Seventh Seal" into an opera, we've had close contact with Ingmar Bergman's legacy, philosophy, and body of work. Bergman loved opera. I've grown to love the opera because it unites all art forms. Being around theater and performers has made me a better photographer. It is all storytelling. Best of all, I get to apply my skills to set design, projection, and photographing for the posters. With Toshiaki and Hisa, we've conceived, photographed, and designed 6 opera posters.

What other interests do you have outside of your work?
Spending time with my family: my husband João and our daughter Indira. I love running and breathing in nature—it's great for clearing my mind. I actively keep our friend circles nurtured. Real time friendships are really important to me. Also, though we are New Yorkers, we try to go to our home in Brazil once a year.

What do you value most?
Love. It's the miracle of life.

What would you change if you had to do it all over again?
I wouldn't change anything. Somehow, when you look back, you see that everything you did and felt led to this moment. You know, you wouldn't even be able to think about how you would change the past if it hadn't occurred as it has. All of it, the suffering and the celebration is part of being alive. What we call "the past" is sort of an abstract thing; so, instead I work to see each day and each moment as a new creation. Of course, this is easier said than done.

Where do you seek inspiration?
With an open mind and curiosity, every encounter can be a source of inspiration. I'm inspired by nature, feminist theory, theater and dance, fashion, through studying great photographers and painters. It's just as inspiring to go to NYC's art museums and galleries as it is to walk on the city's streets or to stay home with my family. My husband João inspires me daily - composing for opera is a feat!

How do you define success?
I'm always striving to push myself to explore and develop my craft further. I predict that I will continue to have this aspect of me that is searching, creating new goals, and deepening my dreams. That said, I think that I am currently experiencing one of my great milestones of success, which is feeling confident in my abilities and career, and having a family.

Where do you see yourself in the future?
I see myself further enhancing and synthesizing the separate projects that I have been spinning. By that I mean using my experiences with the opera and "pure art" to make my commercial work more moving and, vice versa, using my commercial work to make my art more impactful. By juggling between these two worlds, I'm able to self-critique and art direct more clearly. I see myself having bigger projects that provide some source of comfort, vision, and healing for these difficult times that we are all facing globally.

Athena Azevedo athenaazevedo.carbonmade.com
See her Graphis Master Portfolio on graphis.com.

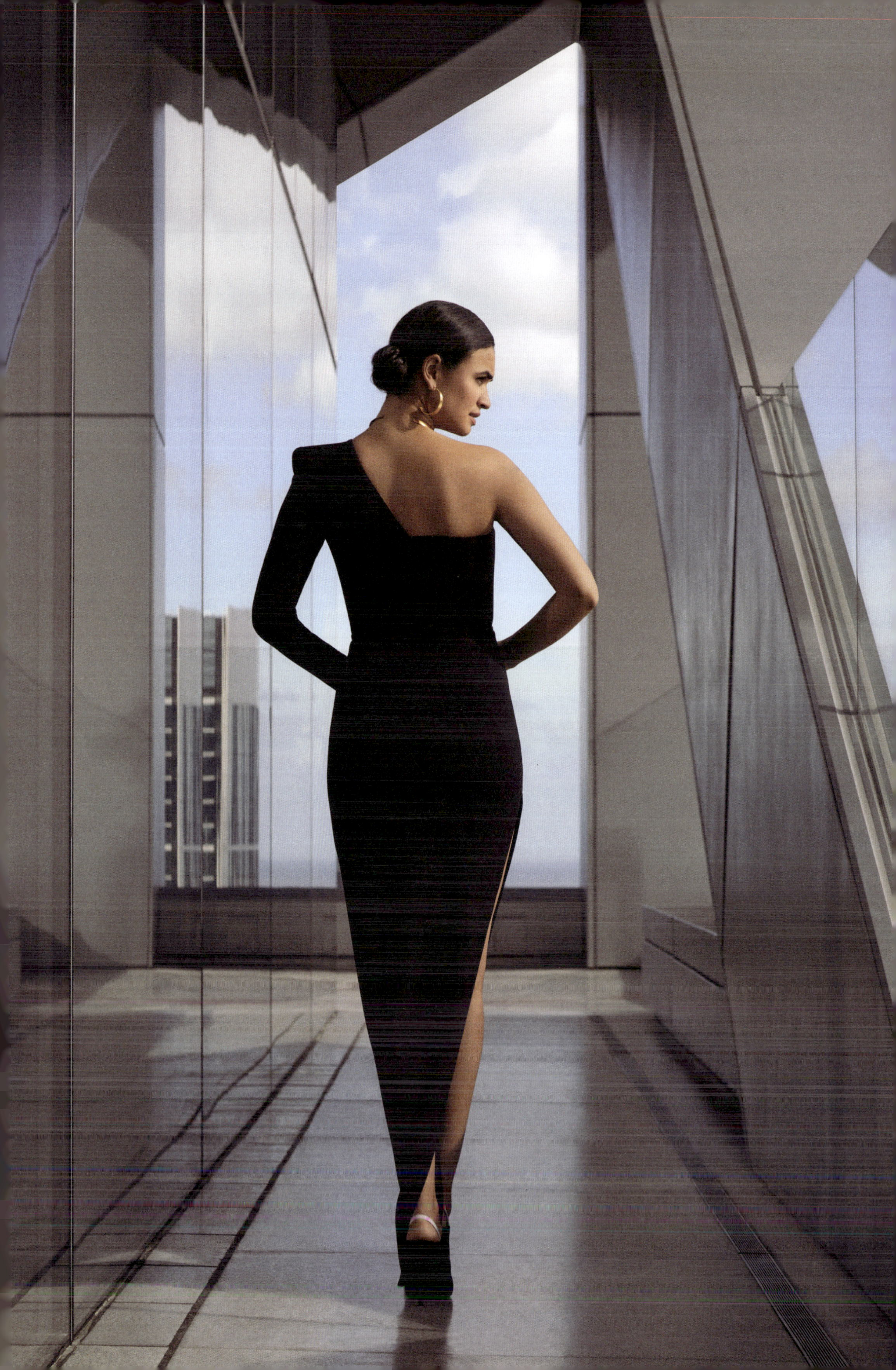

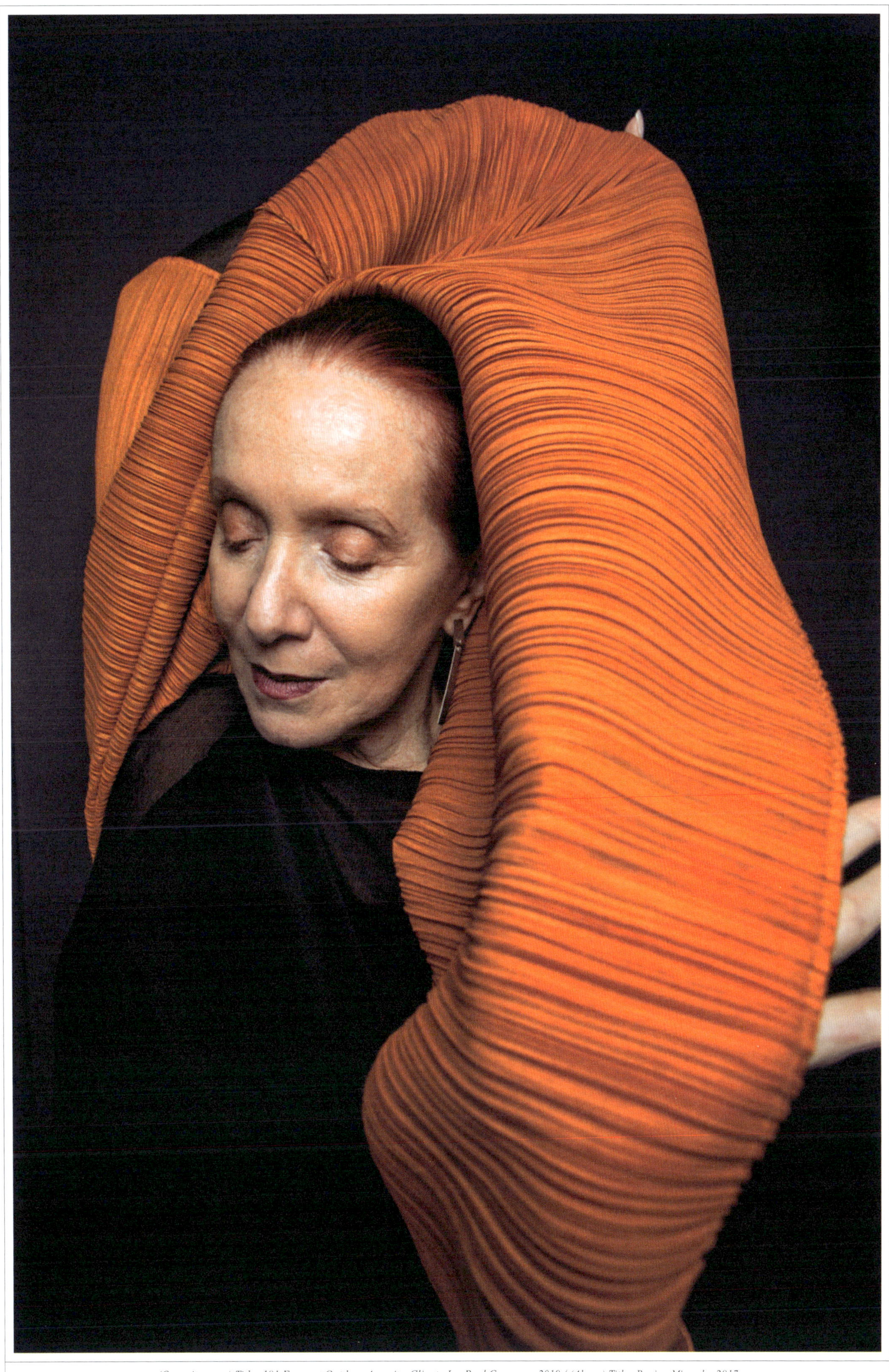

(Opposite page) Title: 181 Fremont Outdoor Amenity, Client: Jay Paul Company, 2019 / (Above) Title: Regina Miranda, 2017

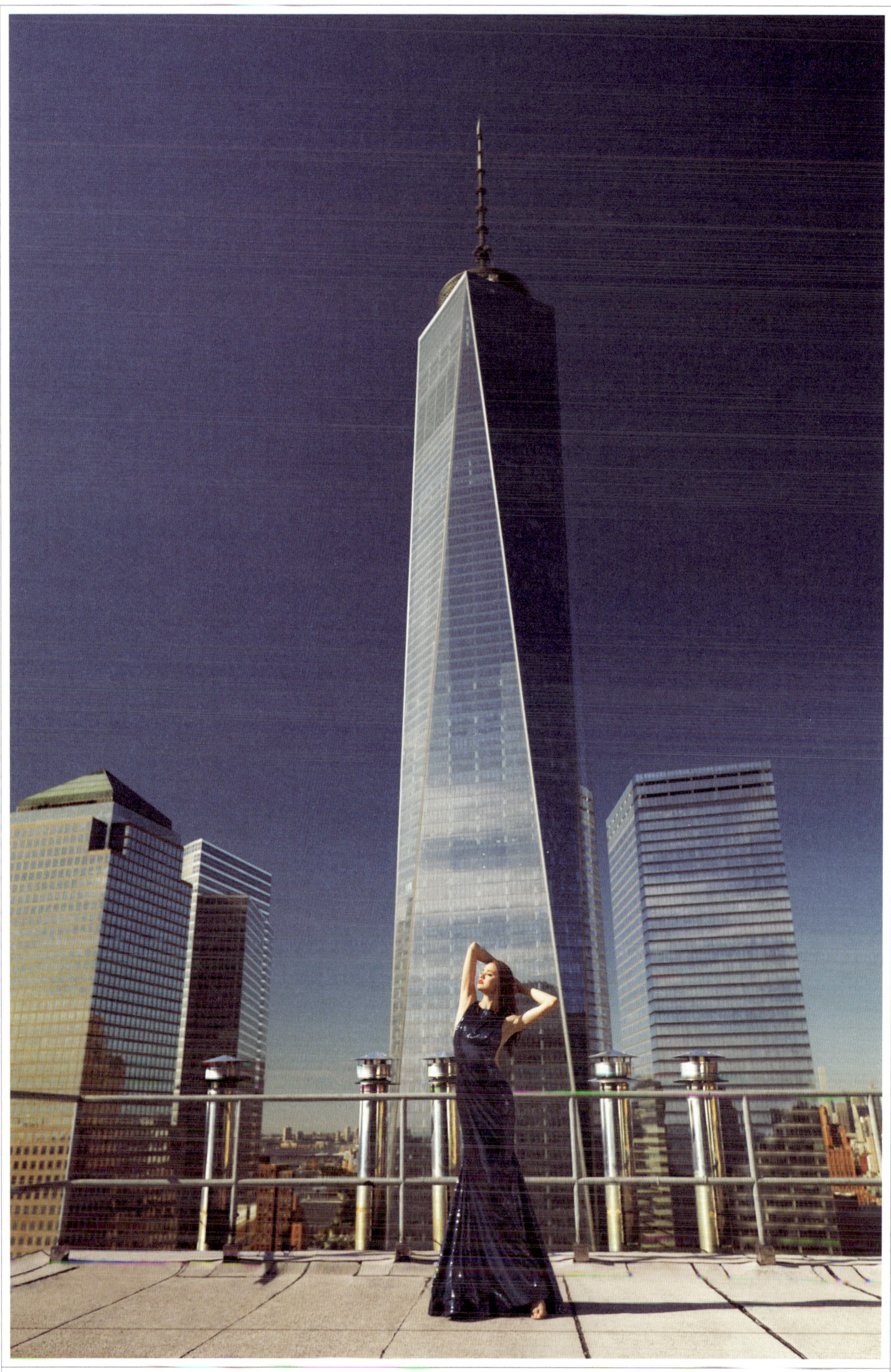

Title: Tower One Muse, Client: IGI US, 2016

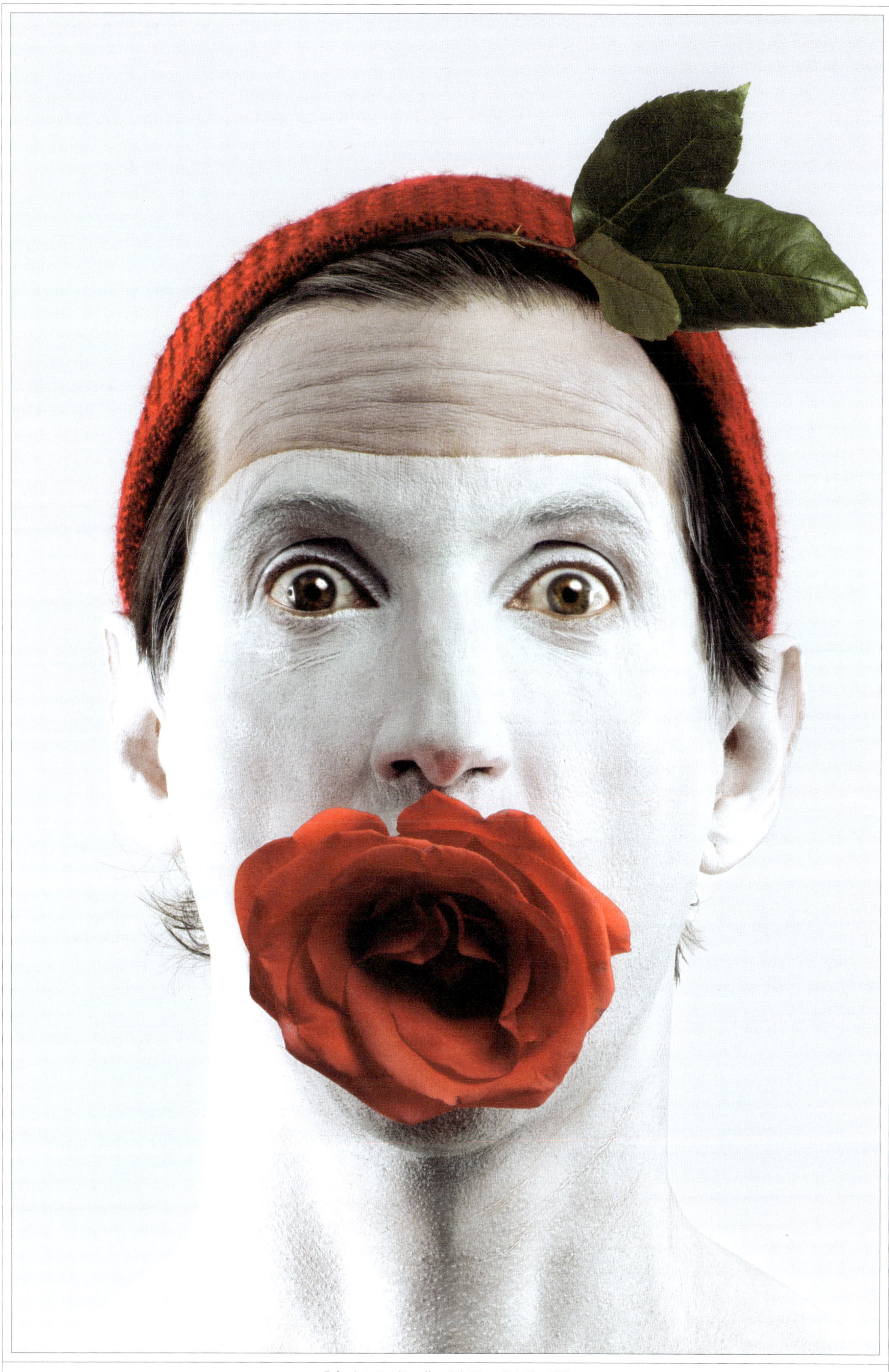

Title: João MacDowell as Jof, Client: Epic Eye, 2017

Vincent Junier: Creations; Never Replication

VINCENT ALWAYS IMPRESSES WITH THE IMAGINATIVE QUALITY OF HIS CREATIONS. HE AVOIDS THE TRAP OF REPETITION AND PREFERS TO PROPOSE NEW IDEAS, EVEN TAKING RISKS.

François Borderie, *Artistic Director at Epoka, à Paris.*

WORKING WITH HIM ON VARIOUS PROJECTS FOR CLINIQUE WAS A GREAT EXPERIENCE. HIS USE OF COMPOSITION AND LIGHTING CREATES A FLAWLESS IMAGE THAT FUSES COMMERCIAL AND ARTISTICS.

Jen Kever, *Art Director at Clinique EMEA*

VINCENT HAS MARRIED THE QUIRKY SENSE OF HUMOR IN HIS PLAYFUL SCULPTURES WITH HIS STILL LIFES. HIS CLEVER SENSE OF COMPOSITION, COLOR, AND HIS TECHNICAL PROWESS ELEVATE HIS PHOTOGRAPHY TO THE HIGHEST LEVEL.

Adam Savitch, *Photographer*

HIS BRAIN IS ALWAYS THINKING, ALWAYS WORKING ON THE NEXT PHOTOSHOOT. HE'S AN AMAZING PHOTOGRAPHER, AND HAS BEAUTIFUL IDEAS ON HOW TO COMBINE DIFFERENT WORLDS WITH HIS ART.

Tami Eshed, *Founder & Designer, T-Squared*

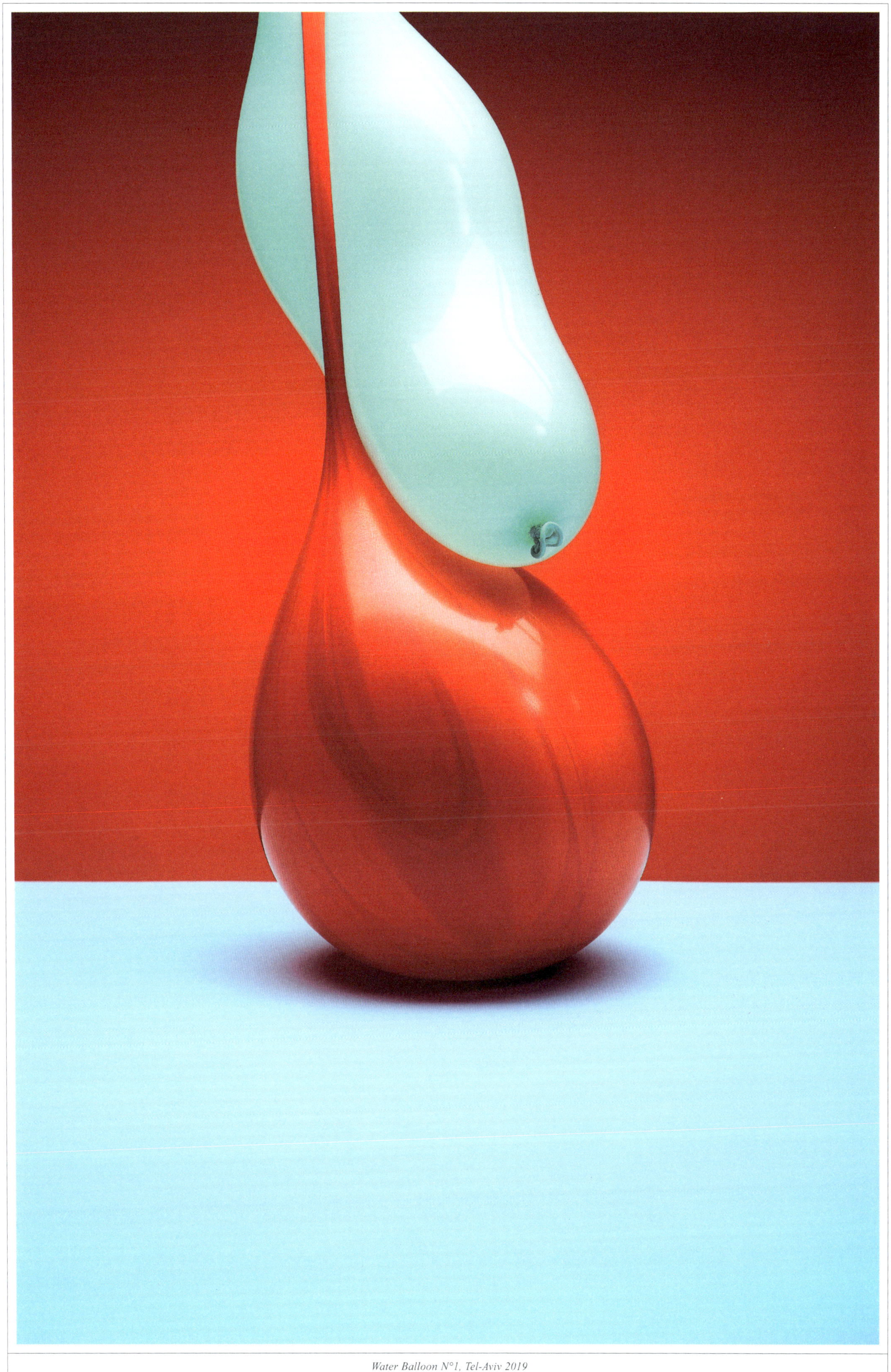

Water Balloon N°1, Tel-Aviv 2019

Vincent Junier is an excellent still-life photographer with whom I have had the pleasure of working regularly. From his training as a graphic designer comes his great mastery of composition and color schemes. And from his experience as a creative director, he got the habit of thinking of a concept first, and then finding the best and simplest way to illustrate it. ■ Vincent is a purist photographer for whom the image is made almost entirely during the shoot. He remains attached to this craft conception of his work and only moderately uses the facilities offered by post-production. ■ Vincent is fascinated by improbable mixtures of materials. In his pictures, objects become unified and connected to one another. His imagination is always renewed. His work is bright, graphic, and strange, always at the border between graphics and photography.

THE MOST IMPORTANT THING FOR ME IS TO CREATE, NOT TO REPRODUCE OR REMAKE. START FROM A VAGUE IDEA, AND LET IT GROW AND TRANSFORM INTO A CONCEPT, AN IMAGE.

Vincent Junier, *Photographer*

HIS ADEPT AND CREATIVE USE OF COLOR, MIXED WITH A CLEVER USE OF TEXTURE AND EYE-CATCHING ELEMENTS, ENCHANTS WHILE MAINTAINING HIS SIGNATURE STYLE THAT CHARMS.

Jan Kalish, *Photographer*

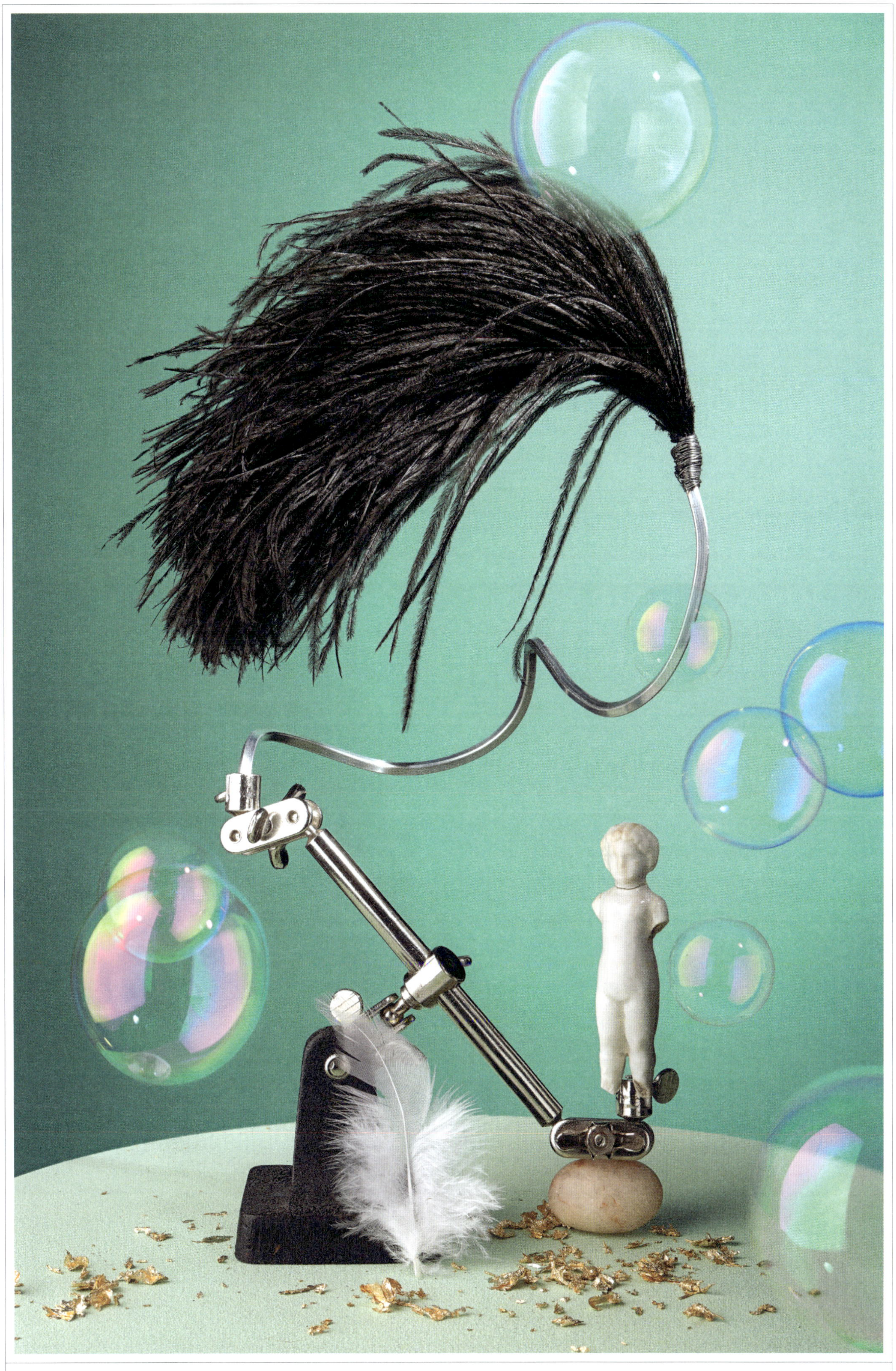

Bubbles, Paris 2018

What inspired or motivated you into your career?
The most important thing for me is to create, not to reproduce or remake. Start from a vague idea, and let it grow and transform it into a concept, an image. Regardless of the medium used, it is the creation process and the result that is important.

What is your work philosophy?
Do your best, don't follow the easy way and if you fail try, again.

Who is or was your greatest mentor?
There are two. Hilton Mcconnico, set designer and artistic director for more than 20 films but also architect, photographer and interior designer. I met him in the '90s and on these sides I understood that as an artist, there is more than one way to express my creativity.

The second is Michel Journiac, a French artist who was one of my teachers at the art school. He gave me one of the most important goals, "Always be open-minded," and when you love or hate something, try to understand why.

What is it about photography that you are most passionate about?
In still-life photography I'm most passionate about the lighting and compositions that are always different. You need to constantly find solutions for unexpected problems.

What has been your most memorable project?
One of my first ones, for Beaux Art magazine. After 6 months in Barcelona, I returned to Paris to present my book to the art director of the magazine. At the end of my presentation, he asked me if I was interested in getting some photos of Gaudy's architecture, but without the assurance of being published. So I went back to Barcelona for a week, and finally I published 6 pages including 3 full pages, and received a lot of money to pay the bills.

What is the most difficult challenge you've had to overcome?
Lead, assist, grow, and take care of a 12-person team, and while at the same time doing my own creations. Fortunately, it only lasted 10 years.

Who were some of your greatest past influences?
When I was young I had access to many art books that a cousin gave me, paintings, photography, and graphic catalogues. It's from there that I drew my first influences and my desire to become creative. I especially remember two books, one about the Russian constructivism, especially the affichists like Rodchenko, Lissitzky and Lavinskii. The other from the Gamma agency and amazing photographers like Raymond Depardon, Gilles Caron, and Marie Laure de Decker. When you spend as much time as I do looking and looking at the same books it ends up influencing your look.

How did you become interested in graphic design?
In a very unexpected way, in 1991 or '92 I don't remember exactly, I did a portrait of Didier Derlich, a very famous French astrologue at the time. When he saw the result he called me and asked me to design the cover for a 12-book collection. I argued that I wasn't able to but he said "don't worry you'll be perfect, it's my job to know the future." Okay, no way out. So I asked my girlfriend at the time who was an art director to give me some tips. The result was that I completed his collection within two years. As I had fun doing this, I took some graphics classes and I gradually continued towards graphic design.

*What made you decide to switch from graphic design
back to photography?*
Five years ago one of my clients for whom I made visual concepts knew that my first job was a photographer. He asked me to shoot his campaign. After saying no for a few weeks, I decided to buy a camera and flash…and said ok let's do it.

What would be your dream assignment?
One with Hermes or Vogue I hope.

Who among your contemporaries today do you most admire?
Nick Knight for his creativity. Richard Pierce for his capacity to put magic in his work. Karel Martens for his incredible talent. The Neubau studio in Berlin, I'm in love with the way they use typography and black and white. There are so many talents, it's impossible to name everybody. Take a look at my Instagram to see the people I admire.

*Who have been some of your favorite people
or clients you have worked with?*
As graphic designer I would say the Bank of Luxembourg. For 8 years, I made the annual reports around the same theme: flowers. It was a great challenge. As a photographer, I would say Darphin from the Estée Lauder company, because they gave me the opportunity to came back to photography. A enormous proof of trust or unconsciousness.

*What are the most important ingredients you require
from a client to do successful work?*
Trust, lots of exchanges, and a good brief.

What is your proudest professional achievement?
My last exhibition in Israel at the Eretz Israel Museum about plastic waste on Israeli beach, and the windows at Hotel Coste in Paris with my collages.

What is the greatest satisfaction you get from your work?
Not feeling like I'm working, but doing what I love.

"ALWAYS BE OPEN-MINDED," AND WHEN YOU LOVE OR HATE SOMETHING, TRY TO UNDERSTAND WHY.

Vincent Junier, *Photographer*

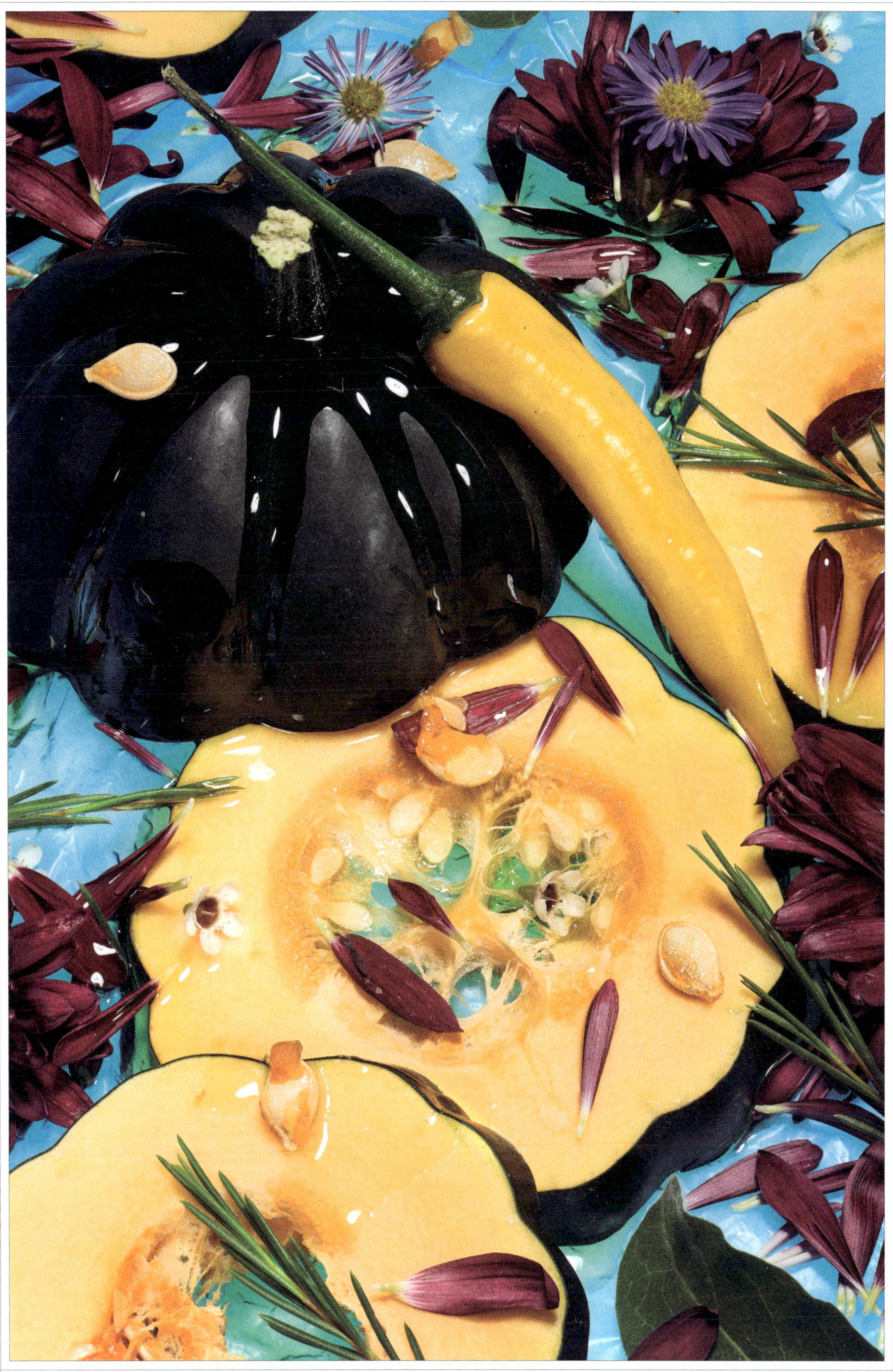

Souk-Hacarmel N°2, Tel-Aviv 2019

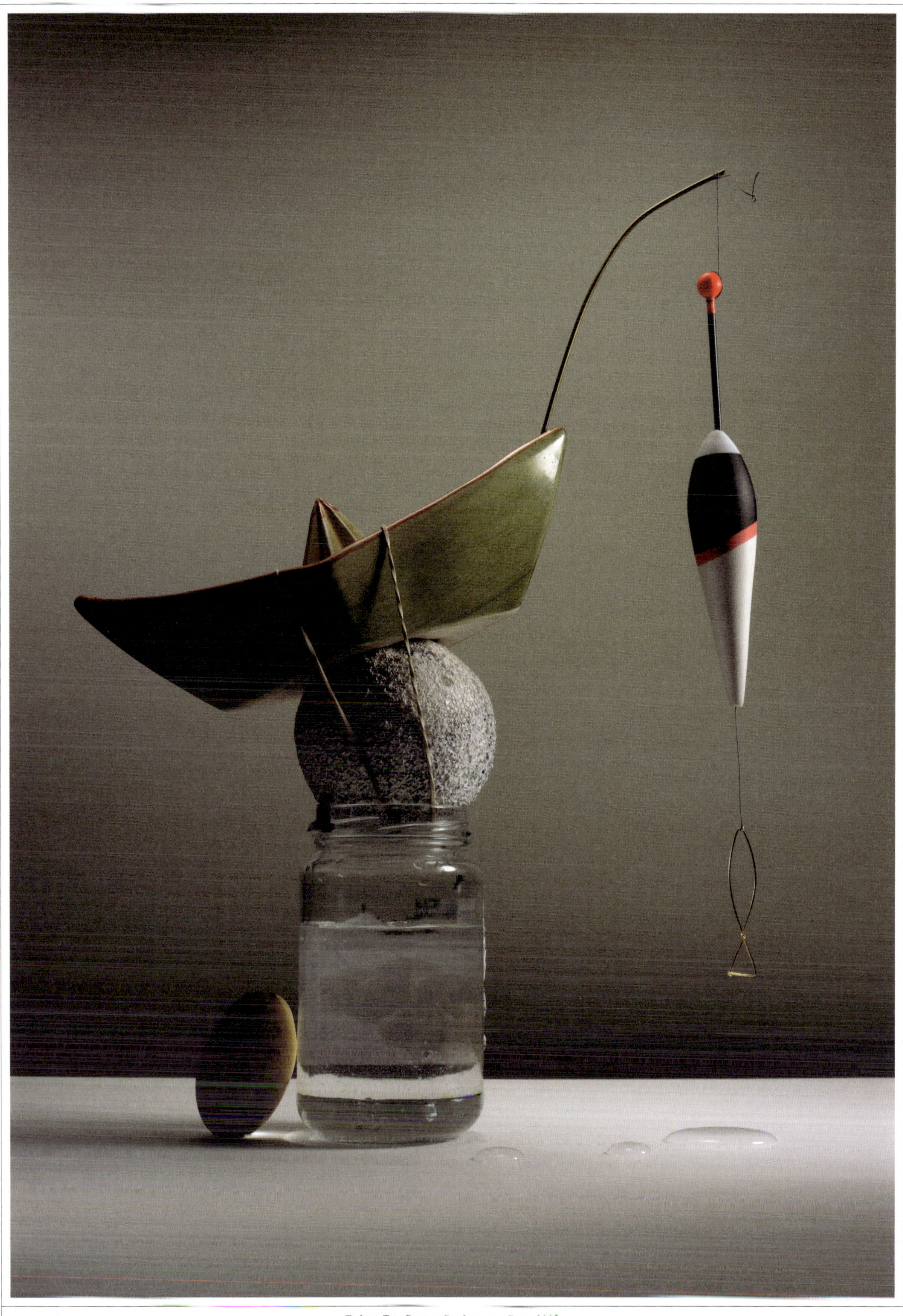

Fishing Trip During Confinement, Paris 2018

DO YOUR BEST, DON'T FOLLOW THE EASY WAY. AND IF YOU FAIL, TRY AGAIN.

Vincent Junier, *Photographer*

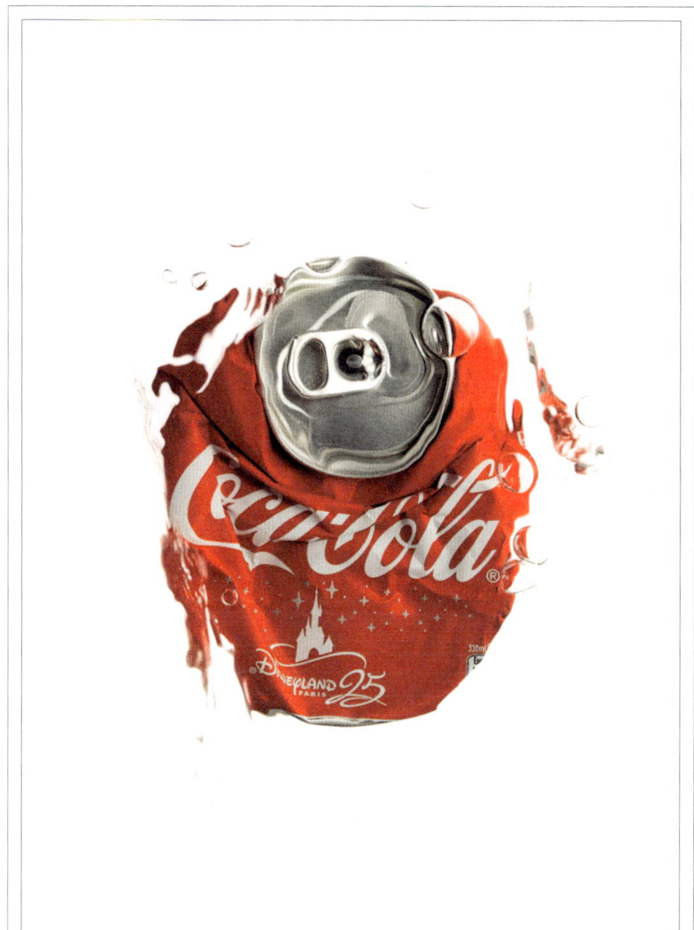

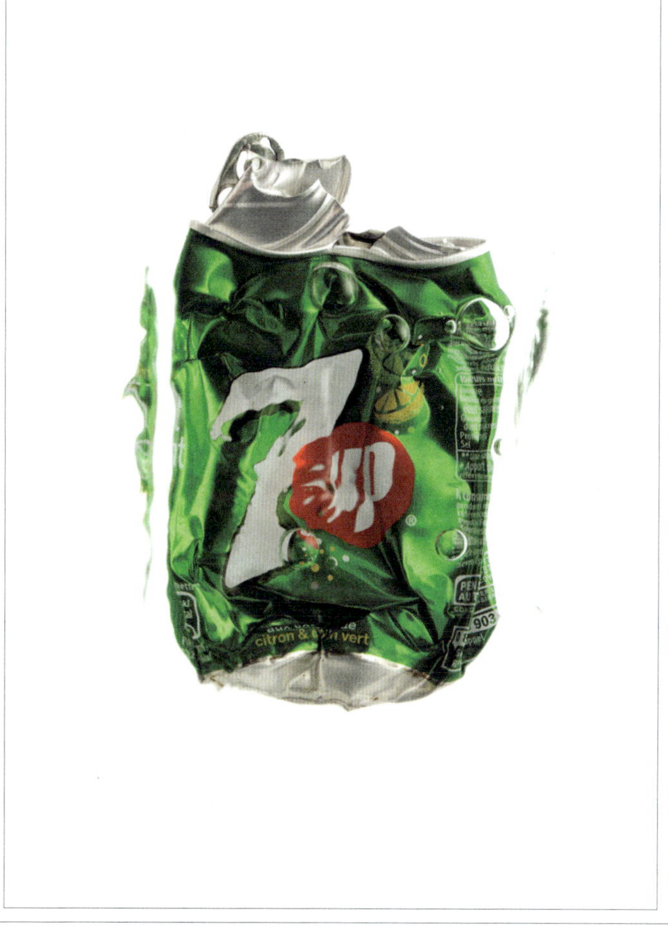

Crushed Can, Paris 2018

What professional goals do you still have for yourself?
Learn and practice again and again

What do you wish you had known when you first started out?
I always knew it wouldn't be easy, but I didn't know how hard it would be sometimes.

What advice would you have for students starting out today?
Follow your dream. If you want to be a creative, don't ask your parents if it's a good idea, but first be sure you love the rice and noodles.

What interests do you have outside of your work?
Climbing to clear my head, traveling, reading, listening to music, jazz or pop when I'm cool, trans and techno to break my head, making collages, going to art exhibitions, watching movies and series. I don't like to stay too inactive.

What do you value most?
The discovery and the unexpected.

What would you change if you had to do it all over again?
Nothing except trust myself more. And I would try to be a better creative director for my team.

Where do you seek inspiration?
Most of the time inspiration comes from my everyday life, an image, a color, people on the street; I let my mind wander. I've noticed that the more you work, the easier inspiration comes. But I have to admit, when I'm stuck on a subject, I go on Pinterest and instagram.

How do you define success?
The capacity of doing what you want in your life.

Where do you see yourself in the future?
Somewhere in the world surrounded and working with the people that I love.

Vincent Junier www.vincentjunier.com

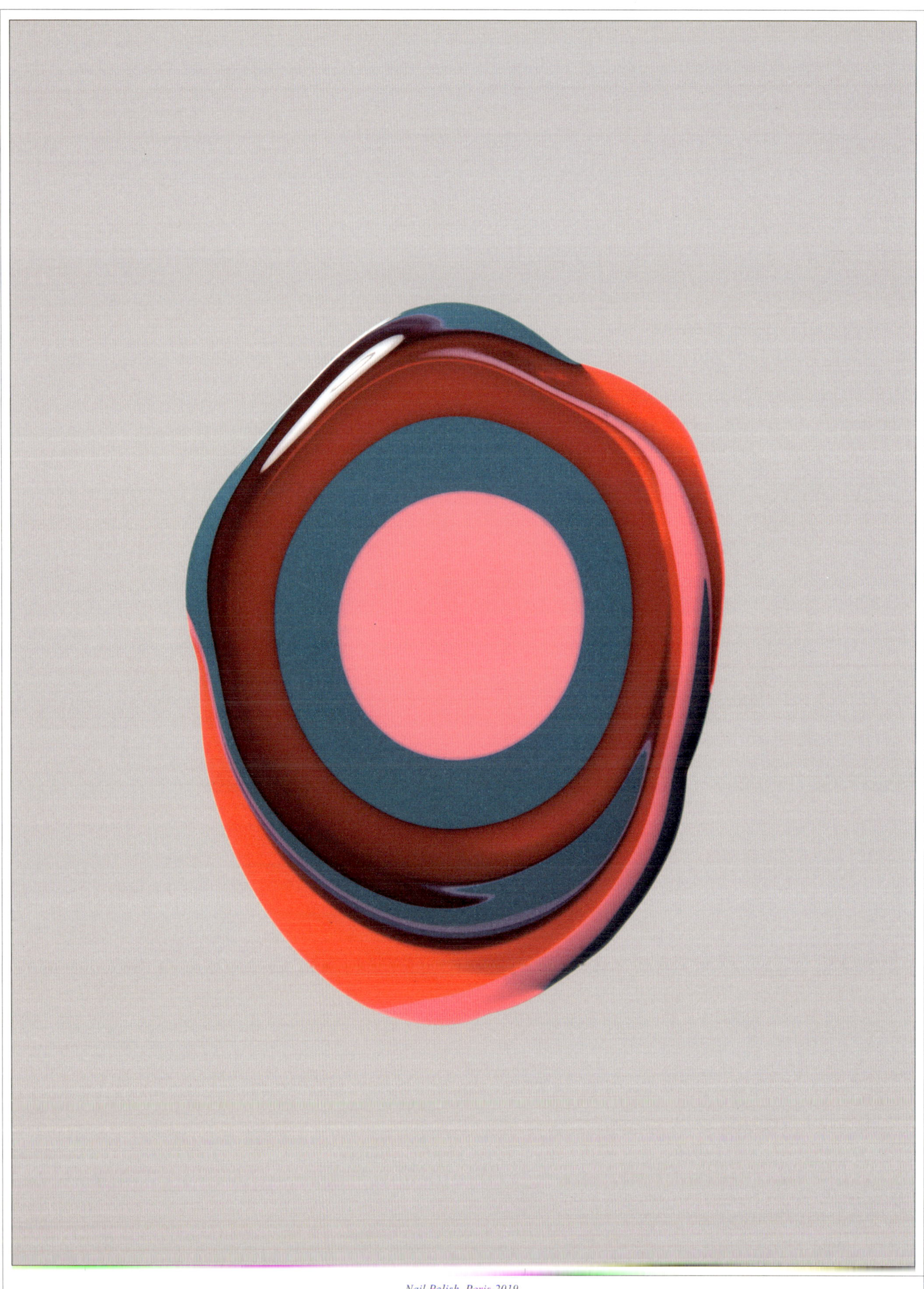

Nail Polish, Paris 2019

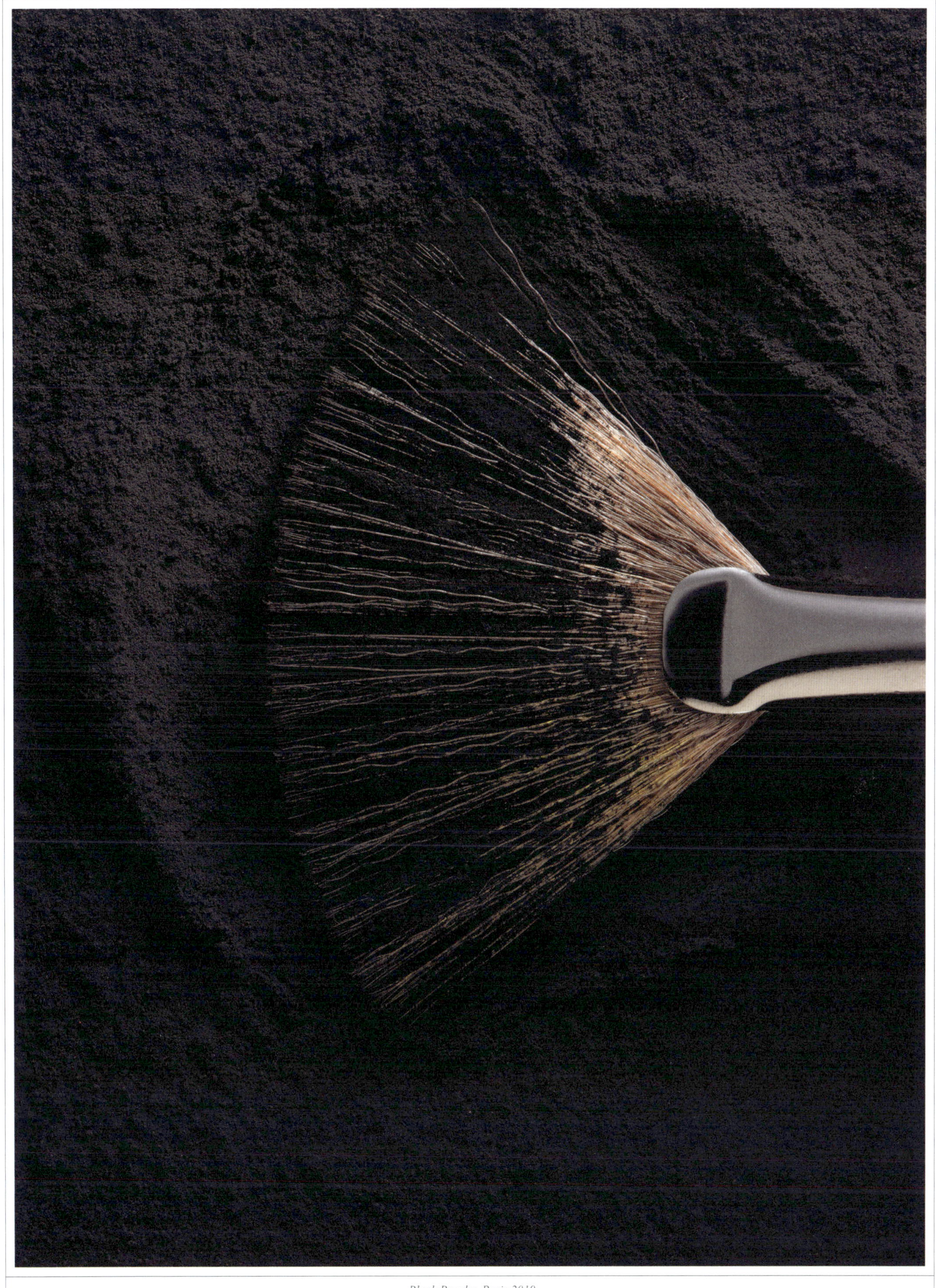

Black Powder, Paris 2019

90 JOHN MATTOS / USA

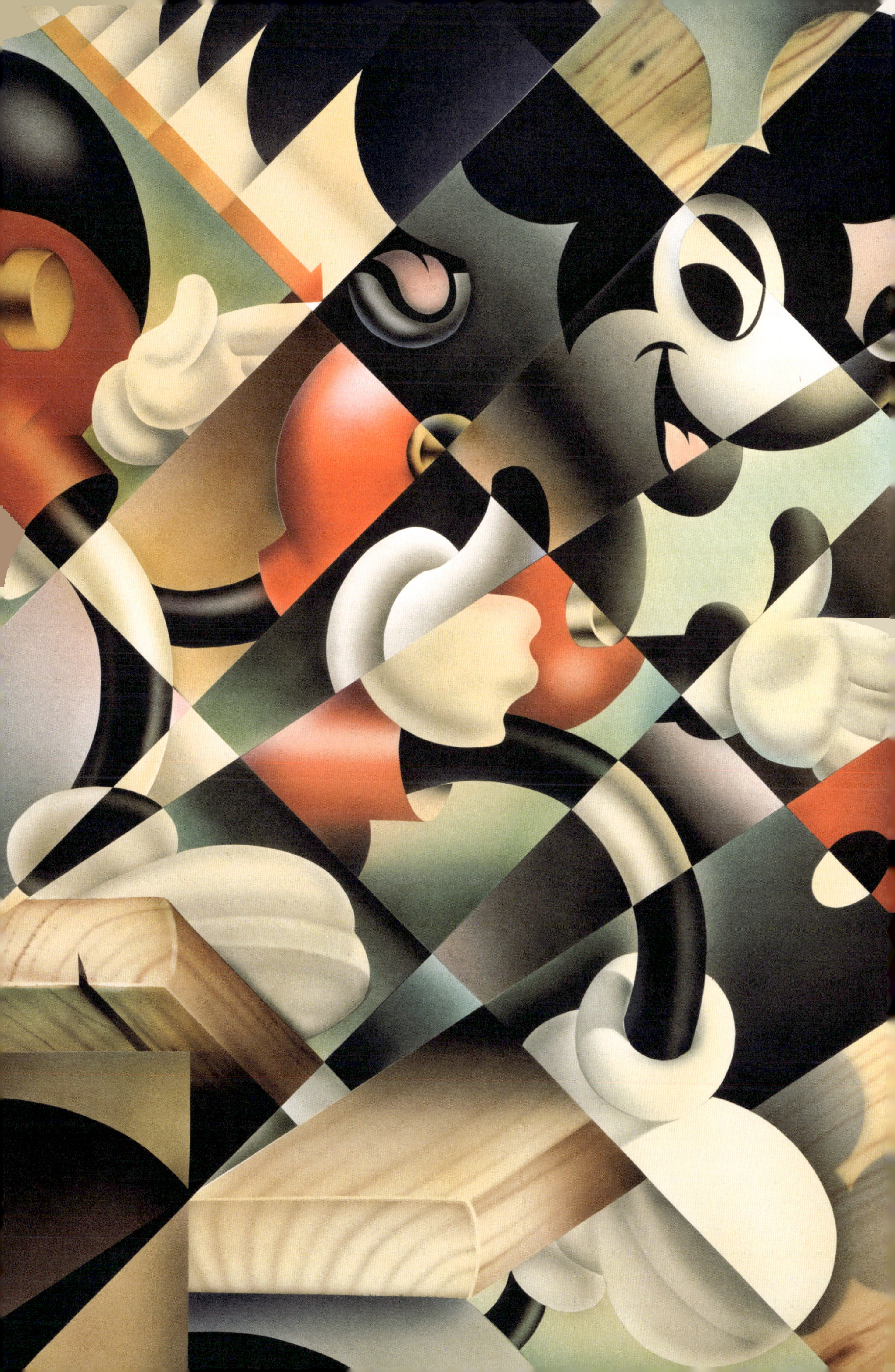

John Mattos: A Larger Than Life Point-of-View

JOHN DOES NOT DO ORDINARY. HE DOES MONUMENTAL, UNFORGETTABLE, HEROIC, DRAMATIC, LARGER-THAN-LIFE IMAGES THAT DEMAND ATTENTION. IT'S BEEN AN HONOR TO HAVE HAD THE OPPORTUNITY TO WORK WITH HIM.

Kit Hinrichs, *Principal & Creative Director, Studio Hinrichs*

JOHN AND I GO WAY BACK TO ARTCENTER AS STUDENTS IN THE EARLY 70'S. HIS GRAPHIC WORK HAS ALWAYS BEEN MEMORABLE, DRAMATIC, PERFECTLY CRAFTED, AND POWERFUL. I AM PROUD OF HIM, LIKE A BROTHER.

Michael Schwab, *Graphic Designer, Michael Schwab Studio*

I HAVE ADMIRED THE STRIKING DESIGN AND MODERN TAKE IN JOHN'S ART DECO-INSPIRED IMAGES FOR MANY YEARS.

Dan Cosgrove, *Illustrator, Graphis Master*

JOHN IS ONE OF THE MOST INTUITIVE AND INSIGHTFUL ARTISTS I HAVE WORKED WITH. WHEN YOU GIVE HIM A BRIEF HE COMES BACK WITH IT BOTH ENHANCED AND DEVELOPED TO A LEVEL YOU HADN'T EVEN DREAMED OF.

Jeremy King, *Co-Founder and CEO of Corbin & King*

MATTOS' ART DECO WORKS HAVE CREATED INDELIBLE RETRO-STYLE IMAGES FOR AMERICAN FILMS, MAJOR SPORTS EVENTS AND CELEBRATIONS OF ICONIC INDIVIDUALS, ARCHITECTURE, PRODUCTS AND CELEBRATIONS.

John Asher, *Editor, Kentucky Derby*

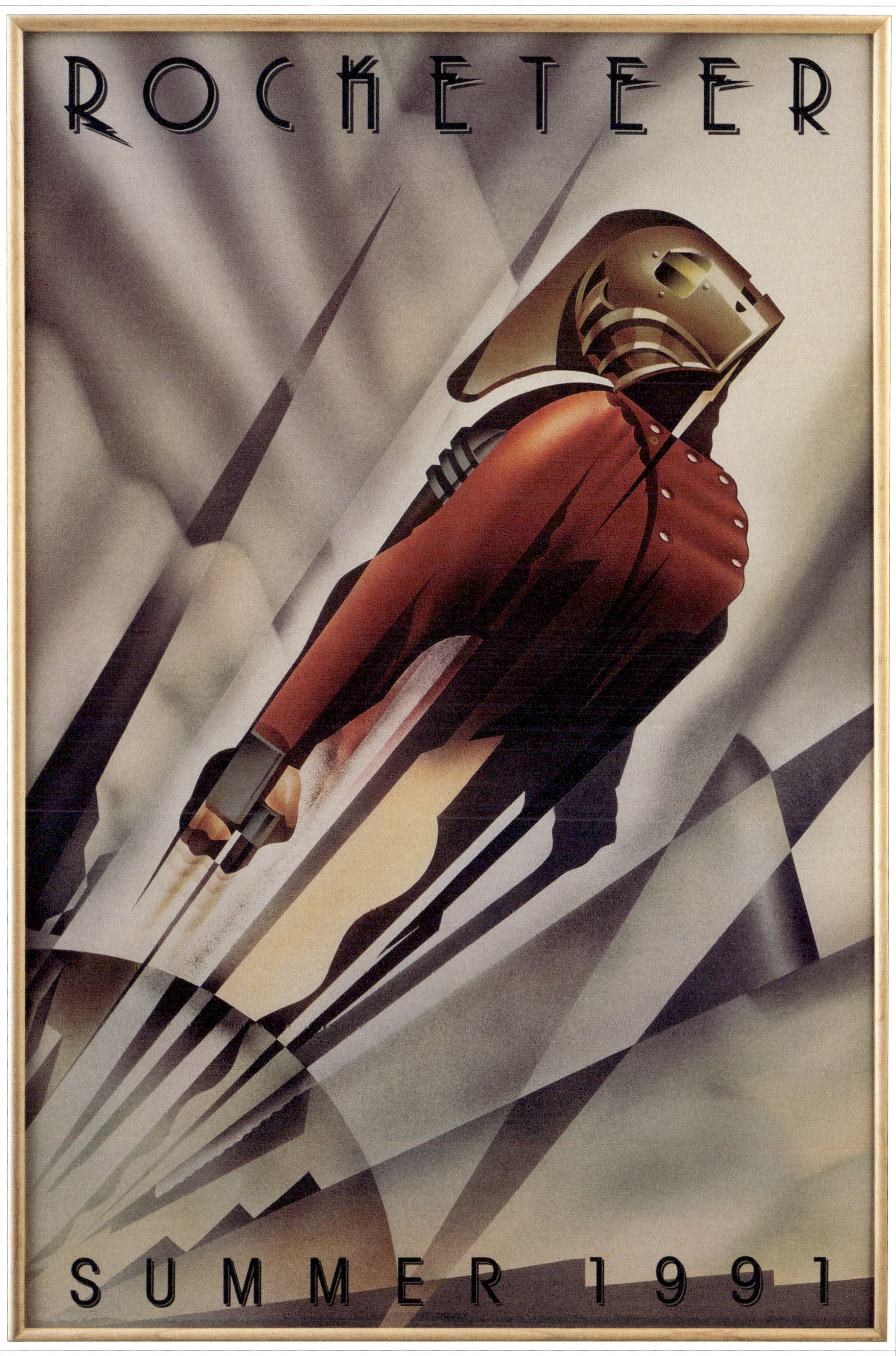

(Page 89) Mickey Descending a Stairway / (Above) Rocketeer

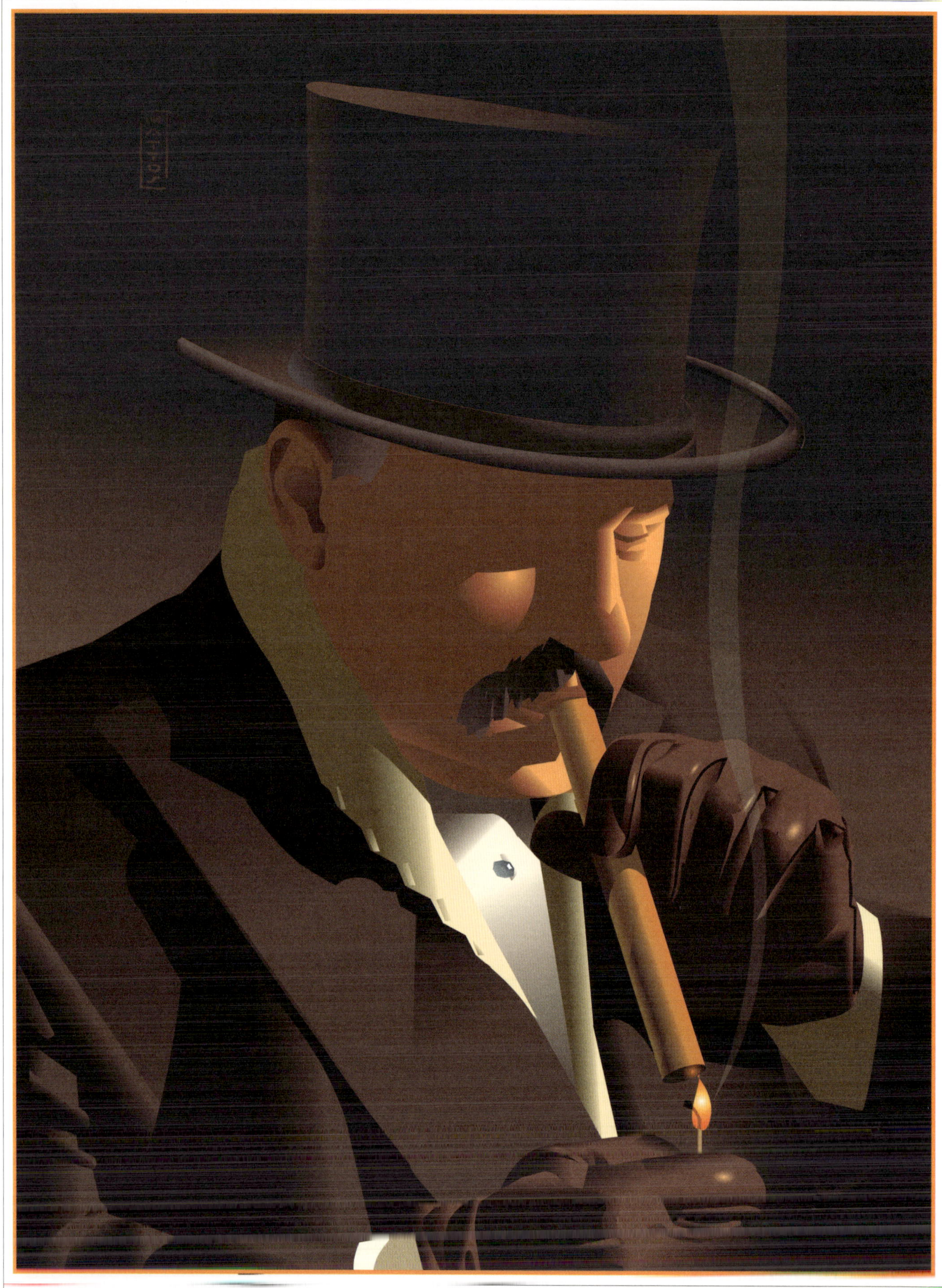

JP Morgan Portrait

Introduction by **Charles E. White III** *Illustrator, Olio Inc.*

John Mattos and I go a long way back, and I mean a long way back. I have loved his work for a very long time. It seems his inspiration came from some of my favorite illustrators and designers, two of them being Ludwig Hohlwein from the early 20th century, and Cassandre from the 1930's Art Deco period. Both of them are very famous artists in their own right. John has taken that inspiration and made it his own. With his elegant design sensibility, he creates beautiful images that have a hint of nostalgia yet are very current at the same time, which makes his work seem timeless. In times like these, it is tough being an illustrator. I am proud of John and his being able to keep producing such a beautiful body of work.

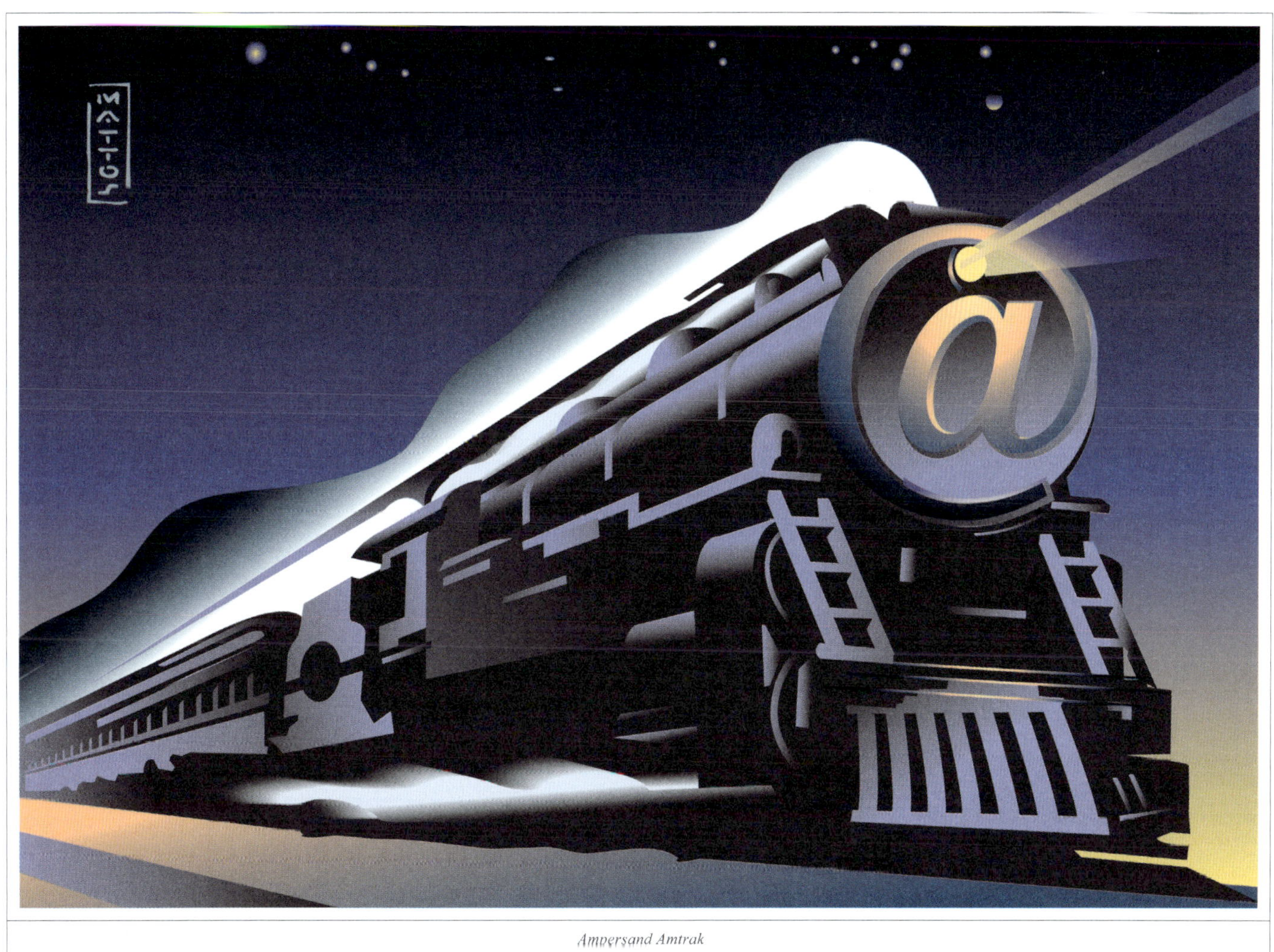

Ampersand Amtrak

JOHN MATTOS' WORK IS A VISUAL FEAST.
IT IS BEAUTIFULLY ERA-DRIVEN AND TIMELESS.

B. Martin Pedersen, *Designer*

What inspired or motivated you into your career?
I've always drawn pictures. As a teenager, I did the typical evaluation of strengths and weaknesses, this led me to Art Center College of Design in Southern California. In that illustration program, there were 2 distinct groups; The "Westport School" - Peak, English, Fuchs, etc., or the "Pushpin School" Glaser, Chwast, Paul Davis, etc. My desire to do airbrush led to a 3rd way for me. I saw this as a way to make pure photographs of ideas. This was 1971 and all that Chrome palm-tree bubble-gum bent-knuckle realism did not exist... yet...

Part of my interest in airbrush was generated by my comfort with the hardware surrounding this demanding craft. I was right at home with the odd equipment: hoses, compressors, knives, air regulators. It was very much like the hardware in my family's dairy barn in Empire, CA. In fact, the DeVilbiss company in Chicago made milking machines, and in down time made airbrushes and industrial spray equipment.

What is your work philosophy?
I keep a sketchbook going always. It has notes, sketches, jokes, recipes, and observations. These are simple reminders of ideas that can be developed later. When a potential solution to a project pre-exists in my sketchbook, I can bring greater enthusiasm to that project.

Who is or was your greatest mentor?
As a student, the Great Charlie White III. As I became a working adult and artist, Nathan Oliveira. White was conceptually sophisticated with remarkable craft.

Upon graduation, I had the opportunity to work with the brilliant Peter Palombi, and later, the talented John Alvin. These were sink-or-swim, take-no-prisoners learning experiences; these were not "apprenticeships" or internships, these were "we're gonna get this done in the next 12 hours, and it's gonna be great" work marathons. I certainly learned to manage stress and got a priceless, up-close view of their professional high-standard, high-wire acts.

What is it about illustration that you are most passionate about?
Uh oh. The word "Passion" implies a choleric approach to illustration that is just not in my tool kit.

What has been your most memorable project?
Nine large-scale murals for a 5-star Hotel in Mayfair, London and 70 supporting caricatures. I got to work with Jeremy King of King/Corbin. Sir Jeremy certainly knew how to work with artists. He had more than one portrait of himself done by Lucien Freud and wasn't like a character in a Pinter play, he WAS a character written into a play by Harold Pinter. He had a bril-

liant way of keeping the project on track and bringing in his necessary input. He would invent a character named "Jimmy Beaumont," give him a back story so there were standards and rules, then we would have wonderful discussions and debates. For example, would J Beaumont approve of dog racing? (Not really, but he would know where to place a bet on a dog race.)

What is the most difficult challenge you've had to overcome?
Transition from analog to digital. I was lucky in that I had an existing analog style, so I had a clear goal in the digital world.

Who were some of your greatest past influences?
They were J.C. Leyendecker, Norman Wilkerson, Ludwig Hohlwein, and Donald Deskey.

Who among your contemporaries today do you most admire?
Some that I admire are: Robert Hunt for grit, wit, and sheer brush mileage determination. Brian Stauffer for brilliant original concepts. He had a Steinberg-like ability to find visual solutions that no one saw, but after Stauffer shows you, you think "of course." Mark Ulriksen - if illustration was baseball, Mark always gets on base. Ward Schumaker and I have gone through the Graphis Annuals page by page, and our taste and comments about what we are seeing are consistently diametrically opposed. I have great admiration for Ward, even though he's dead wrong in his crackpot opinions.

What would be your dream assignment?
Any project where my interests and the commission line up.

You've done work for film and corporate clients among others. Is there a specific field you enjoy most?
Not really.

Who have been some of your favorite people or clients you have worked with?
Kit Hinrichs. By coincidence, he is a neighbor here in Northbeach, SF., so he probably feels like he has to hire me every so often in case he runs into me at the grocery. Kit can draw and think. He has a wonderful, indirect way of moving a project forward. He might say, "of course you will get some reference for those hands in this sketch before you go to finish," or "is this merely indication, or do you intend to paint it like this?" Better yet, "are you working in a new style that is hurried and grounded in indifference?" I love working with this guy.

What are the most important ingredients you require from a client to do successful work?
Clarity and the ability to "make the leap" from sketch to final art.

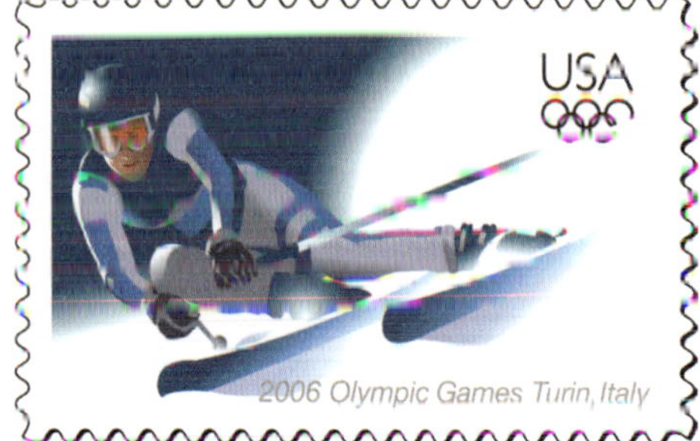

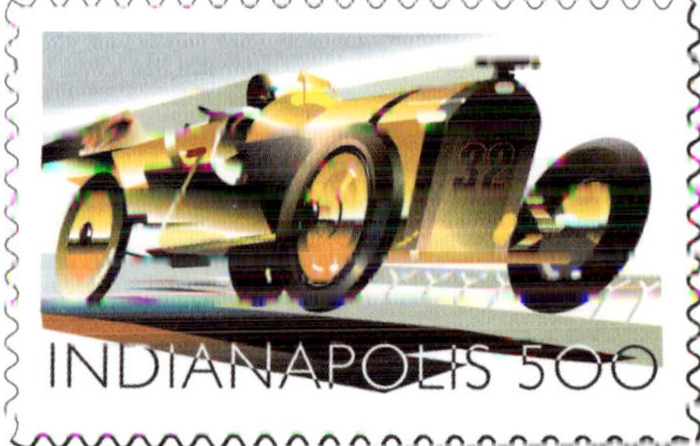

(Left) Olympic Commemorative Stamp / (Right) 100 Years of Racing

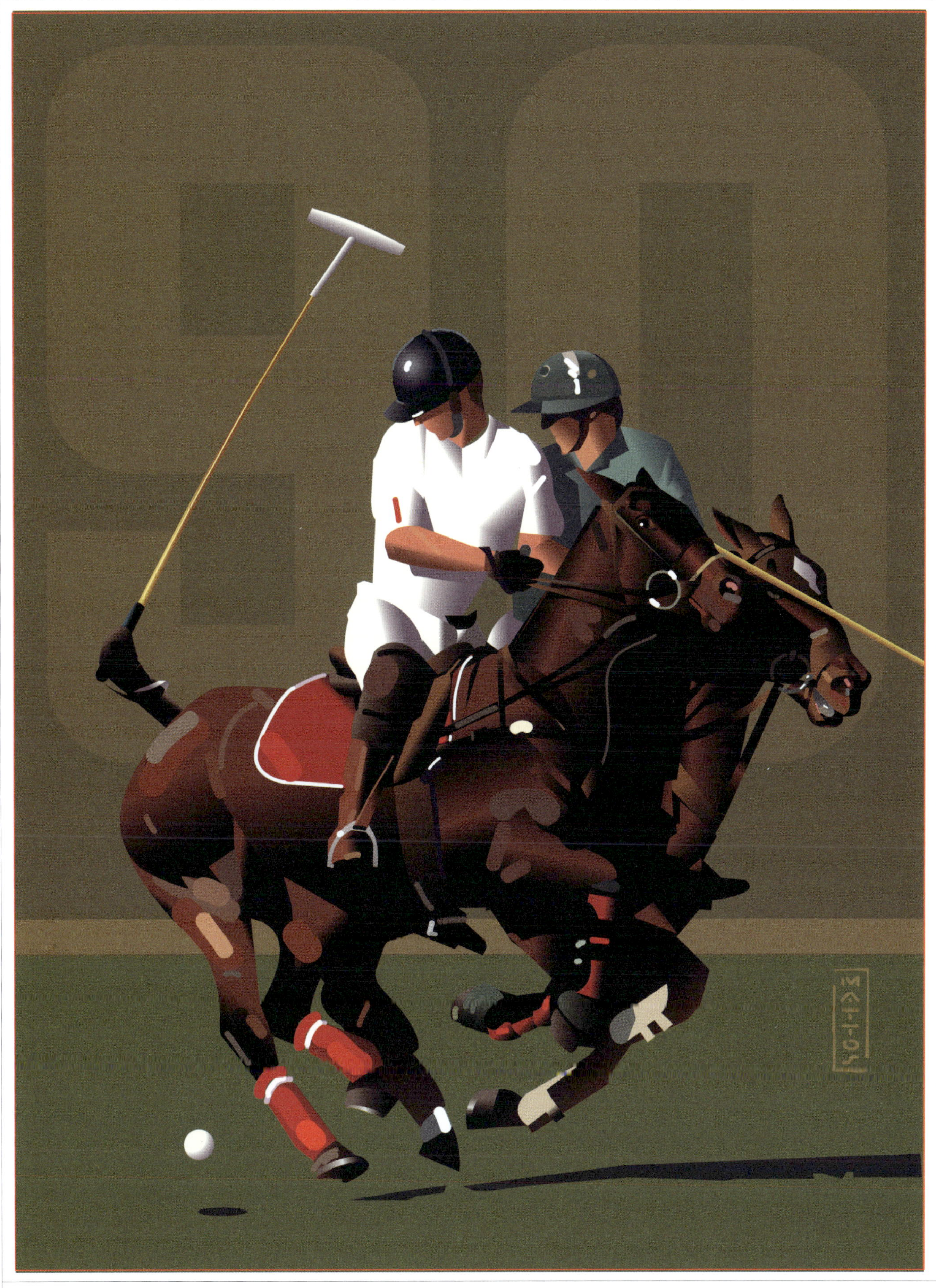

A Handy Horse

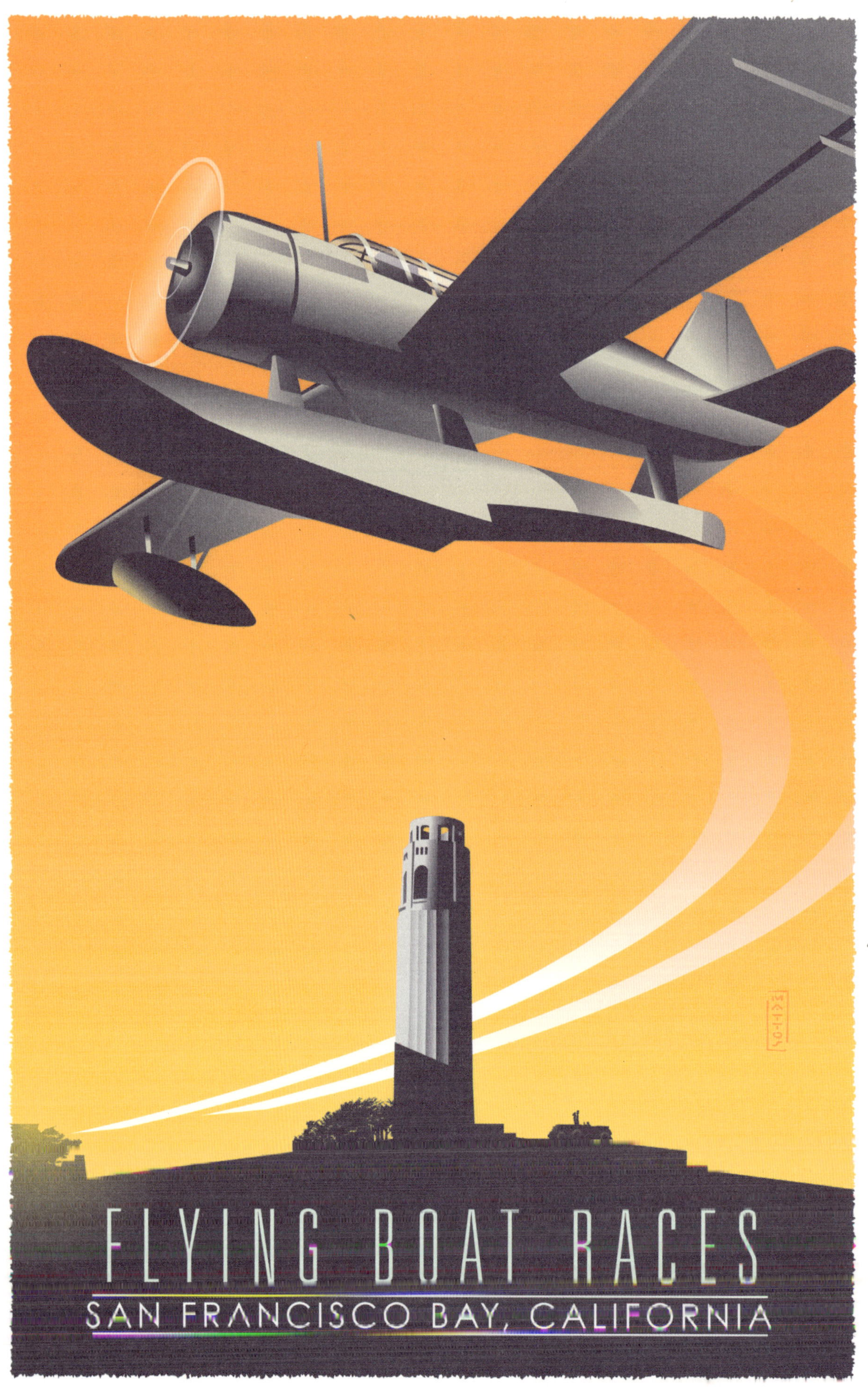

Flying Boat Races

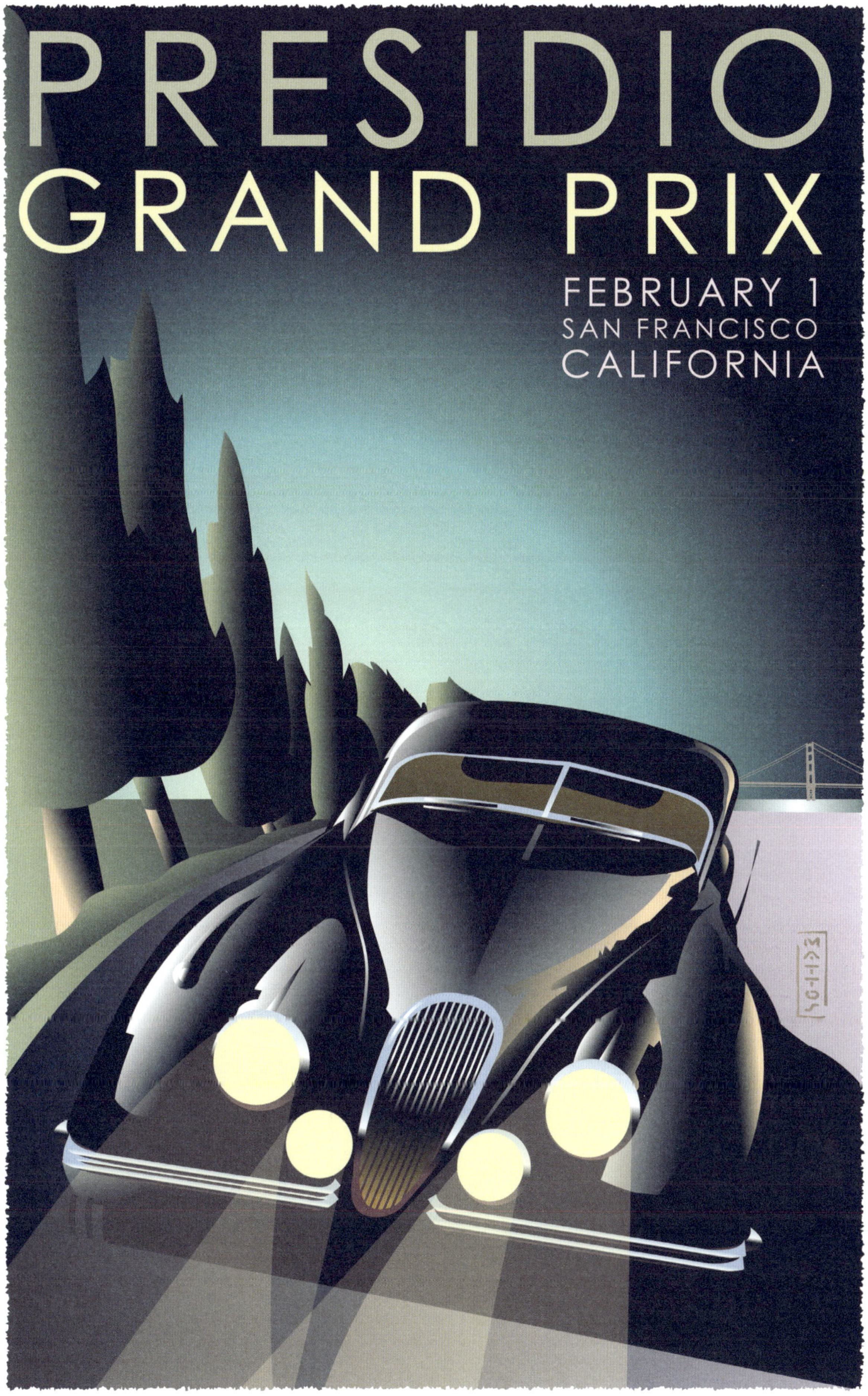

Presidio Grand Prix

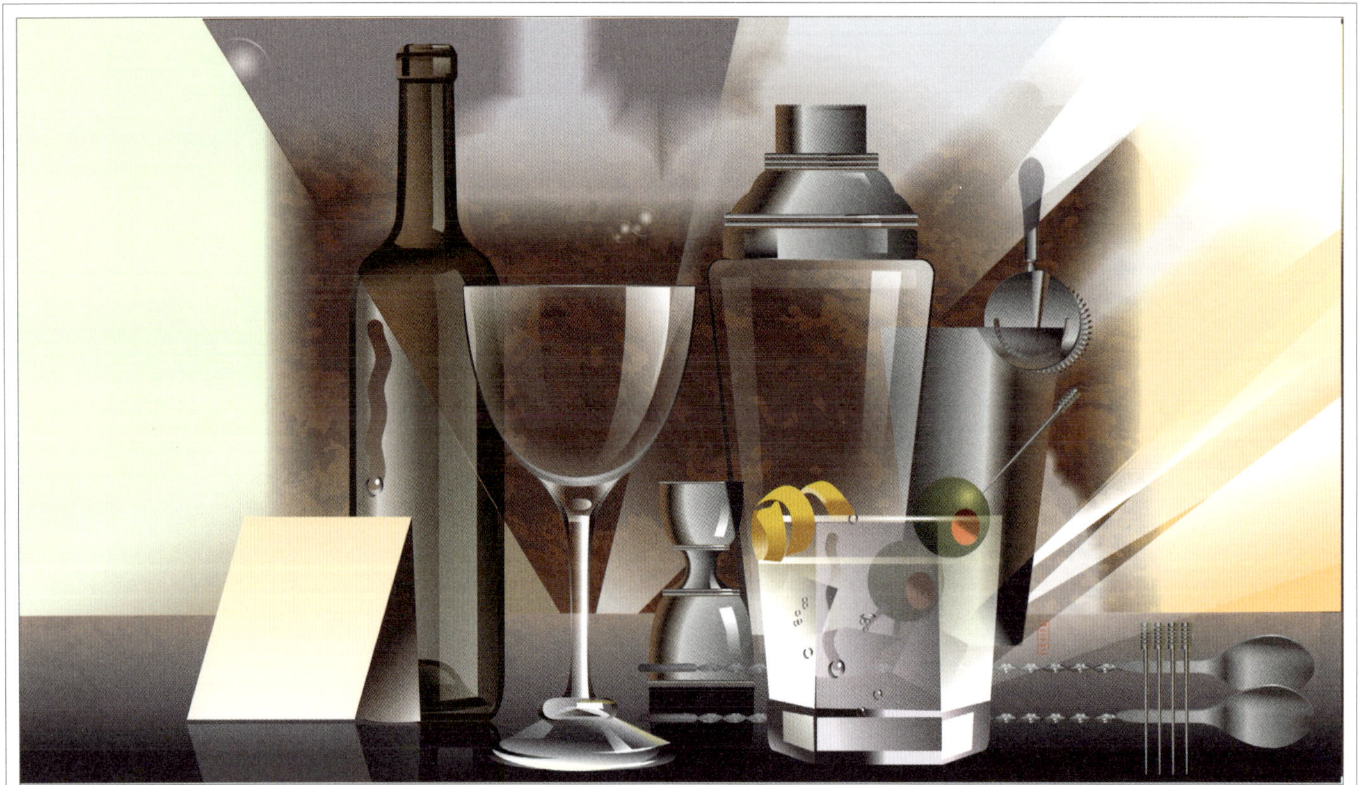

Martini Arrangement

What is your proudest professional achievement?
Right now it's probably 7 murals used in a Netflix series "The Good Cop." The movie poster "Rocketeer" was selected as one of the 100 best movie posters of all time but I didn't get a statuette.

What is the greatest satisfaction you get from your work?
Aesthetically? Making a harmonious series of shapes that fit together in a beautiful and surprising way.

What part of your work do you find most demanding?
My medium, Adobe illustrator, is cold, simplistic, and wants to provide a sameness of edges and surface. Getting some humanity and a "touched by a human hand" feeling into the artwork is most demanding.

What professional goals do you still have for yourself?
I've never cracked that nut "The New Yorker."

*What is something you wish you had known
when you first started out?*
Art Directors aren't always right.

What advice would you have for students starting out today?
Get a point of view.

What interests do you have outside of your work?
I play bass locally on Thursday nights. I have a folding boat that provides some frightening and thrilling moments out on the San Francisco Bay and gives a unique perspective on my seaport home town.

What do you value most?
At this point, it's time - having discretionary time.

What would you change if you had to do it all over again?
I would not waste time revising stillborn, bonehead projects.

Where do you seek inspiration?
Strangely, in reading; biographies, odd science journals, histories. I also like those little intros in coffee-table picture books.

How do you define success?
I'm not a freudian, but I do value love from intimates and family, and recognition from peers.

Where do you see yourself in the future?
I live on a hillside one-half block from Coit Tower in San Francisco. I did the "Preserve Coit Tower" Art. I have sweeping views that include the Golden Gate Bridge. I got to do the 75th anniversary bridge poster. I can see Alcatraz. I did the art for the GGNRA "Save the Rock" campaign and did the maps and illustrated the walk-around infographics there. I can hear the nearby Joe DiMaggio playground, I did their logo. North Beach Library - logo and artwork. Every morning, I see kids on their way to school wearing sweatshirts and tees with my fundraiser art for Garfield school up the hill. I like it here and see myself here in the future.

John Mattos www.johnmattos.com,
richardsolomon.com/artists/john-mattos
See his Graphis Master Portfolio on graphis.com.

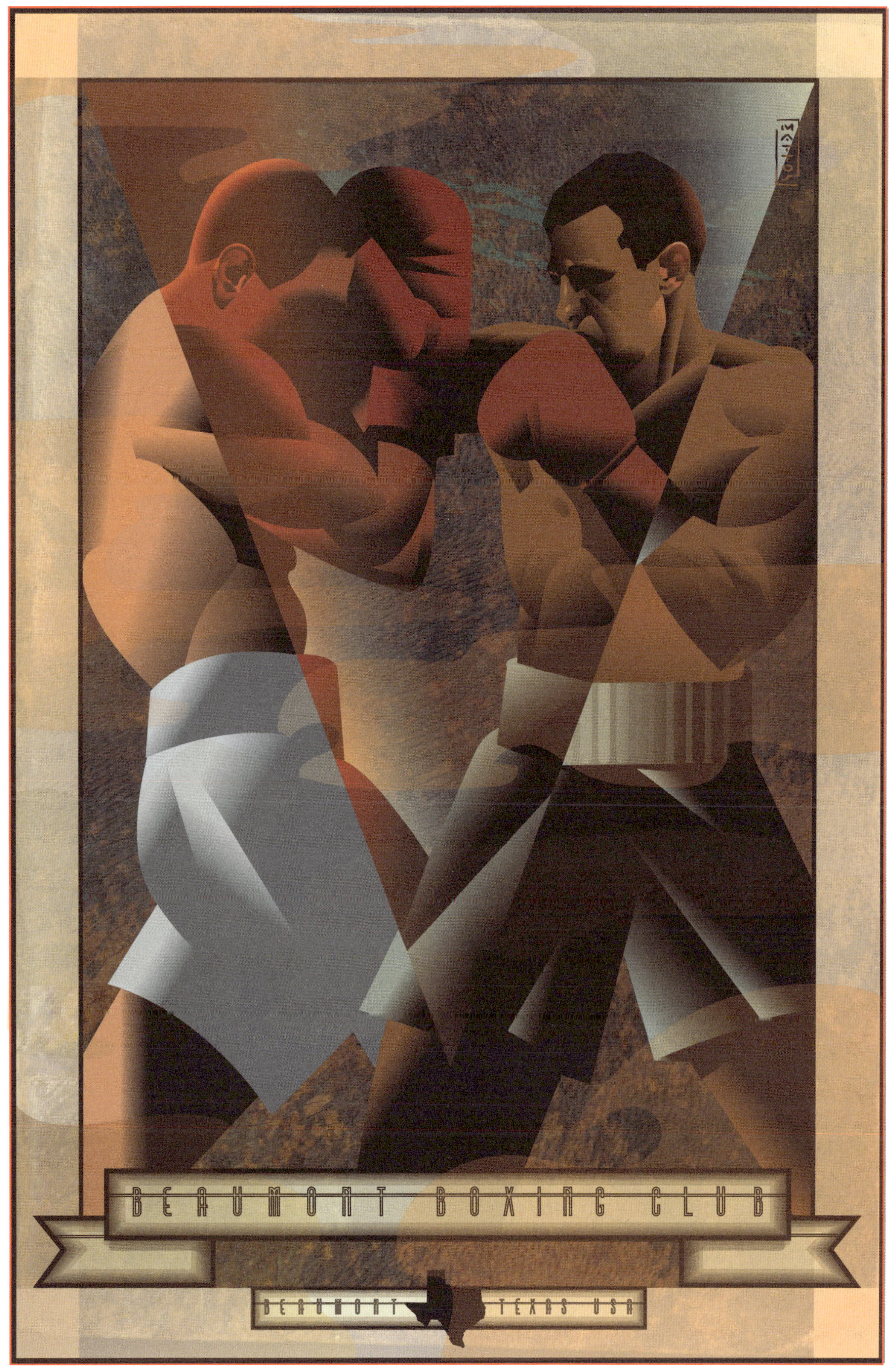

Beaumont Boxing Club

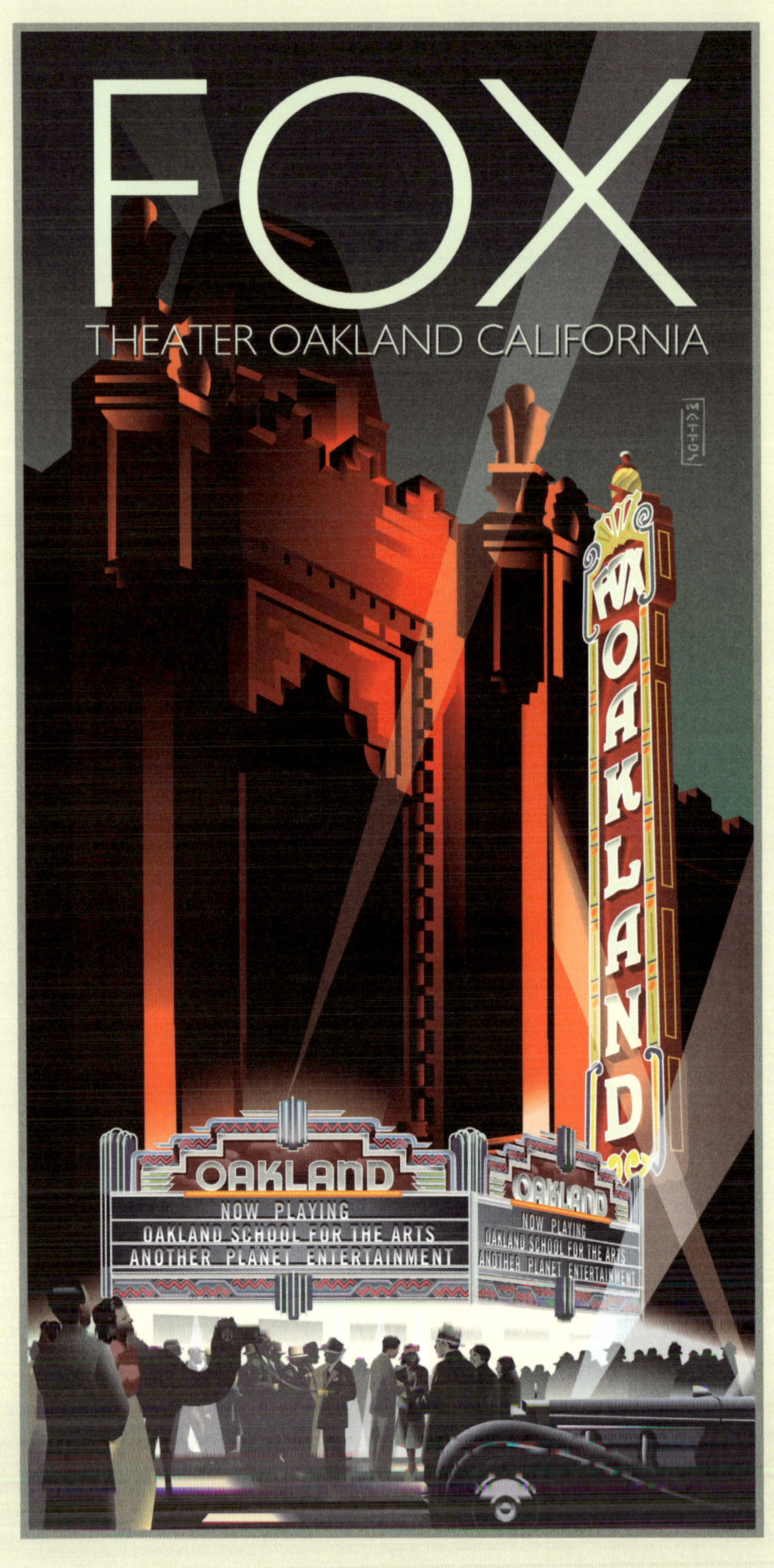

Fox Oakland Poster

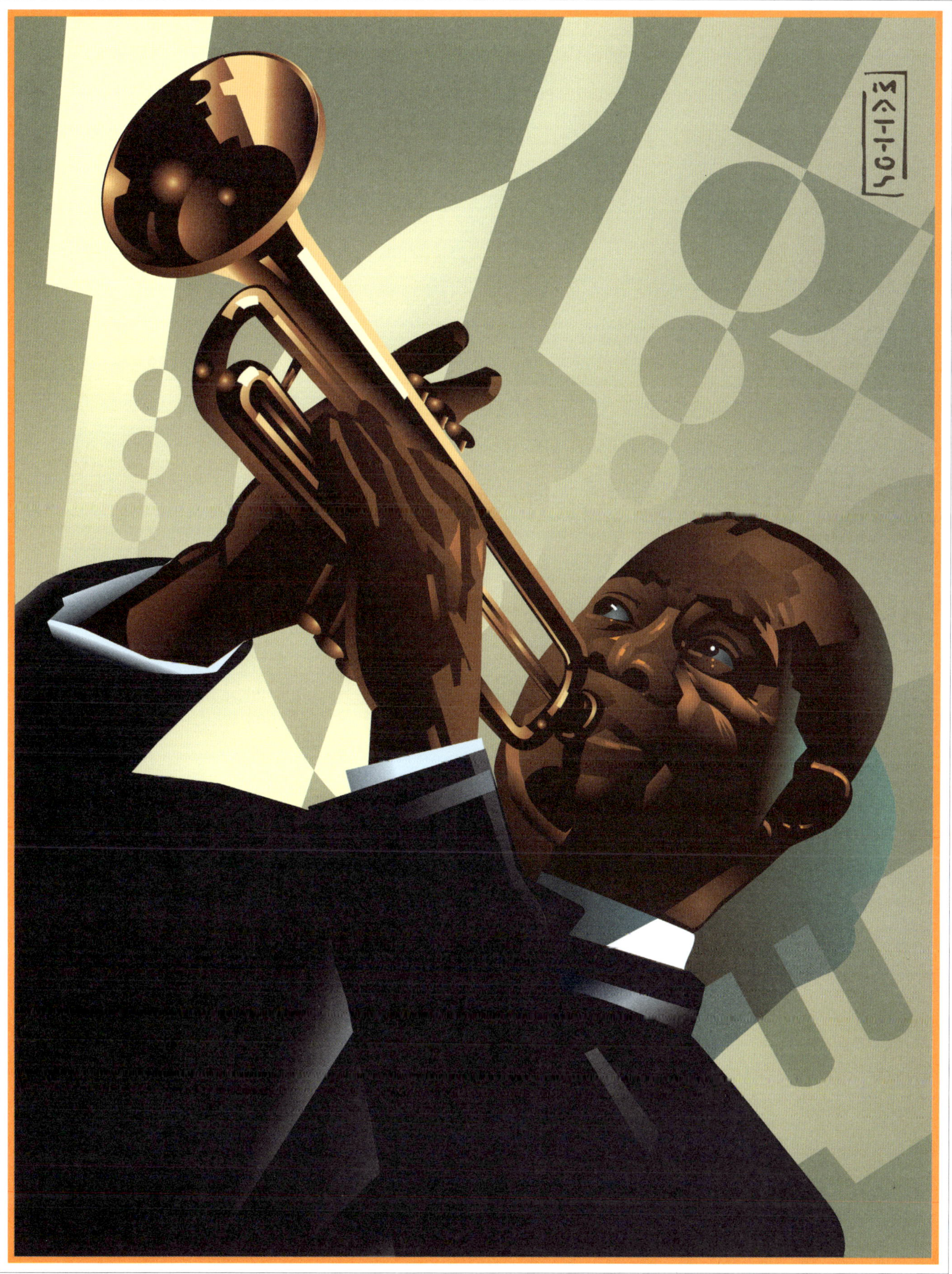

Louis Armstrong Portrait

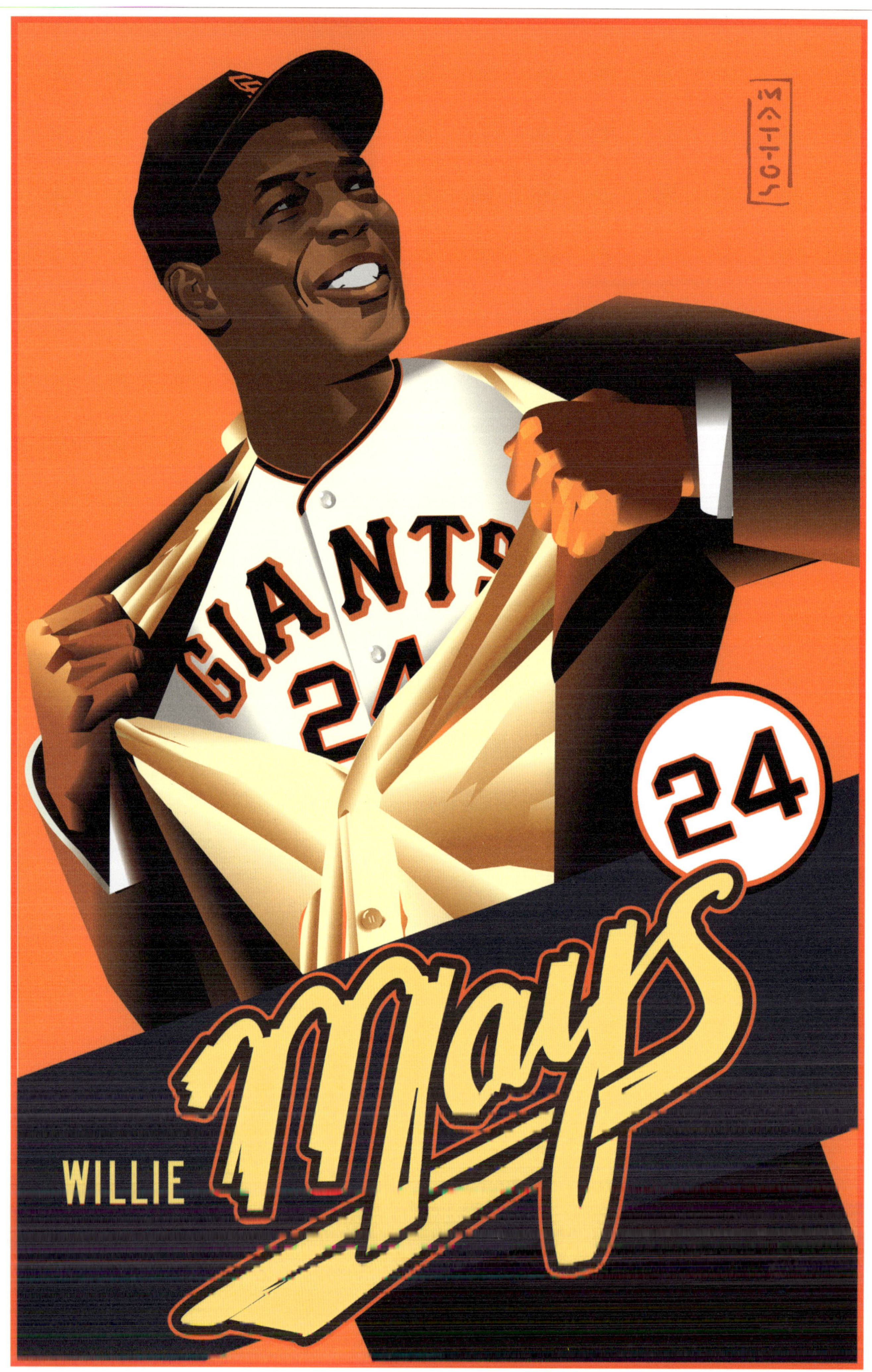

Willie Mays Portrait

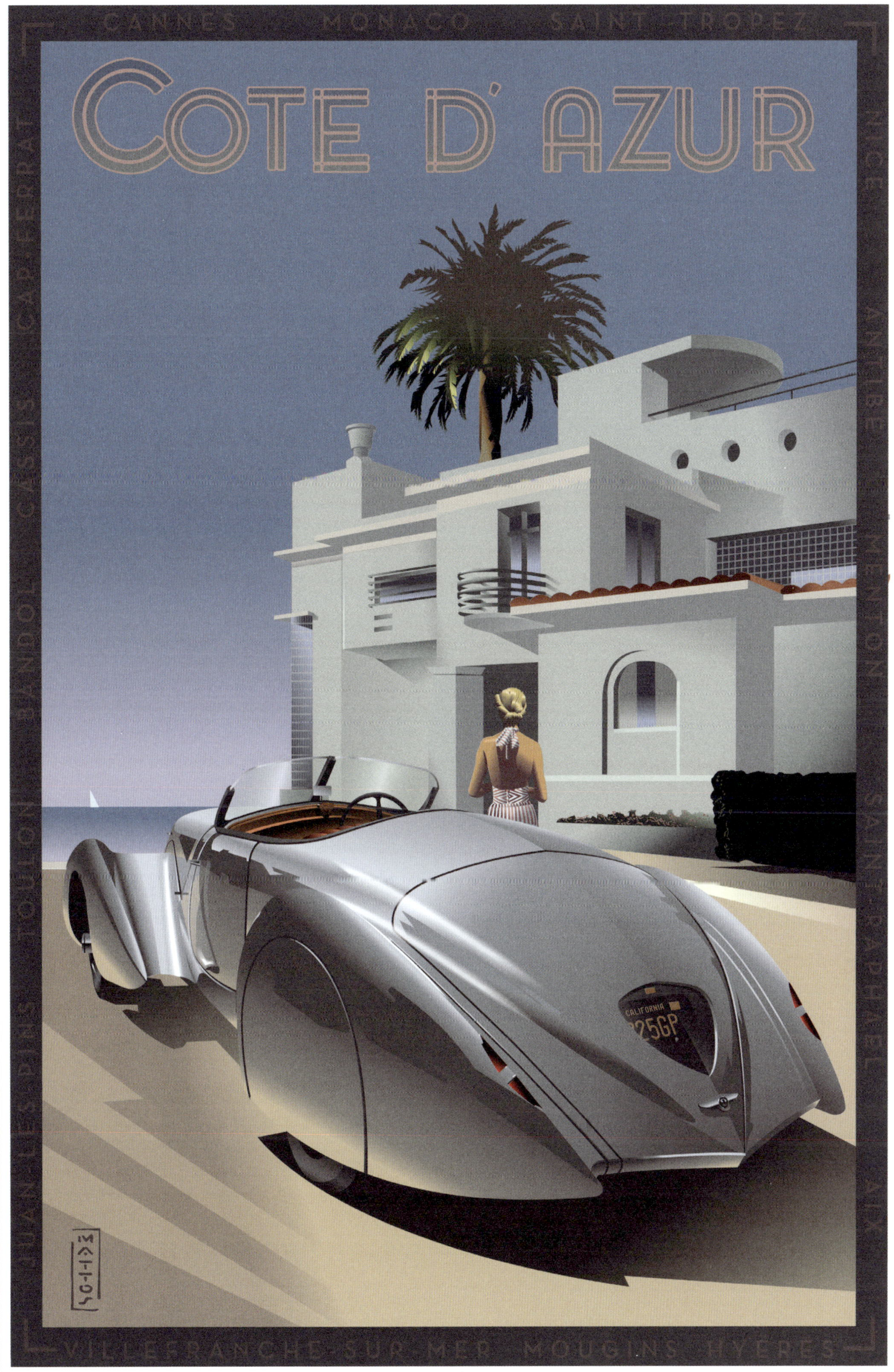

Gary Moore Bentley

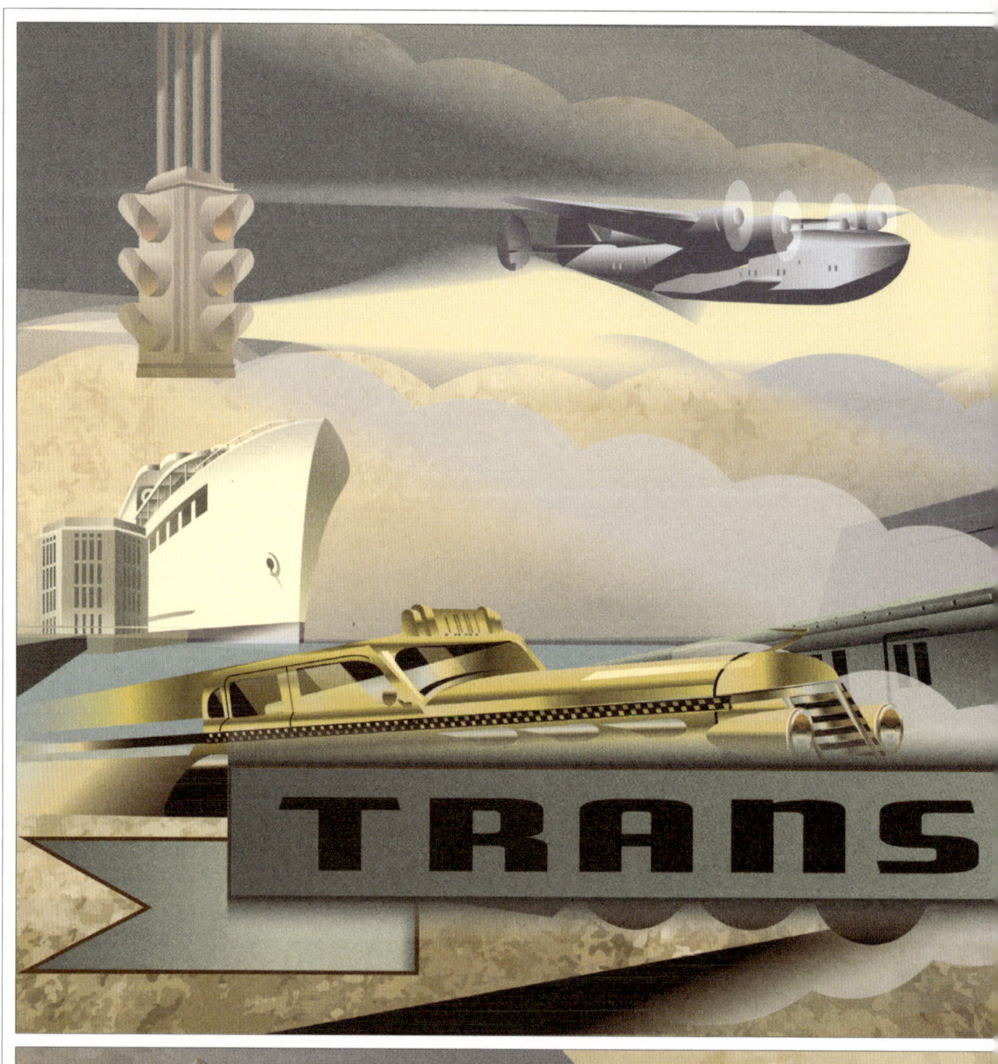
TRANS

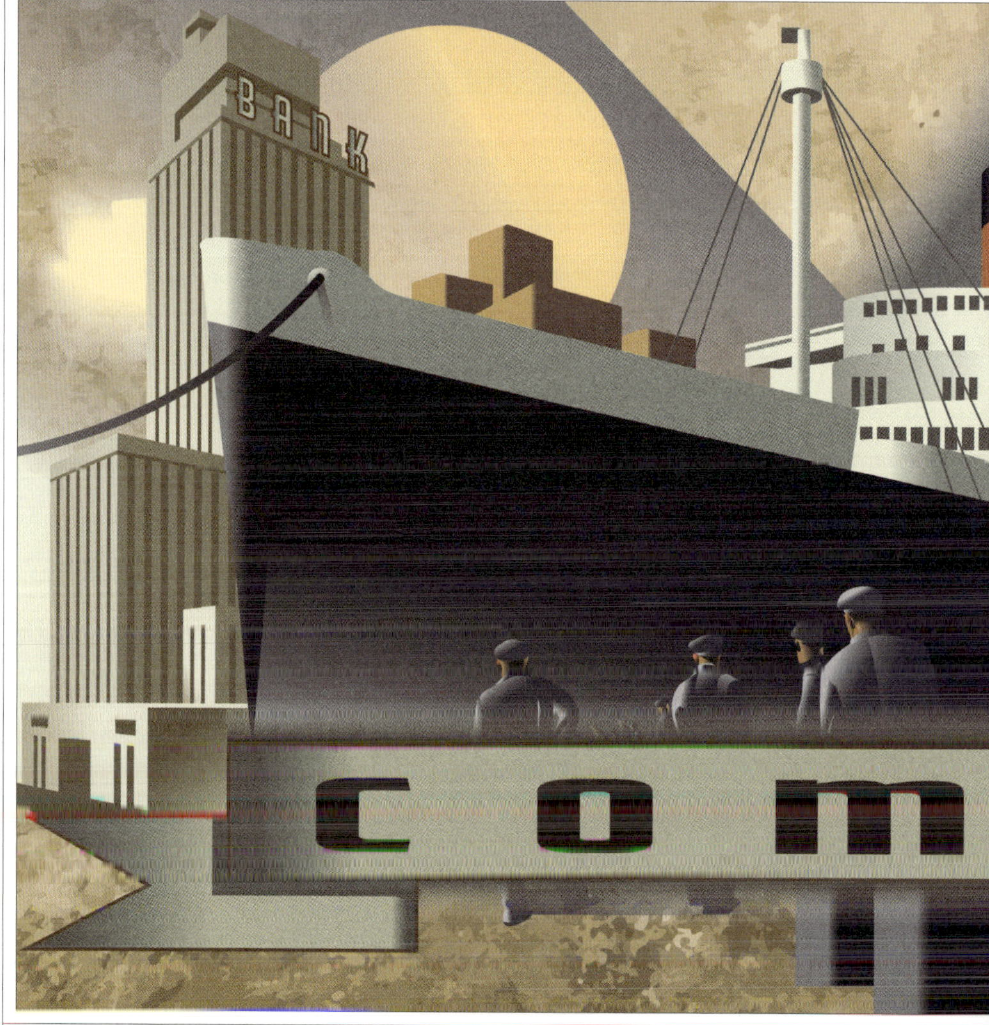
BANK
COM

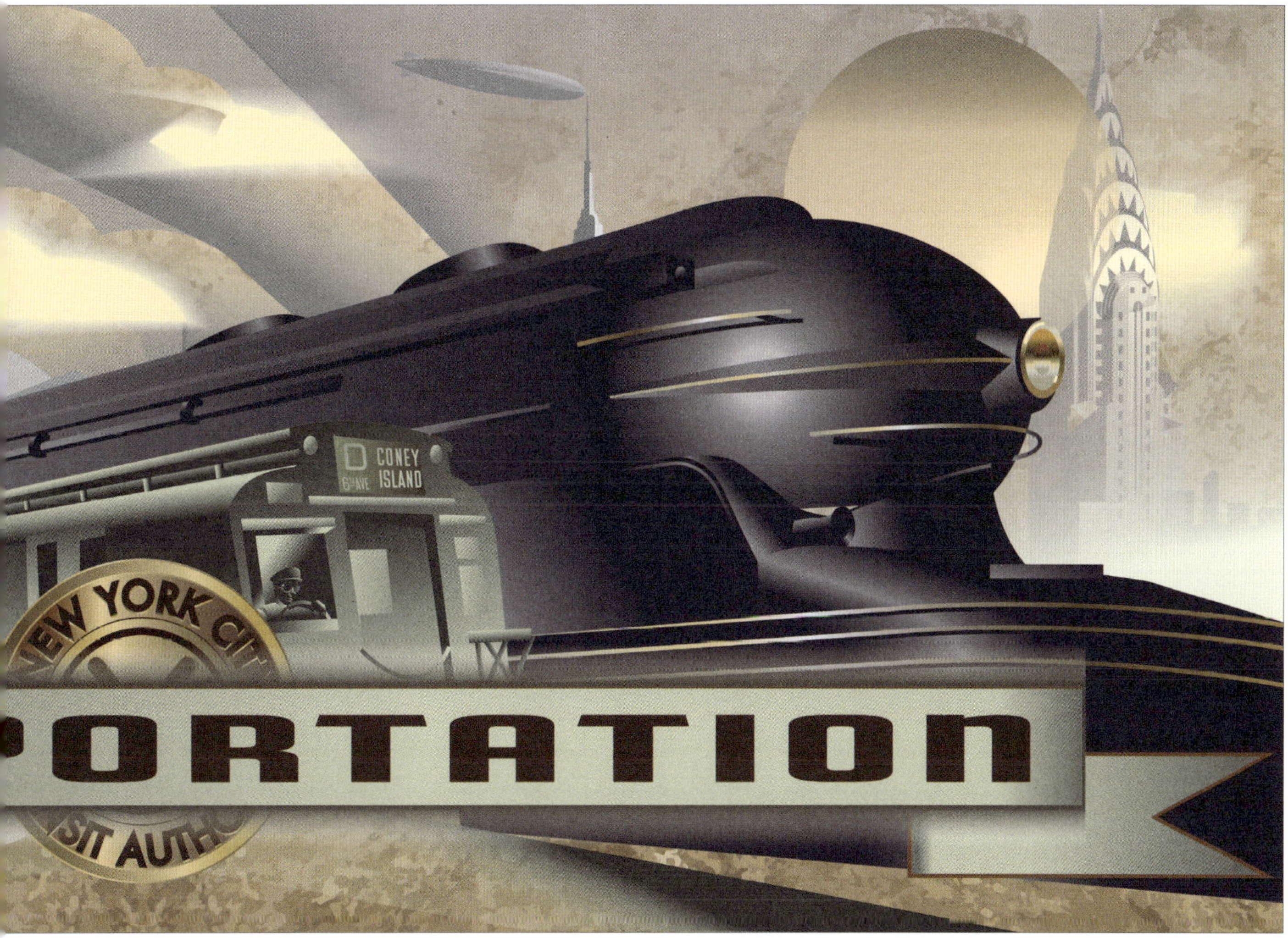

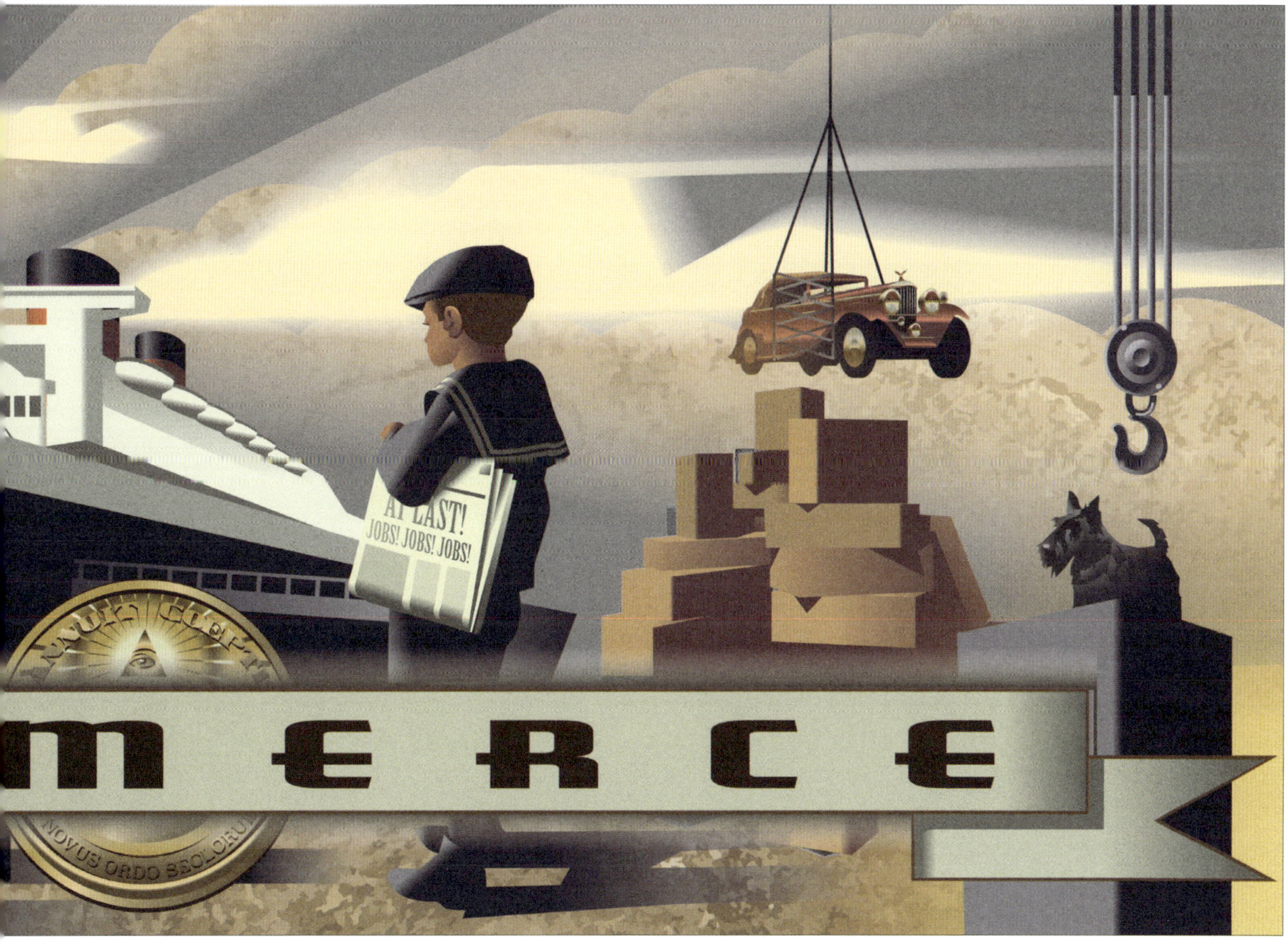

(Top) Netflix Transportation Mural / (Bottom) Netflix Commerce Mural

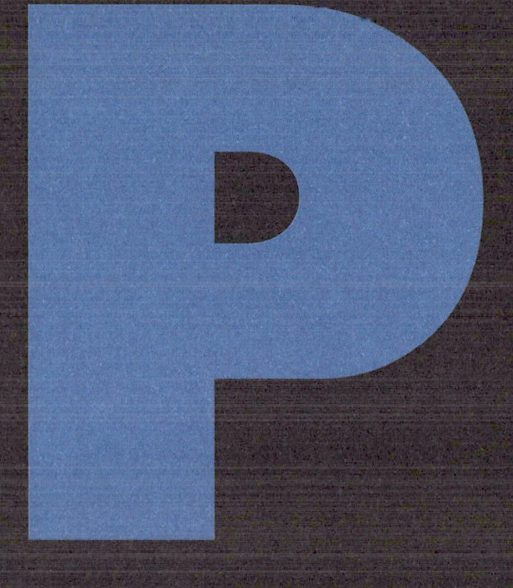

P

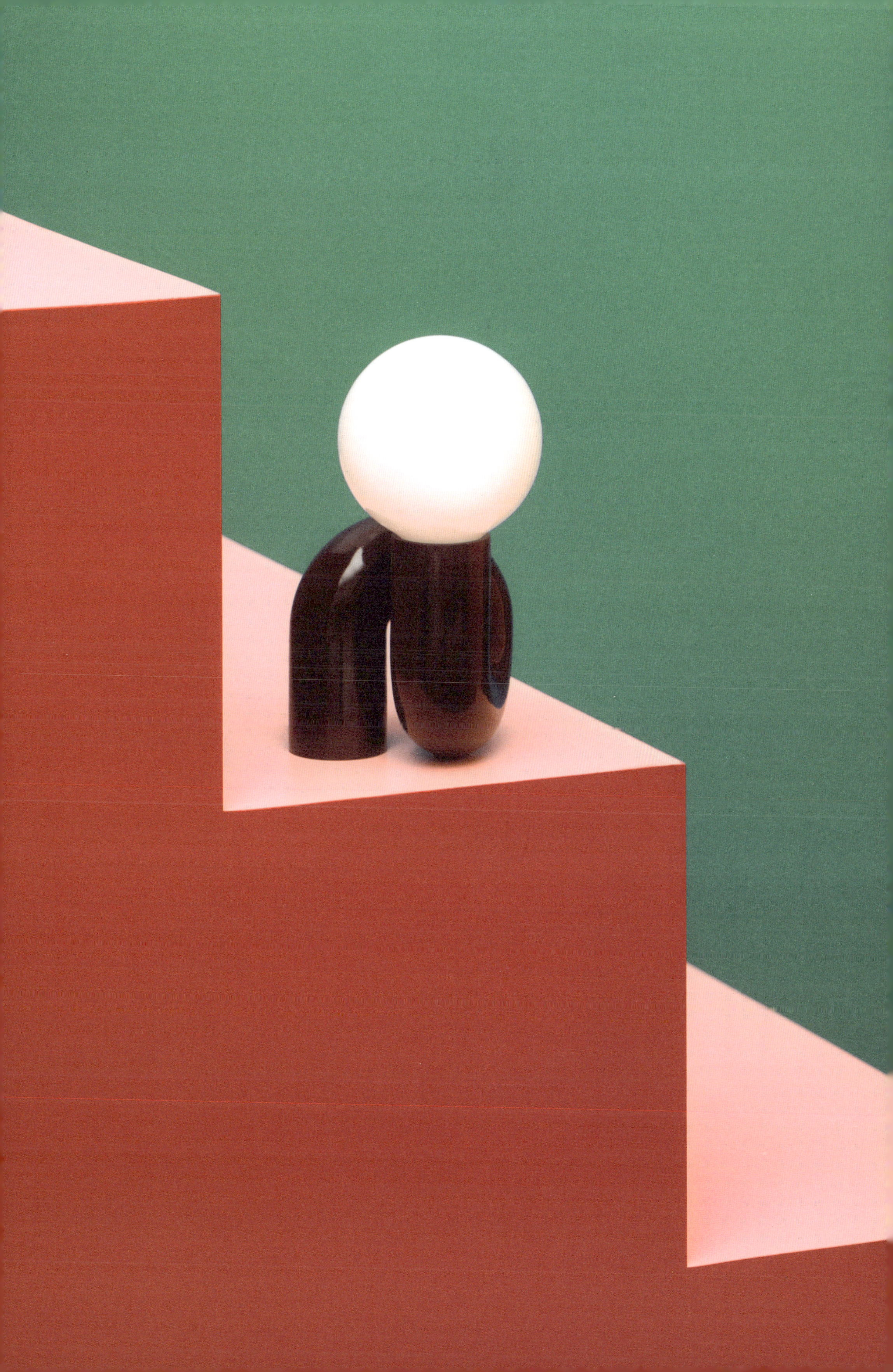

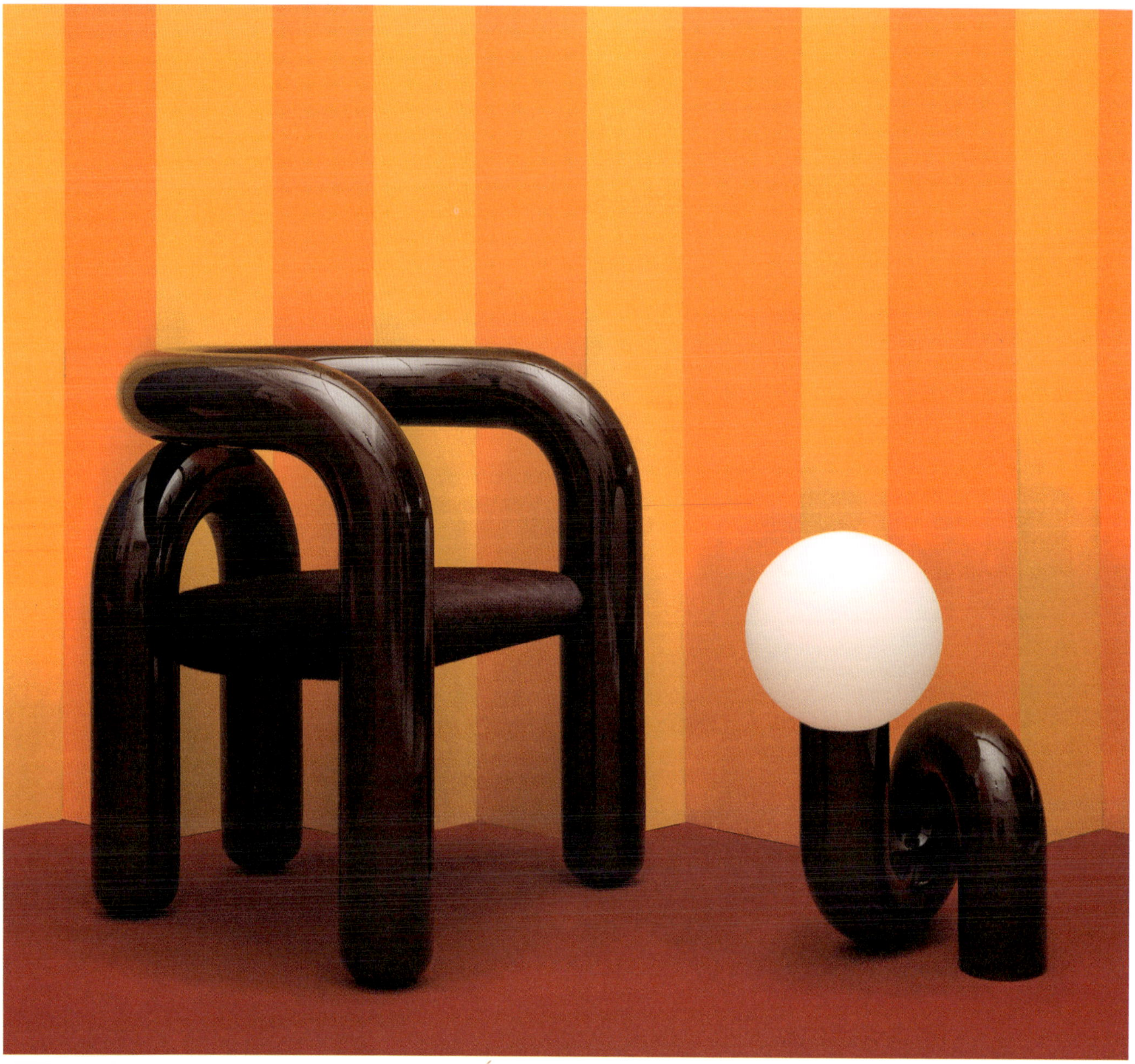

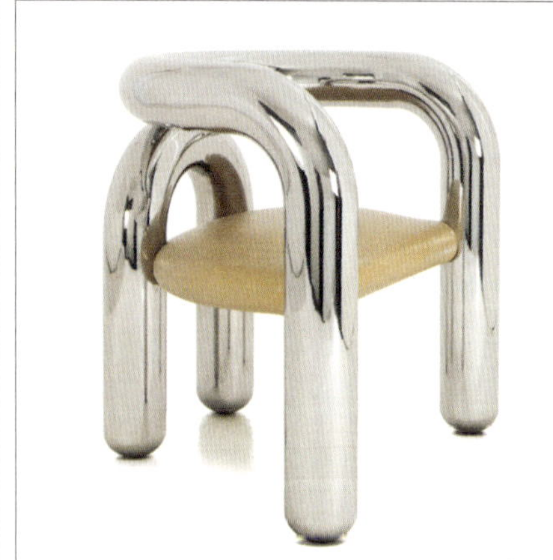

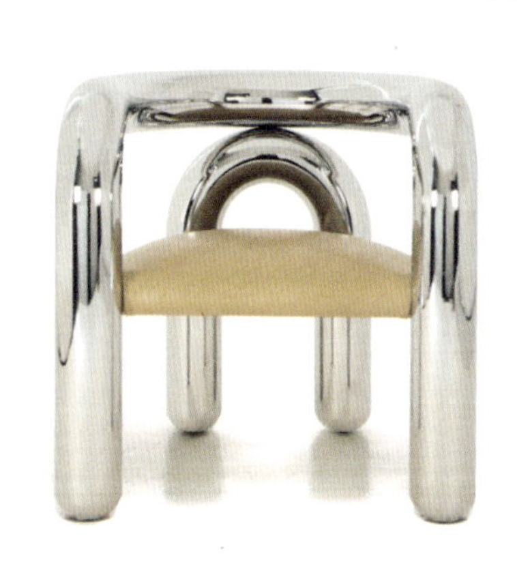

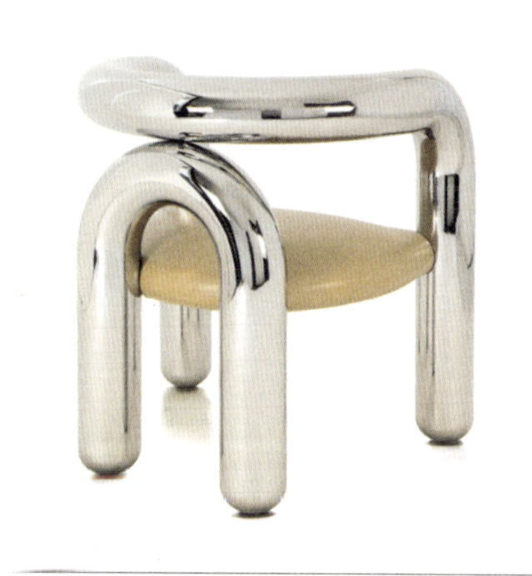

JUMBO Neotenic Collection

This Neotenic lounge chair, priced at $14,000.00, features thick, whimsical curves in its metal arms. The chair comes in an array of fabrics and colors ranging in price, and is part of a series of Neotenic furniture from the designers Monling Lee and Justin Donnelly at the award-winning studio, Jumbo NYC. The full Neotenic collection features the chair, a sconce, a floor light, and a table light, each featuring the same smooth, thick curves and rounded edges. As a finalist in Interior Design Magazine's 2018 NYC Design Awards, its "clumsy" features are meant to bring out our childlike nature. The NYC Gallery, Matter, says the chair allows us to "see ourselves in our surroundings." According to designer Justin Donnelly, its round and cute design "limits our higher brain functions in the presence of childlike or cartoonish things, easing back on adult judgement and anxiety." Cuteness and the relaxed state of mind it brings is the aim for this luxury piece of furniture, which is a rare aesthetic in the design world. Perhaps the Neotenic lounge chair will bring a new turn to childhood in interior design.

ElectraMeccanica is an electric vehicle manufacturer that is looking to the future of affordable and futuristic models. The latest innovation comes in the form of the 2021 ElectraMeccanica SOLO. A single-occupancy vehicle that turns the typical compact driving model on its head. With three-wheels, SOLO combines the best of both worlds of a car and a motorcycle. The SOLO is determined to be the affordable option for single drivers, and a mobile solution for sustainable energy.

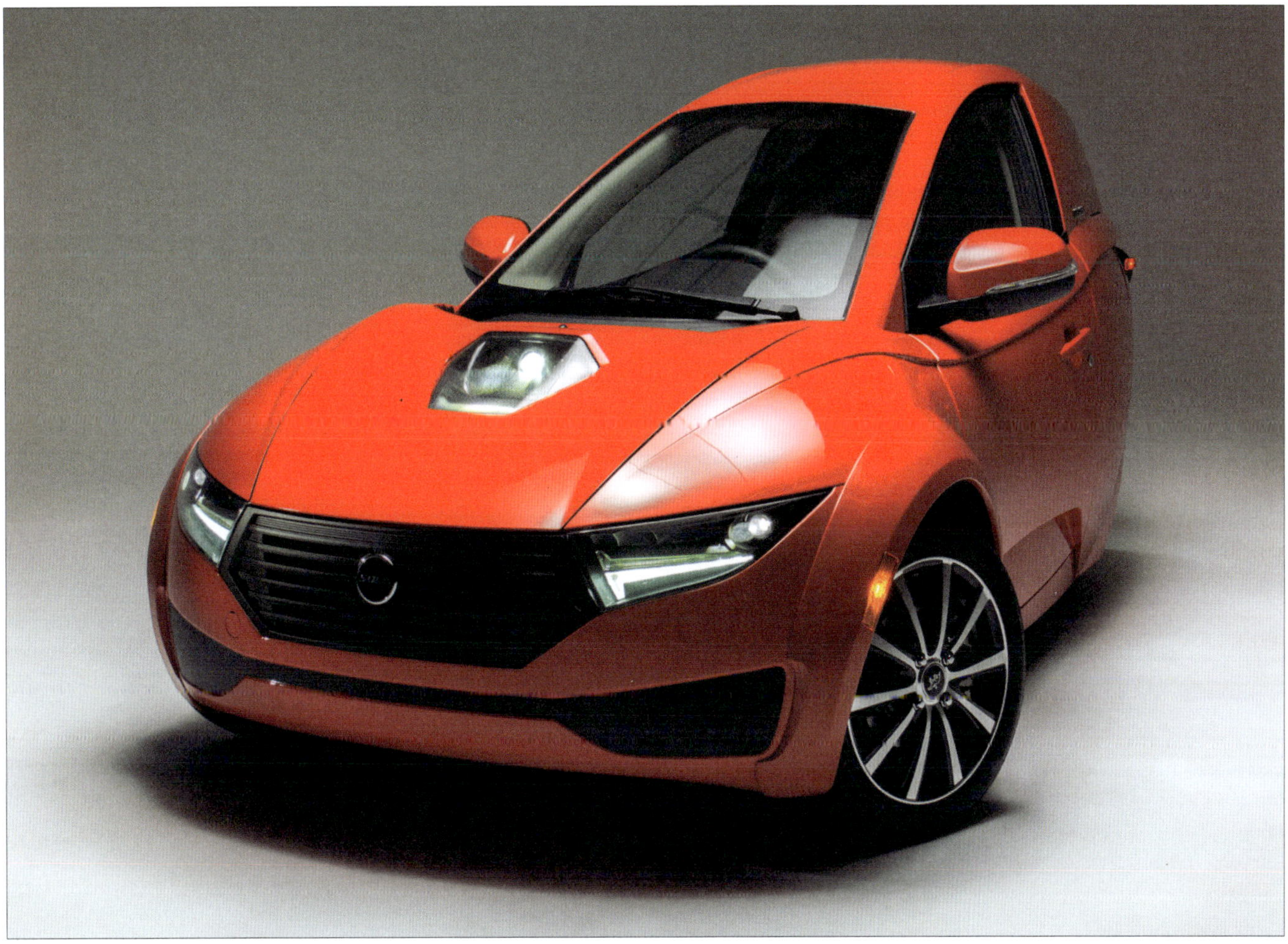

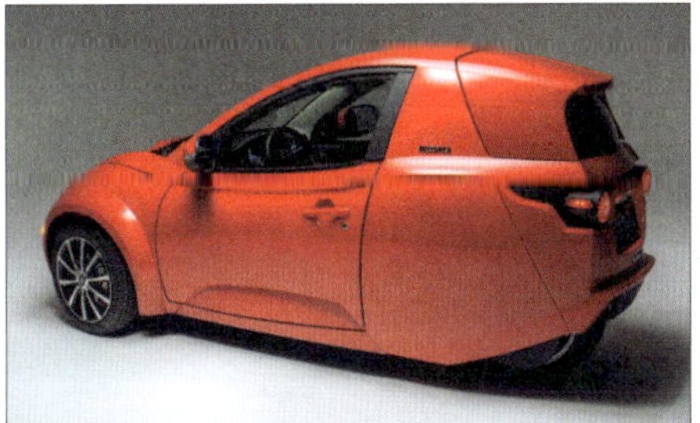

(Top) SOLO Horizontal Side View / (Bottom) Solo Rear Side View

Speed: 80 mph, goes from 0-60 in 10 seconds	**Battery:** 17.3 kWh NCA	LED headlamps	Cluster
Range: 100 miles	**Standard Features.**	Heated seat	Rearview camera
Full Charge: Less than 4 hrs using 220V outlets	3 Colors: Electric Red, Raven Black, and Arctic White	Bluetooth stereo with USB and LCD Digital Instrument	Cargo Space: 5 cubic ft

According to ElectraMeccanica, 119 million people in North America commute using personal cars, while as much as 105 million of those people commute by themselves without passengers. The SOLO removes the unused seating and is perfect for commuters who travel on their own. The SOLO is completely electric powered, reducing their carbon footprint by eliminating the need for gas. With more and more public charge stations popping up at malls and parking lots, the SOLO can be taken almost anywhere, including the highways.

The design of the SOLO from the front looks like your typical car, with headlights and a hood. But at the back, the combustion engine has been removed, along with the passenger seats, turning into a three-wheeled vehicle. The SOLO is just as safe as a standard car, with side impact protection, and front and rear crumple zones. The SOLO offers a unique driving experience with zero emissions, zero noise and zero time wasted at the pump - drastically reducing cost from your wallet. Pre-orders for the SOLO are available on the ElectraMeccanica website.

PERHAPS THE MOST IMPRESSIVE PART OF THE SOLO EXPERIENCE IS THAT YOU CAN INSTANTLY FORGET THAT YOU'RE IN A THREE-WHEELER.

Jeff Zurschmeide, *Freelance Writer, Digital Trends*

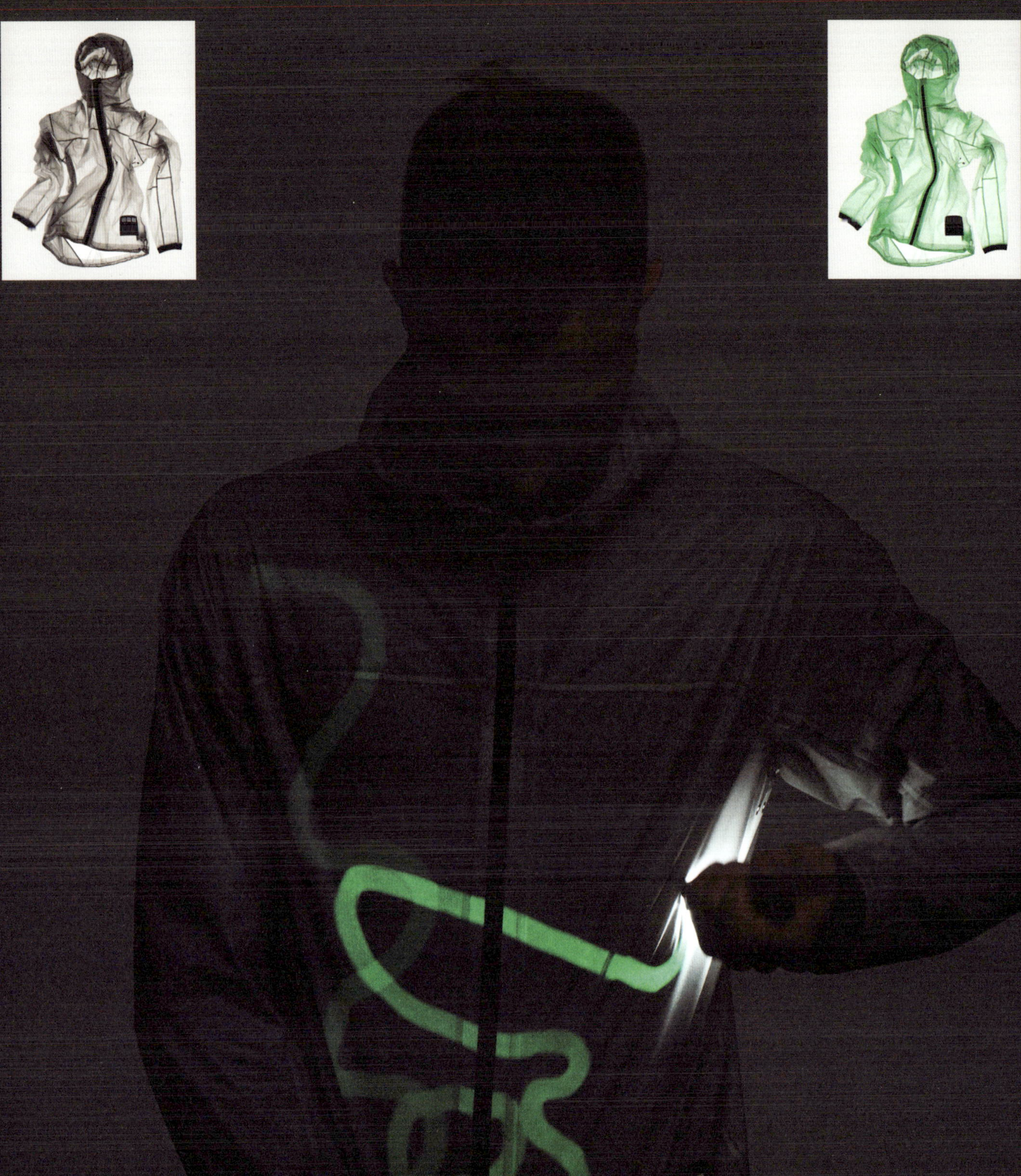

Opposite: Vollebak's solar charged jacket was named one of the winners of Time Magazine's Best Inventions of 2018. With Vollebak's intention of creating clothing for the future, the jacket runs on solar energy that converts into emanating light that glows in the dark. Due to the phosphorescent compound within the jacket's lining, it is able to store all forms of light and emit them over time. Fully charged, the jacket gives off a luminous green glow like "Kryptonite" that will last up to 12 hours. When not charged, it is semi-translucent and becomes darker or lighter based on the clothing underneath. The jacket is also waterproof, stretchy, breathable, and lightweight. Perfect for athletic activities, or even just as a fashion statement. No wonder this is called the "Swiss-army knife" of jackets.

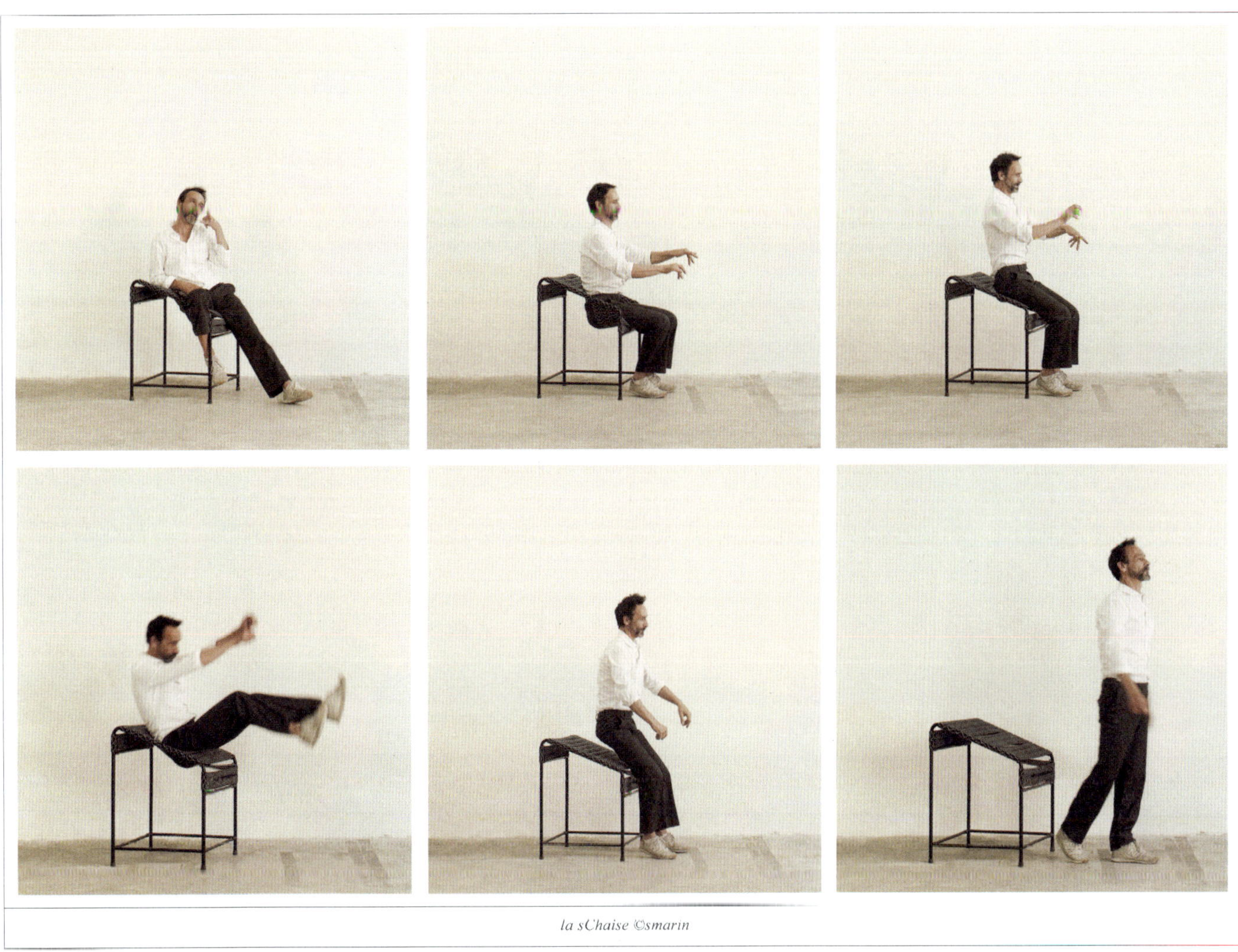

la sChaise ©smarin

Above: One of the most difficult office struggles is the ability to continue sitting in your flat, uncomfortable office chair for hours and hours on end. However, Smarin has a solution for that; their "sChaise" is, as their website describes, "a new therapeutic object through mechanics." ■ The chair is made with a steel frame and fabric, resistant, elastic straps; all materials having been made in France. Because the seat has that allowance for rebound with the elastic straps, it makes the chair much more ergonomic than any other flat office chair that you've experienced. Along with the chair being incredibly comfortable, it also promotes better posture and good blood circulation because of the better flexibility your spine will feel. Your back will thank you when you've sat in the sChaise.

A

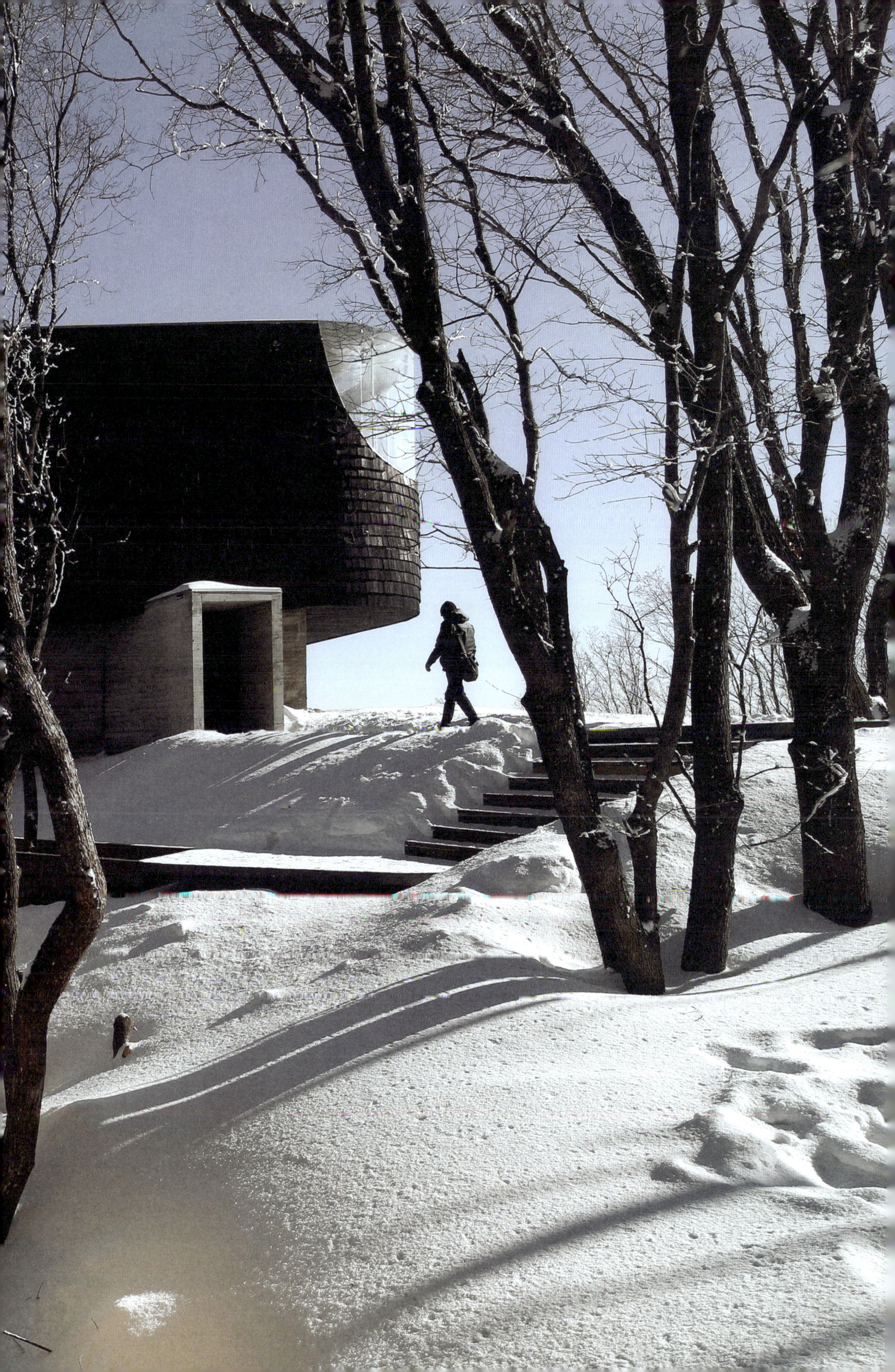

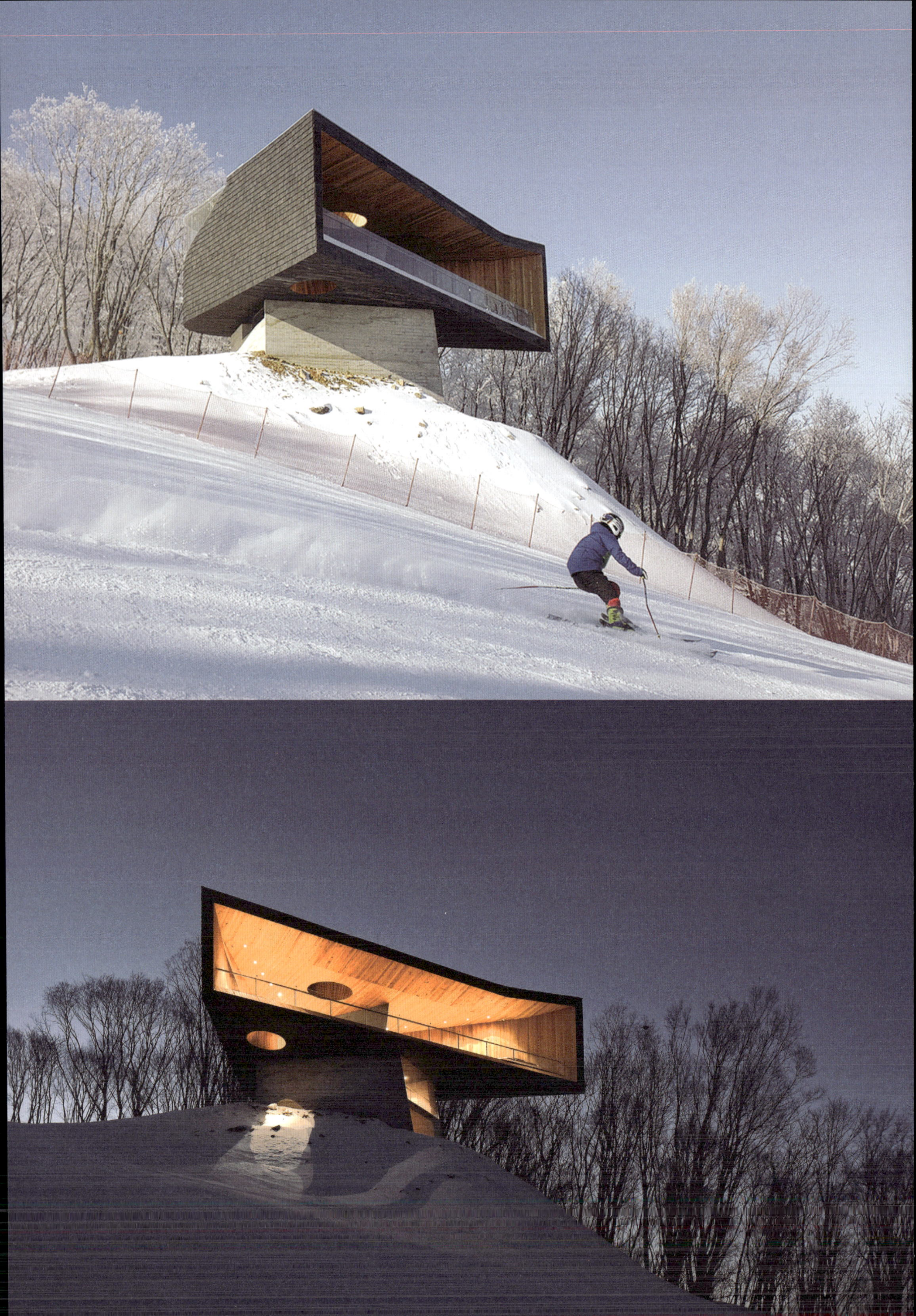

Located in Jilin, China, at Songhua Lake Resort, is a structure called Stage of Forest. The location and shape of the stage took a lot of planning; the architects at META-Project had to determine the site condition in order to reduce the impact for plant life that already lived there, and to make sure the view of the stage stood out.

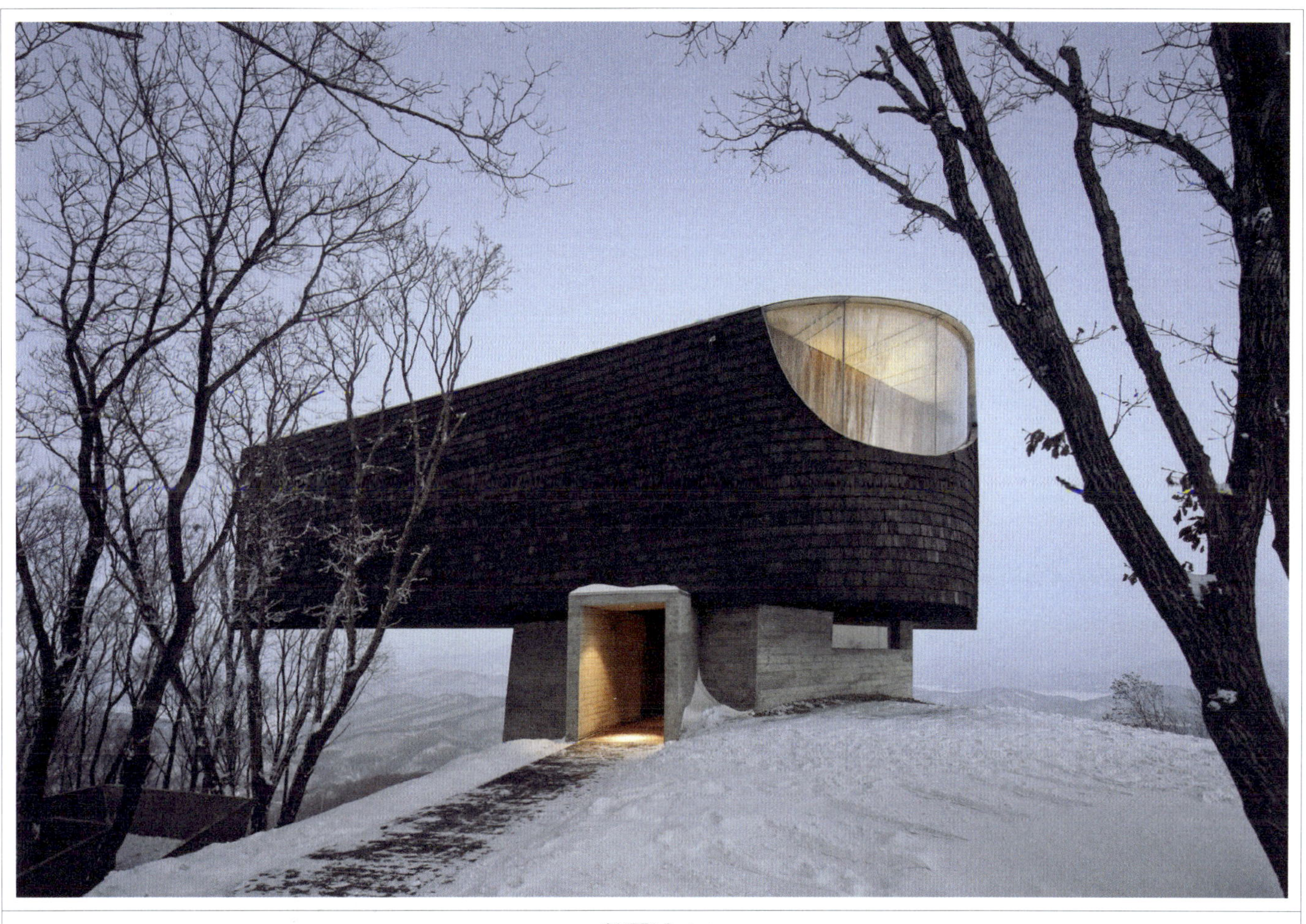

©META-Project

Placed on a hillside between the forest and a slope, the final product sits on a hill facing the Songhua Lake. It can be seen by visitors coming from two different ways, from the ski-slope and from the trail in the forest. The structure does not block the view of the nature surrounding it, but rather becomes a part of a landscape. Since from a distance, it is horizontal, and up close it is vertical, the building has a twisted look depending on the perspective.

When seen at a distance, the stage is a dark stone simply floating in the landscape, with a concrete base underneath it. When seen at a closer view, you can see more of the details; it is covered with rough charred cedar shingles, and the concrete base has a wooden texture. Inside the structure, there is a narrow staircase that leads to the stage, which gives you a panoramic view of the entire landscape. There are also oval openings inside, one on the floor and one on the roof. The one on the floor allows you to see below the stage, and you can interact with the people outside. The opening on the roof brings in sunlight and some snowflakes in the winter. The walls inside are red cedar, and are very colorful and vibrant compared to the outside.

When creating the "Stage of Forest," META-Project believes that working in nature is a new way for humans and nature to interact. This structure is not just used to view the landscape, but can be used for public events, exhibitions, and meetings. META-Project wants to encourage people to explore their relationship with nature, while working within nature.

THE "STAGE OF FOREST" IS INTENDED TO STIMULATE PEOPLE TO EXPLORE THEIR RELATIONSHIP WITH NATURE, AND TO BECOME PART OF NATURE ITSELF.

META-Project, *meta-project.org*

USA architect, Nina Edwards Anker, founded nea studio in 2006, focusing on architecture and interiors. She is the architect behind the beach house, "Cocoon," located in Southampton, Long Island, New York. The house is laid out in the shape of an "L," forming what looks like a co-

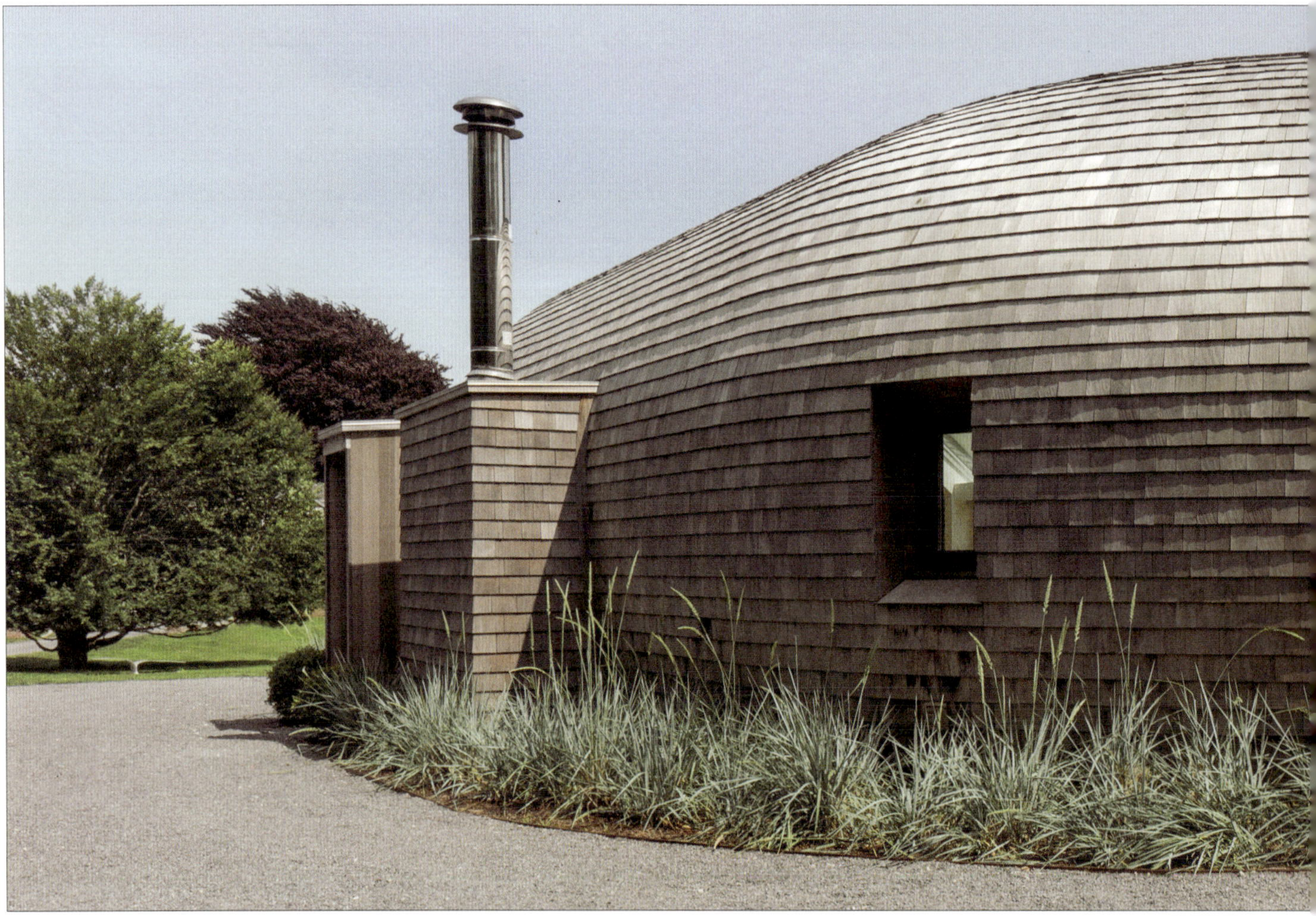

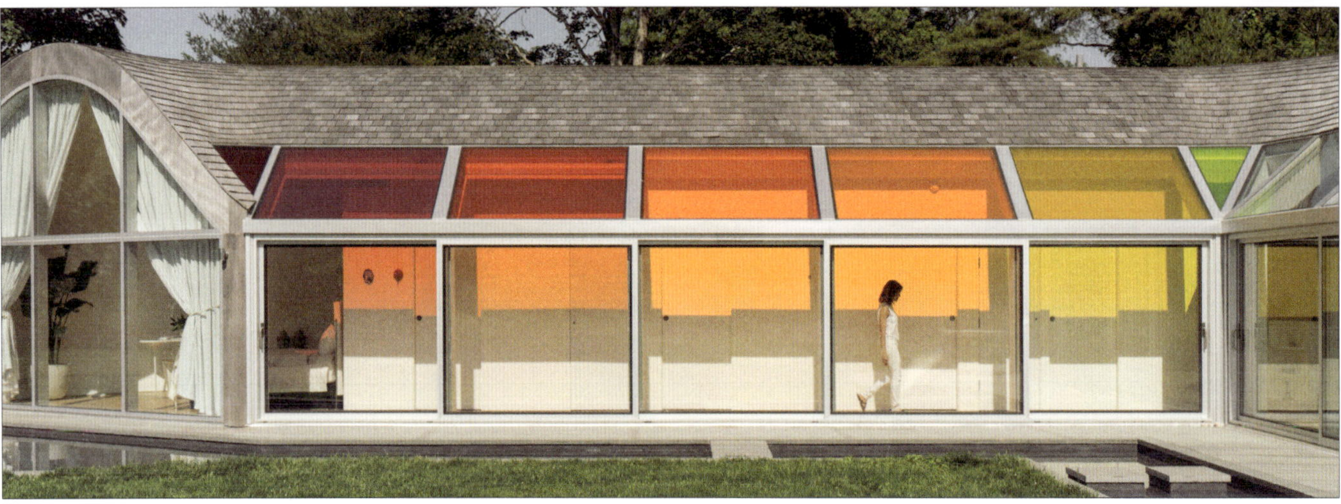

Anker set a goal to create an incredibly sustainable house, and now the Cocoon has a Gold LEED-certification to prove that! Not only is the house powered by solar energy, but it is surrounded by native plants, utilizes rainwater recycling, and stores the sun's heat in the back wall of the house in order for the house to be heated using passive heating. Additionally, there is no structural steel used whatsoever in the house, the house only has timber. Not using structural steel is both helpful for the natural surroundings to reduce carbon emissions as well as for the human lungs.

The back wall, in addition to being the vessel for storing their passive heating, wraps around the house, actually acting as the front of the house facing the rest of the neighborhood. The back wall is where the name "Cocoon" derives from in that this wall curves around the house, forming a cocoon. With the back wall facing the rest of their neighborhood, its cedar shingle cladding that wraps around the house blends in with the architectural material palette of their historical neighborhood beautifully. The house has a relatively small footprint, standing at 16-feet high and just one story. It is dwarfed by the neighboring trees.

coon from the front of the house. The Cocoon's distinct shape was not only meant for aesthetics, though; the house is laid out in the cocoon-like formation in order to maximize daylight and solar energy, something that Anker is passionate about.

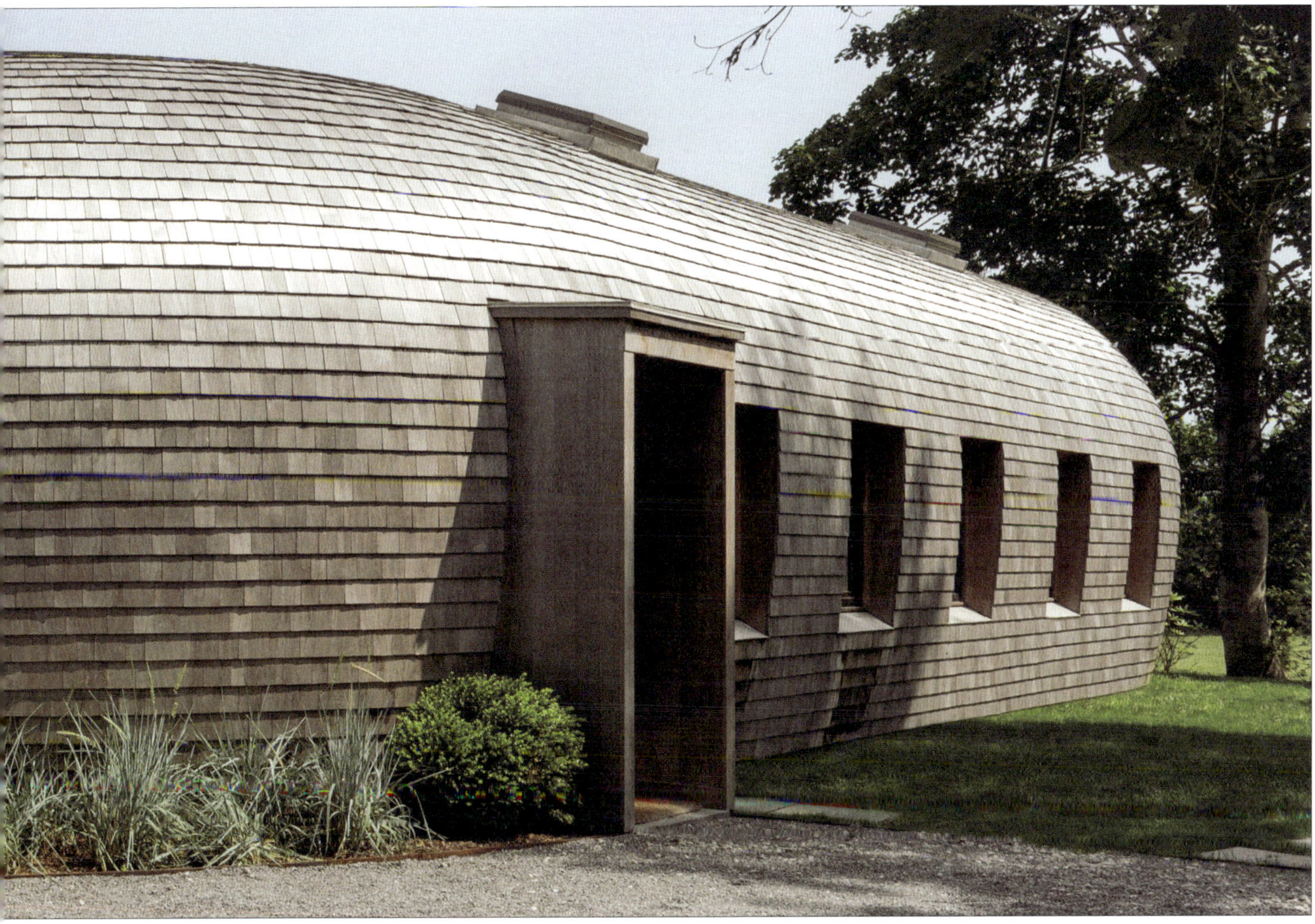

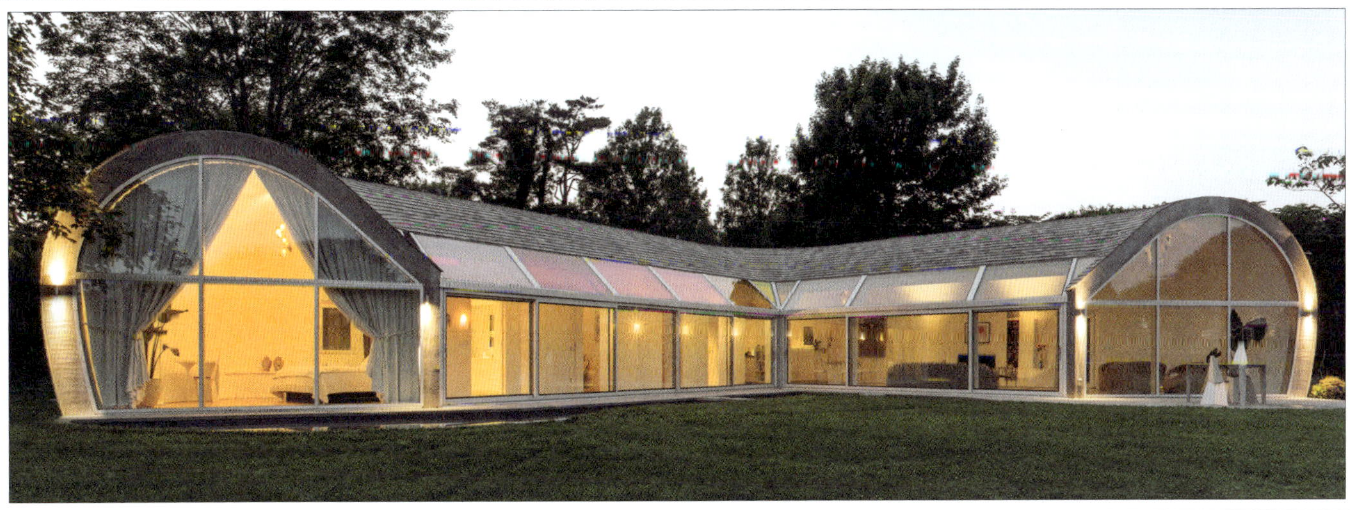

Images by Caylon Hackwith

As the back wall faces the rest of their neighborhood, their inner walls face the south, with a view of the beautiful natural wildlife preserve on the wetland. These walls are completely made of glass, filling the house with natural light all year round. This house is always filled with light and color though because of the colored skylights that are installed throughout the floor plan. Across the entire house are colored skylights based on the color theory of Goethe. In this color theory, the importance is put on how sunlight reflects light; Goethe's color wheel is still in rainbow order, but reads "good," underneath yellow, indicating that this color is a neutral, happy tone. This color theory was used by J.M. Williams Turner in his 19th century paintings of sunlight above water. Edwards Anker used vermilion red skylights over the bedroom to represent sunset and rest and a deep yellow skylight in the living room to represent activity. As you walk from the bedroom to the living room, the skylights slowly transition from red to yellow to symbolize the energy of a new day.

Nina Edwards Anker says that her focus is on creating an alternative to cookie-cutter sameness, the hedges and manicured lawns typical of the Hamptons.

Lundhagem and Atelier Oslo present the revolutionary Deichman Bjørvika Library in Oslo, Norway. Originally slated to open in March 2020, the library features six floors of reading with a cinema and auditorium in the basement. The library is situated next to an opera house on the scenic Oslo waterfront, and although the land itself is small, the building makes up for it with a cantilever structure, its upper stories jutting out above the water.

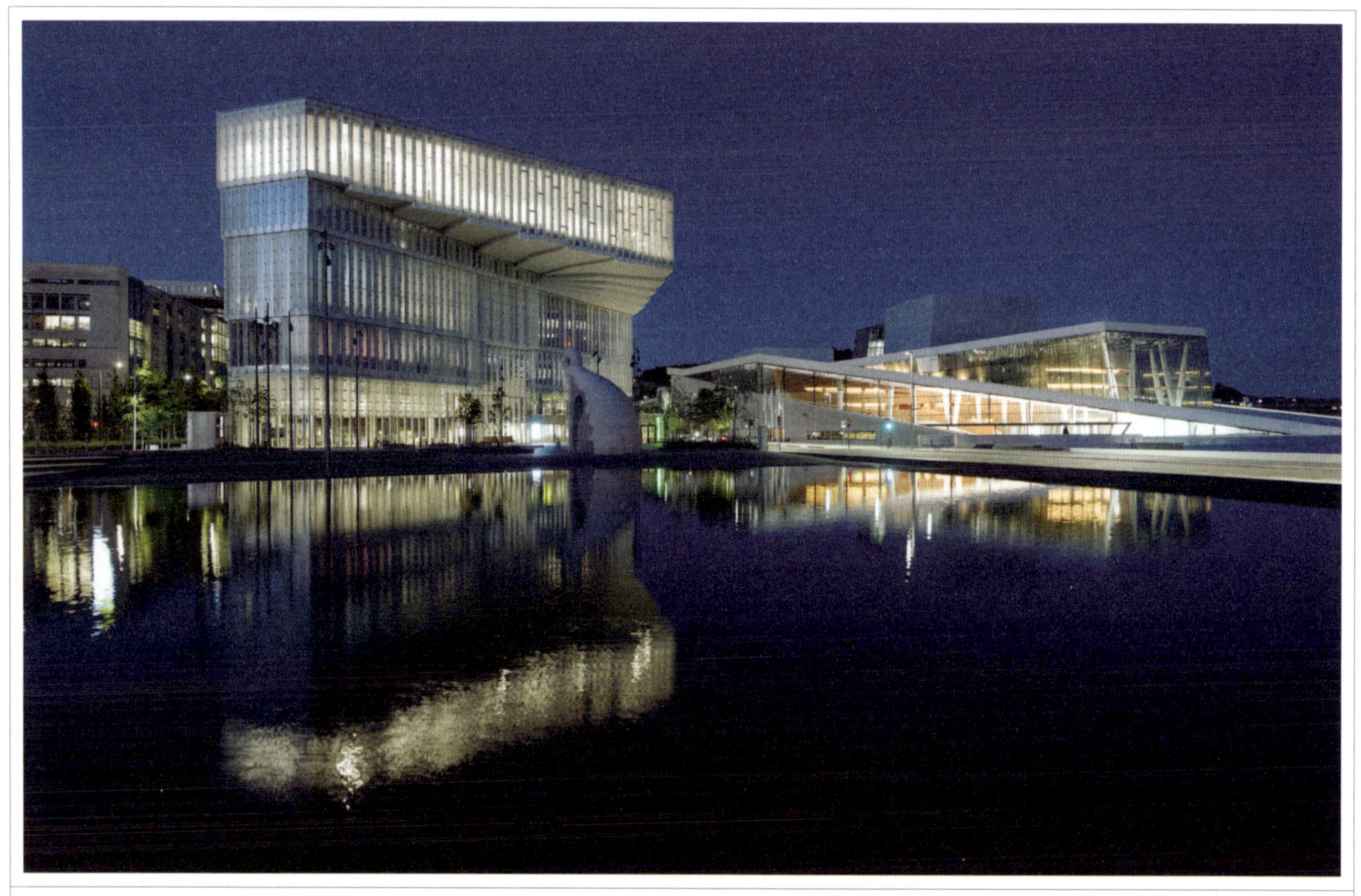

Photo: Einar Aslaksen

450,000 books make their home in this new library. The library receives its name from Carl Deichman, who started the library's collections by donating the first books back in 1785. The library is expertly crafted with the height of entertainment in mind; each floor is broken into smaller sections so that the library itself feels secular and neat despite its overwhelming height. Atelier Oslo says of the building's interior design, "Even though the books still have a strong presence, this library is designed first and foremost as a place for people."

The books are organized starting with the childrens' section, gaming rooms, and mini theatres in the lower floors, rising up to science and non-fiction in the higher floors. Everything is set up so the library becomes quieter as visitors take escalators higher and higher up. Study rooms are built with beautiful contrasting white and black minimalistic color schemes and great floor-length panoramic windows designed to let in as much light as possible. At the highest floor, the library boasts the Future Art Project, a collection of writings started in 2014. Each year, one selected author will publish a piece of writing to be displayed in the library in 2114.

Deichman Bjørvika Library encourages visitors to explore and make themselves at home with its bright natural lighting and welcoming, open corridors. "The interior opens for exploration like in a forest, where you are constantly invited around the next corner to discover new areas of the library," says architect Lundhagem. The Library itself also features a cafe with a terrace and its own restaurant, Centropa. The invitation is truly felt throughout the building's interior design, as the children's reading rooms feature bold splashes of color. Visitors worldwide will find the Deichman Bjørvika Library an easy addition to their traveling bucket list.

THE DEICHMANN LIBRARY AIMS TO REDEFINE WHAT A PUBLIC LIBRARY IS AND SHOULD BE.

Quinn Ho, *Oslo's New Library Will Redefine Public Libraries In Europe, Gonomad.com*

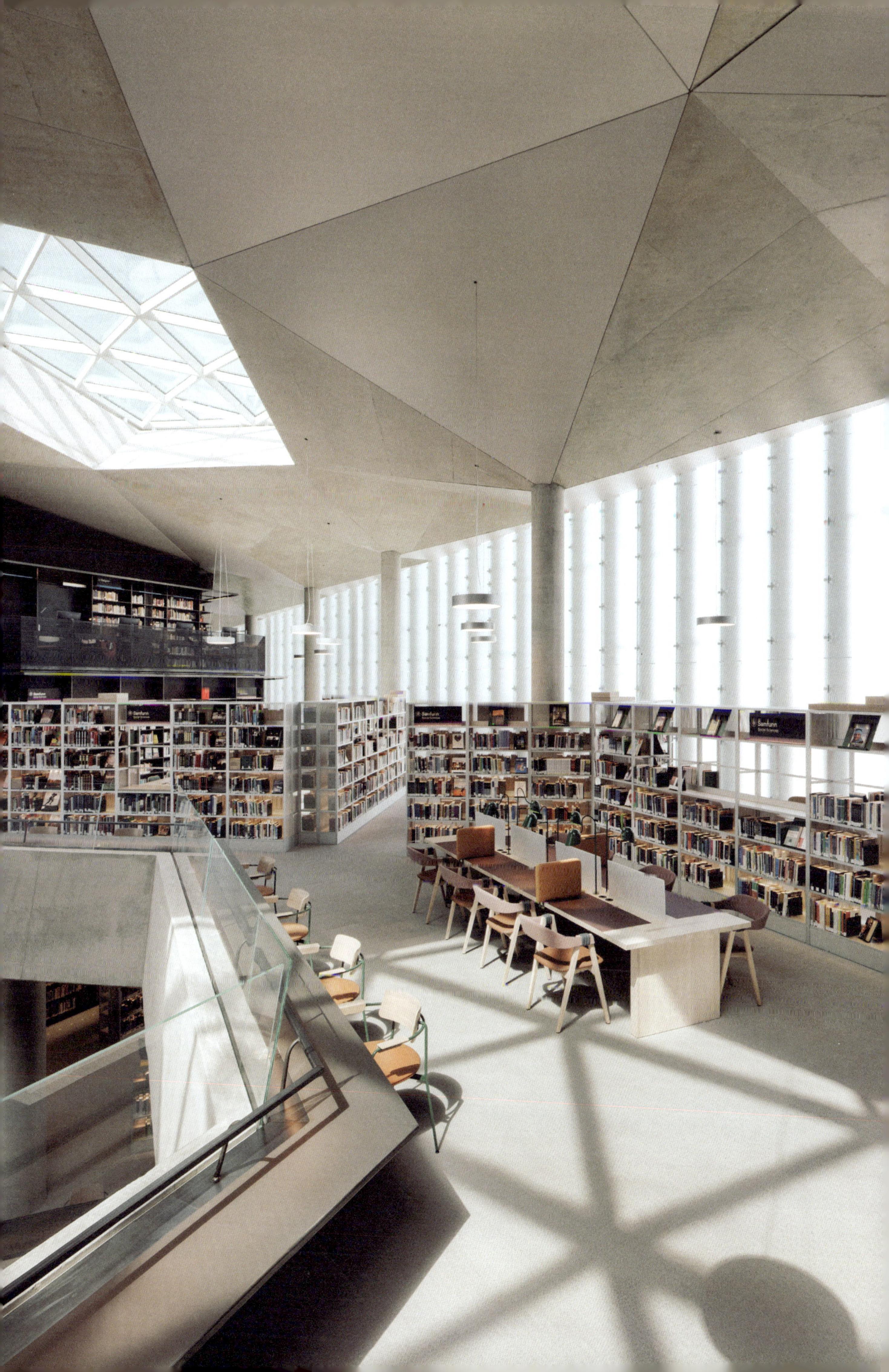

E

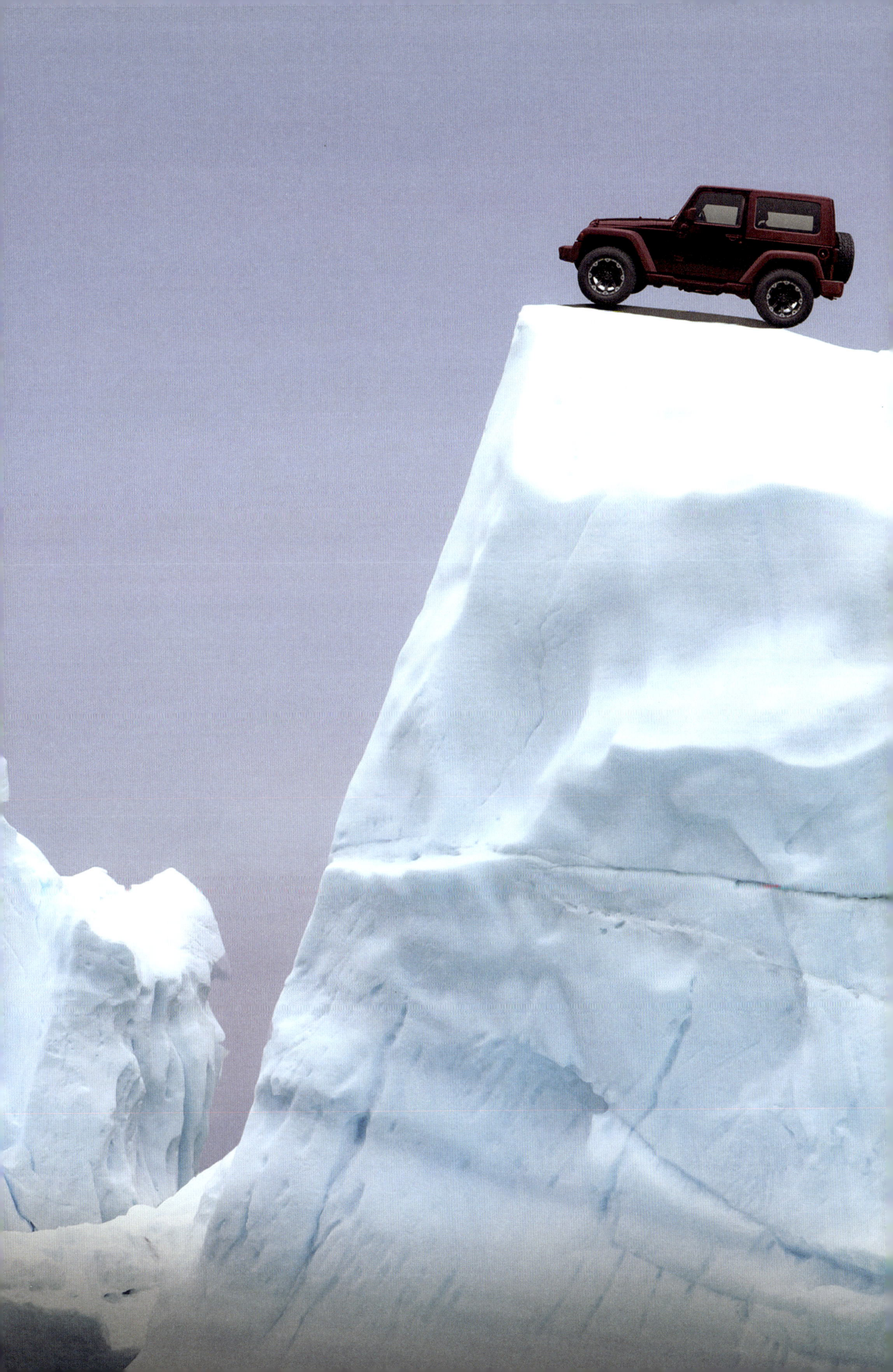

MEL HAS BEEN A TRANSFORMATIONAL ADDITION
TO OUR PORTFOLIO PROGRAM. LIKE ALL GOOD
TEACHERS, SHE'S FOCUSED ON OUR STUDENTS'
SUCCESS. SHE SETS A HIGH BAR, DRIVING
THEM TOWARD IT WITH WARMTH AND HUMANITY.

Kevin O'Neill, *Professor of Practice, Advertising, Syracuse University, The Newhouse School*

SUCCESSFUL ADVERTISING REQUIRES TWO
THINGS, THE FAMILIAR AND THE SURPRISING.
MEL'S STUDENTS ACCOMPLISH THAT AND MORE.
THEIR WORK HAS INTELLIGENCE, CLARITY, AND
WIT. HER STUDENTS HAVE A BRIGHT FUTURE.

Adrian Pulfer, *Platinum-winning Professor at Brigham Young University*

MEL TAUGHT ME TO THINK VISUALLY.
EVEN AS A COPYWRITER, I USE THIS TOOL DAILY.
SO MY SUCCESS IN ADVERTISING IS BECAUSE
MEL TAUGHT ME HOW TO THINK DIFFERENTLY.

Doug Knopf, *Copywriter, BBDO, NYC*

I'VE NOTICED THE WORK OF WHITE'S STUDENTS
FOR YEARS IN GRAPHIS. IT'S BEAUTIFULLY
EXECUTED. SHE BRINGS OUT THE STUDENTS' TRUE
EMOTIONS. BRAVO TO A GREAT EDUCATOR!

Kevin O'Callaghan, *Chair of BFA Advertising/Graphic Design Department, SVA*

MEL IS A DYNAMIC PROFESSOR WHO TRULY
UNDERSTANDS THE EVER-CHANGING MEDIA
LANDSCAPE AND IS A MASTER AT GETTING STUDENTS
READY FOR THE MODERN WORLD OF ADVERTISING.

Taras Wayner, *CCO of Wunderman Thompson in NYC and SU VPA alumni*

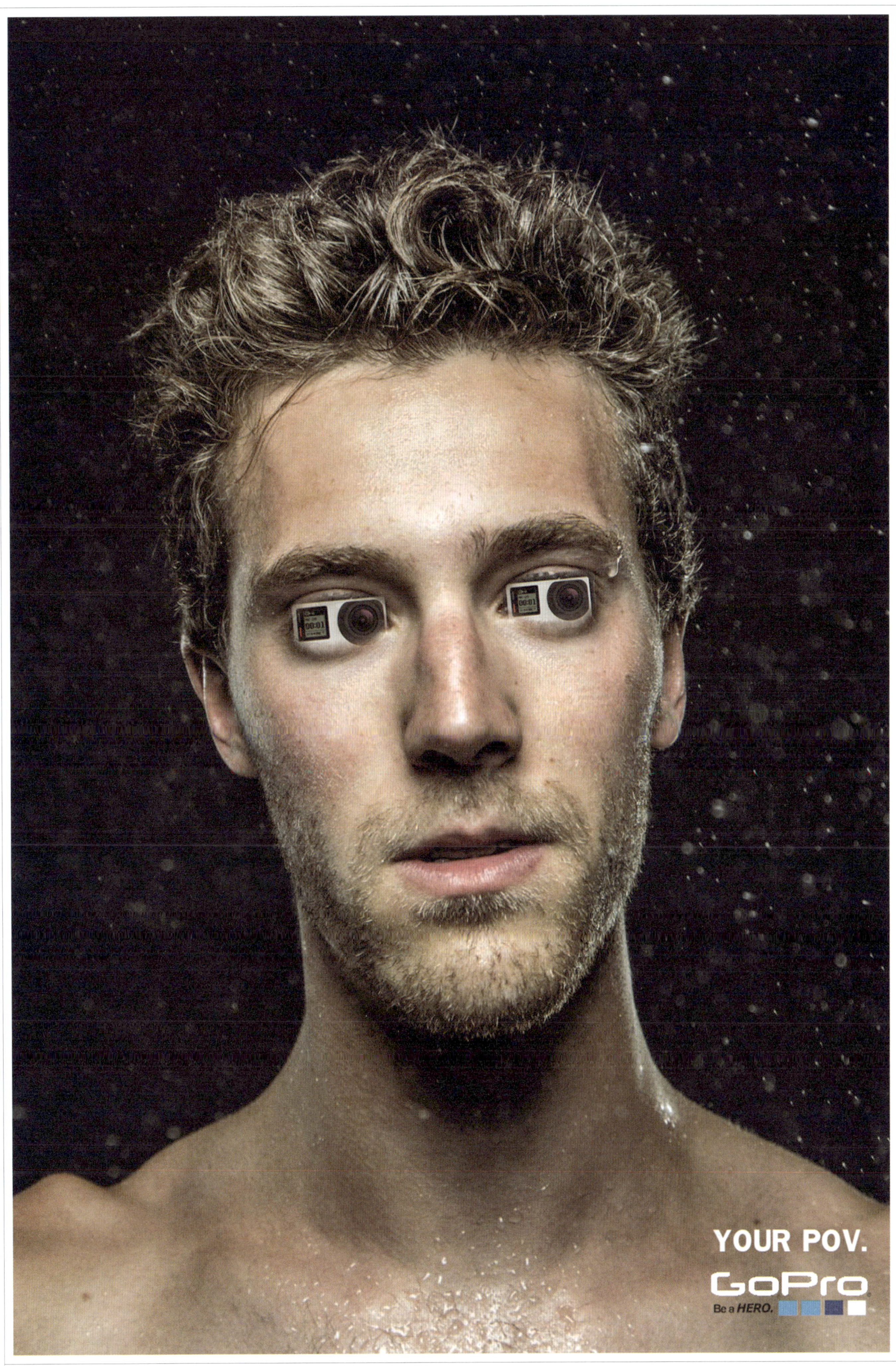

(Page 121) "It's Not Easy to Stop a Jeep," New Talent Annual 2020, Gold-winning student: Zhixin Fan
(Above) "GoPro Your POV," New Talent Annual 2016, Platinum-winning student: Lan Zhang

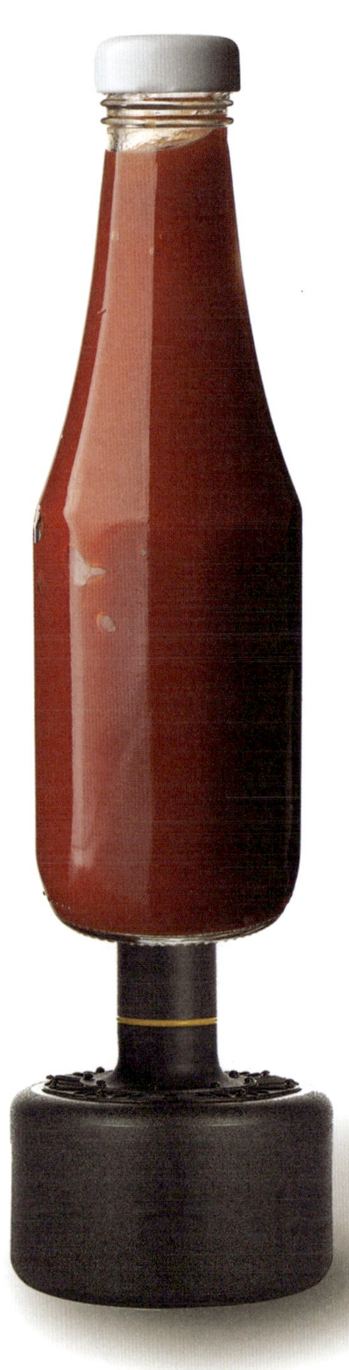
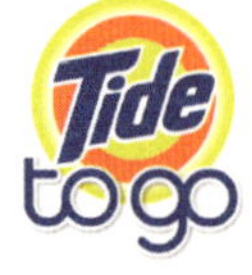

FIGHTS TOUGH STAINS
Tide
to go

Professor Mel White has significantly lifted the standard of our creative sequence since she joined the team five years ago. My colleagues and I would agree that she has been a caring, conscientious, dedicated, demanding, passionate, and responsible teacher with the ultimate goal to keep pushing students to the highest level of their limit. In the past three years, our students have won more than 350 top awards including Graphis New Talent, One Show Young Ones, Cannes Future Lions, Clios, ADC Competition, ADDYs, Ads of the World, Communication Arts Advertising Annual, Creativity International Awards, Lurzers International Archive Student Contest, recently New York Advertising Festival 2020, and others. Her students have been employed as creative talents working at leading ad agencies and top social media companies globally. She is a creative powerhouse who has successfully helped the school build national visibility as one of the most competitive and creative programs across the nation.

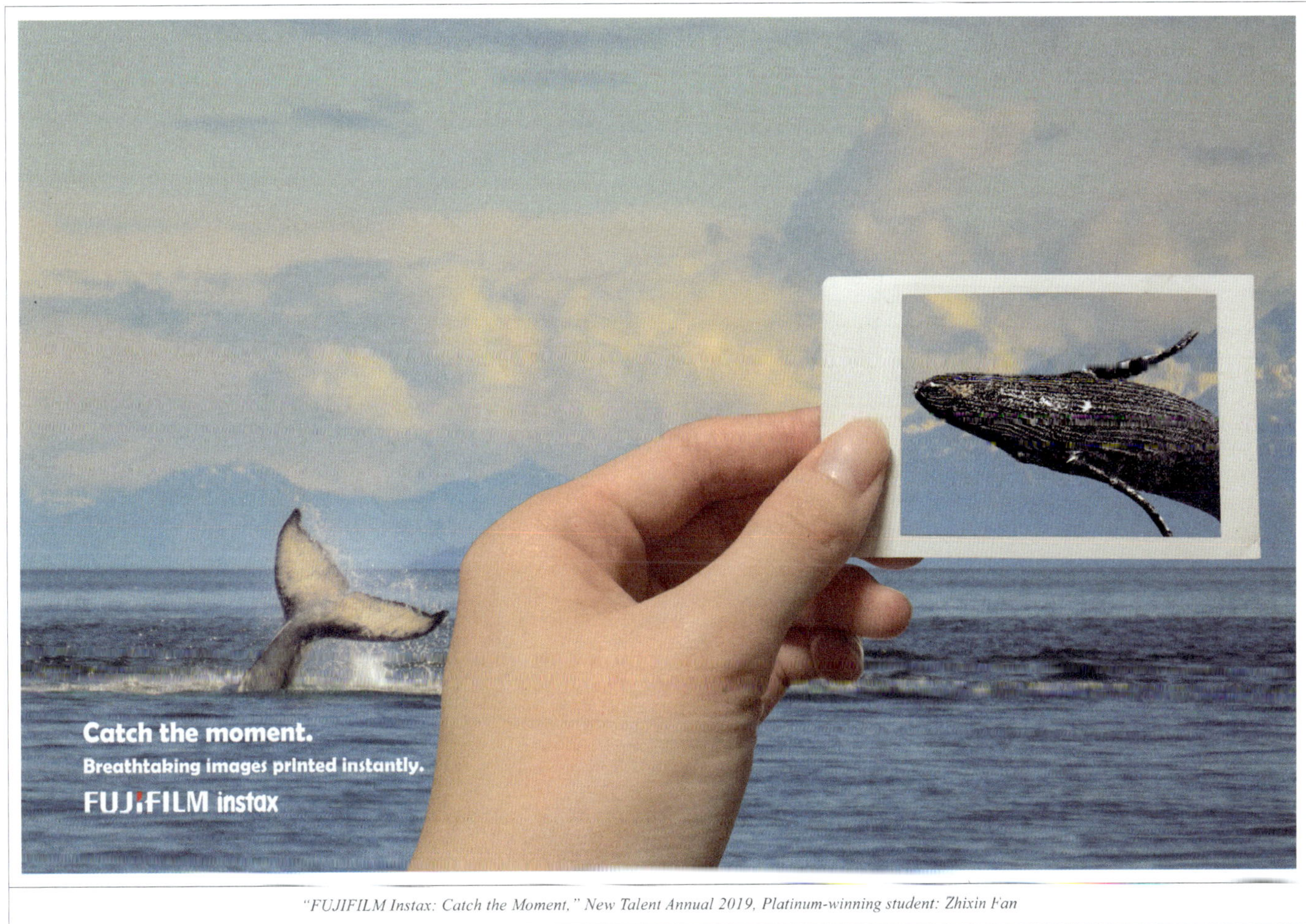

"FUJIFILM Instax: Catch the Moment," New Talent Annual 2019, Platinum-winning student: Zhixin Fan

MEL ENSURES EACH STUDENT WALKS AWAY WITH THE PROFESSIONAL FINESSE TO GET GREAT IDEAS HEARD AND ULTIMATELY CREATED IN A HYPER-COMPETITIVE INDUSTRY.

Kate Sheehan, *Copywriter, 360i, NYC*

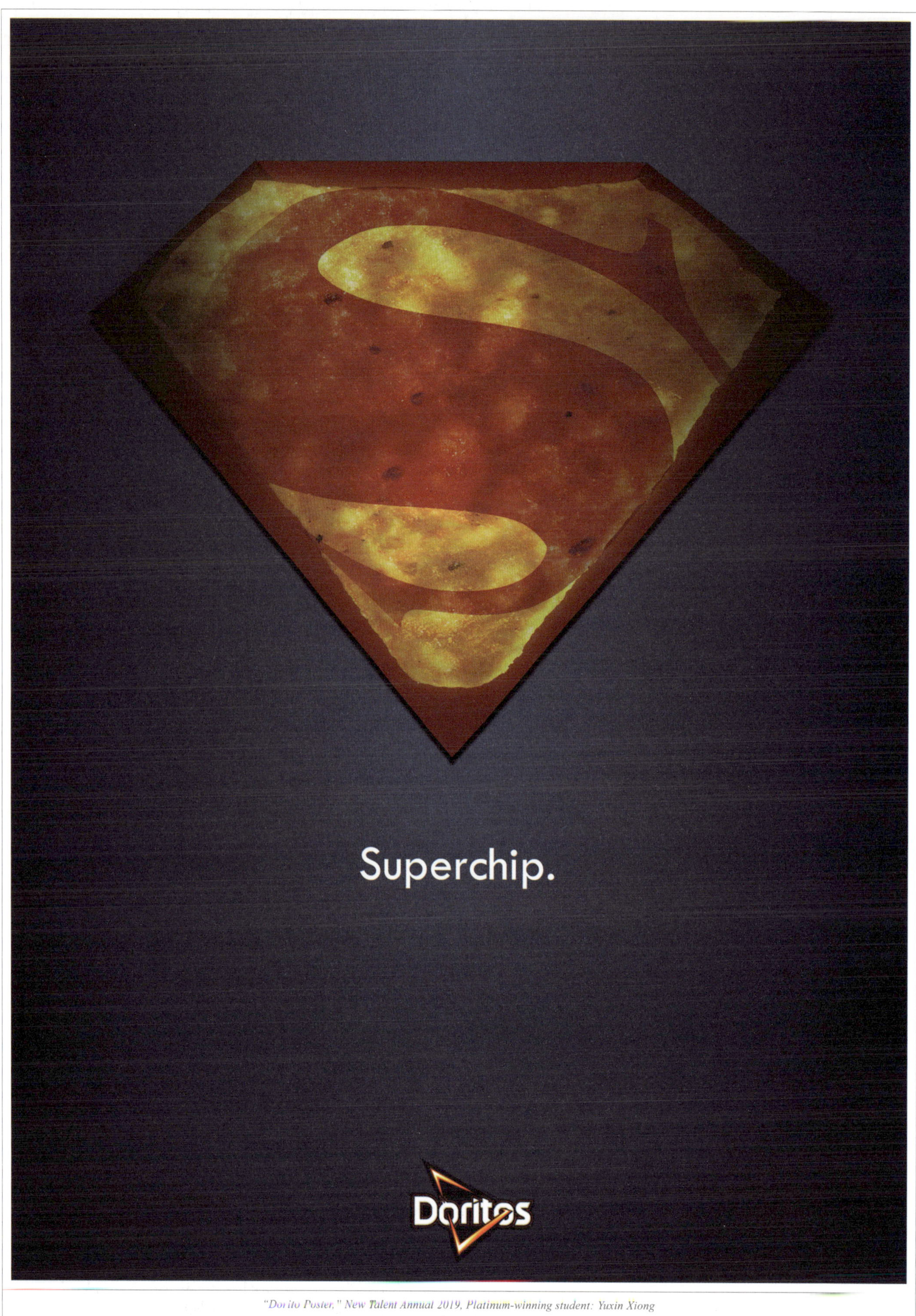

"*Dorito Poster*," New Talent Annual 2019, Platinum-winning student: Yuxin Xiong

What is your process for selecting a student for your class?
The Portfolio I course that I teach at Syracuse University's Newhouse School is the first creative advertising course that Newhouse creative advertising students take. For Portfolio I, students need to be interested in exploring the Creative Copywriting and Art Direction Advertising Sequence in the Advertising Major.

Portfolio III, the senior and final creative advertising course of our Portfolio sequence, is robust and serves as the capstone. For Portfolio III, the students are required to finish Portfolio I, be chosen by the creative judges during the Advertising Department Portfolio Review to move on with the rest of the Creative Copywriting and Art Direction Advertising Sequence, finish Portfolio II, and have a portfolio website.

What are the qualifications you require?
Curiosity is key for any art director and copywriter in my classes, as well as, in the industry. Having an innate interest in many topics helps creatives observe peoples' behaviors. They should immerse themselves in anything creative, such as going to art museums, interacting with VR, and following quirky Instagram accounts; and express their creativity through photography, writing, posting, drawing, etc. Immersing themselves in current culture can provide a constant stream of resources to draw upon which can lead to original thinking.

In my class sessions, I create an atmosphere where students can learn with open minds and fully immerse themselves in the world of thinking "big ideas." Instead of talking about creating ads, I focus on problem-solving. In my two Portfolio courses, I work to create learning atmospheres where it is okay to fail conceptually when students take bold risks to create impactful ideas. This is where some of the best learning can occur. Sometimes, I will send creative teams "back to the drawing board", from which they almost always return with deeper, more unexpected, and more relatable ideas. After these students struggle through several rounds of pushing their creative thinking, they get a sense of accomplishment from being able to solve the creative problem from the briefs with their own breakthrough ideas. And that is when, as an educator, I know that they are "getting it", and more importantly, are on the road towards being able to replicate this creative process when they intern or get hired into the ad industry. This is a necessary growth period for creatives in order for them to be successful. It's one thing to have an incredible portfolio, but it's another thing to make sure they can replicate that success when they are hired for an internship or a job and when they build a career.

In my courses, I facilitate lively discussions with the students about each of the ad campaigns from my class presentations. I ask open-ended questions to encourage critical thinking about a campaign's subject matter. This leads to students beginning to think for themselves about what makes some ad campaigns work while others do not. Students also need to be able to develop a working relationship with their creative partner, since the team experience is crucial for success in advertising as a creative. Students need to be open to this type of learning.

What are the disqualifications?
In Portfolio I, the students who do well in the course: embrace the creative process that I teach; are open to feedback on their ideas to push them further; and who work hard. Those are the ones who create impactful portfolios of work and are chosen to move on to Portfolio II and Portfolio III. So, the students essentially become "disqualified" to proceed with the Creative Copywriting and Art Direction Advertising Sequence when their ad campaigns have not reached a place of originality and unexpected thinking. When students have trouble with that, it's usually because they do not have the passion to dig deeper to solve problems with a unique perspective, which involves hours of hard work.

We have had a few students try a second time, which means they build a new portfolio of work on their own. The students who go through this process with serious intent and put in a lot of hours seem to invigorate a passion and stronger work ethic, because those students usually pass the second time. There is no third time option. And once our students reach Portfolio II and Portfolio III, there are no disqualifications for the course.

What might be a typical first assignment?
In Portfolio I, the first big assignment is creating a campaign of three print ads with a big unexpected idea using visual solution advertising, which uses an image to communicate the main concept about the product or service on the brief that they wrote earlier in the course.

I find that print is the easiest way to start off the creative process. It's the limited space that allows the students to focus on big idea creation and not get lost in a medium that has lots of possibilities, like the digital medium. That comes later in the course.

In Portfolio III, to demystify and teach creative advertising students a more thorough understanding of digital, experiential, new technologies, and non-traditional advertising – two campaign assignments are created. These assignments explore this variety of mediums to ensure that students develop a high-degree of familiarity and comfort with creating professional-grade work. Briefs from One Show Young Ones, D&AD New Blood, and Cannes Future Lions are used, and each team needs to deliver ten ideas in the first week. A third campaign assignment primarily uses these new expansive mediums for an integrated campaign with the option of using print medium for some of the pieces. Students are regularly exposed to award-winning advertising in these mediums to encourage bold, possibility thinking.

This course prepares the senior creative advertising students for the industry and focuses on creating breakthrough advertising campaigns and solutions to problems, that help the brand connect with audiences. Long gone are the days in making ads. Now, it's about what kind of experience a brand can create using digital, experiential, and new technologies.

In both courses, students turn in concepting pages, research pages, marker drawings, and clear sentences about their insight, big idea, and execution – the more they can practice the difference between those three, the more successful they will be in shaping their work and presenting. The concepting pages don't have to be the typical pen on paper. They can be written on a whiteboard, sticky notes, note app, bar napkins, your arm, typed; or spoken using the Voice in Chrome Extension to speak your ideas that are changed into text, etc. I have found our creative advertising students like to be creative even in how they concept.

Are real clients suggested?
The One Show Young Ones briefs and the D&AD New Blood briefs tend to be from actual clients. The briefs I write for the integrated campaign are not from actual clients, but they are all actual products and services and not made up. In all of these cases though, there is not an actual client that chimes in with changes. There's time enough for that in the industry for the rest of their careers. Our creative advertising students' portfolios are built on their creativity without the restrictions clients can sometimes place on them. This allows for the students to explore the depths of their creativity, to focus on unique problem solving, and to see how different mediums can play a role in interactivity. This, in turn, shows what the creative advertising

students are capable of, and what they have to offer ad agencies. The students do have budget and production limitations, which means that they need to really focus on how innovative and disruptive the ideas are and how they can be clearly shown.

Might you also ask students to choose a passion of
theirs for the assignment?
Yes, I think it's important for creative students to be able to express themselves using a medium other than advertising, such as through a passion project or personal project, for several reasons. This type of project exercises their creative muscles in different ways than what they're used to when creating ad campaigns. It also gives students a creative outlet to explore areas they have never explored before, and it taps into the artist in all of us. The goal is for creativity to start becoming innate. And by allowing the students to express what they are passionate about; it can help free them to solve problems more creatively for the brand assignments. The creative advertising industry relies on originality. If creative advertising students explore their own original thinking in passion/personal projects, the ad agencies can see just how creative and interesting the students are.

Each student creates their own passion project / personal project in Portfolio III, which shows some of the students' skill sets that are transferable to the industry, such as editing, shooting, sound design, writing, graphic design, kinetic type, etc. I have found that students really enjoy creating this type of project, because they explore something they feel strongly about.

For this project, the students check in with me once to show rough ideas. I just offer guidance, because in the end, the students proceed with the passion/personal project they want to proceed with, since it reflects their passions and interests.

Do you work with students individually? Do you present their
work so that you and the class can participate in criticism?
In my Portfolio III course, to truly prepare the seniors for the ad industry, I designed this course, from scratch, to run like an ad agency with students paired up in art director & copywriter teams. I brief the student teams on challenging assignments for ad campaigns, and the teams present their campaign ideas each week. During these student presentations, the rest of the class writes down answers to questions, which helps them form opinions about which ideas are most effective and why. I only provide feedback after the students in the class share their thoughts about the student team's work, so no one feels like they need to agree with me. Then, the team takes that feedback to further develop their work in the second week. By the third week of each campaign, the team and I meet in my office, because the feedback at that stage tends to be more detail-oriented with attention needed to the craft. This feedback-to-further work model is identical to what these students will experience at advertising agencies.

How do you develop and raise your student's visual
and verbal standards?
As the world continues to become more global, compelling visuals are needed to do more of the heavy lifting to reach audiences and convey product benefits across many languages and cultures. And with continued rapid growth in the digital advertising medium, which relies heavily on visuals to capture peoples' attention, I equip my students with the theory, knowledge, and skills needed for creating unexpected visual solutions to advertising problems to help brands grow.

To help my students develop more nuanced understandings, I created and developed a tool called The Six-Point Visual Solution Advertising Scale, which I used in a research study that is working its way towards publication.
I show examples of ads that represent each of the six points.

The six points are defined as:
1. Ad with 100% Headline Solution with No Visual
2. Ad with 100% Headline Solution with Inconsequential Visual
3. Ad with Headline & Straight Visual Working Together
4. Ad with Visual Solution & Headline/Copy Working Together with Purposefully Modified Visuals
5. Ad with 100% Visual Solution with Inconsequential Copy
6. Ad with 100% Visual Solution with No Copy

The majority of the advertising that wins in the top award shows fall on Point 4 of the Visual Solution Advertising Scale, no matter the medium (digital, experiential, print, outdoor, commercials, etc.). And it's the art director / copywriter teams who are creating the visual solution advertising that sweeps the award shows. This includes a lot of the winners in The Graphis New Talent Annual advertising competition which awards a lot of visual solution advertising.

This Visual Solution Advertising Scale helps our creative advertising students better understand how to create visual solution advertising. And, this emphasis on thinking visually has resulted in a profound increase in student award-wins, internship offers, and full-time jobs for our Newhouse Advertising Majors in the Creative Sequence.

For verbal standards, I teach the copywriters how to write lines for Visual Solution advertising that pays off the visuals, and how to write Headline Solution advertising where the concept is being conveyed through the headline, using insights about the product, product category, and the target audience. Words can be involving; they can take an idea and boil it down to its simplest form; tell a story; give a brand a voice, a perspective; be powerful and disturbing; create tension; be funny; and be impactful.

In Portfolio III, I bring in an award-winning Creative Director / Copywriter guest speaker to present Advanced Copywriting and conduct a challenging in-class writing exercise. I require the writers to read Thomas Kemeny's book "Junior: Writing Your Way Ahead in Advertising". It clearly takes writers through the process of writing instead of talking abstractly about it.

To help the students with their verbal skills when presenting, they have to write their insight in a sentence, big idea in a sentence, and execution ideas in sentences for each campaign. This makes presenting very pointed and takes the "ums" out. The students present their campaigns almost every week in Portfolio III, from initial ideas, developed ideas, to finished pieces. The Portfolio I students also practice presenting.

What percentage of the class reaches award-winning work?
The biggest and most powerful initiative I started at Newhouse was to connect our creative advertising students with the ad industry by starting the Creative Advertising Awards Program in my first semester in the Fall 2015, that I have been building upon every year since. The program quickly changed from zero awards prior to my arrival in Fall 2015, to 17 awards in 2015/2016, and has steadily grown every year (36, 127, 142) to 151 awards this past school year 2019/2020.

The work students created have been winning in these student award shows: The Addys (local, District, and National), Ads of the World, Cannes Future Lions, The Clio Awards, Communications Arts Advertising Awards, Communication Arts Student Showcase, Creativity International Media & Interactive Awards, Creativity International Print & Packaging Awards, D&AD New Blood, Graphis New Talent, Luerzers International Archive, New York Festivals Advertising Awards, The One Club Portfolio Night competition, The One Show Young Ones ADC (Art Directors Club), and The One Show Young Ones Brief competition.

For the 2018 Cannes Future Lions competition, there were 386 participating schools, from 55 countries, with over 2,000 competition participants, and only five winners worldwide.

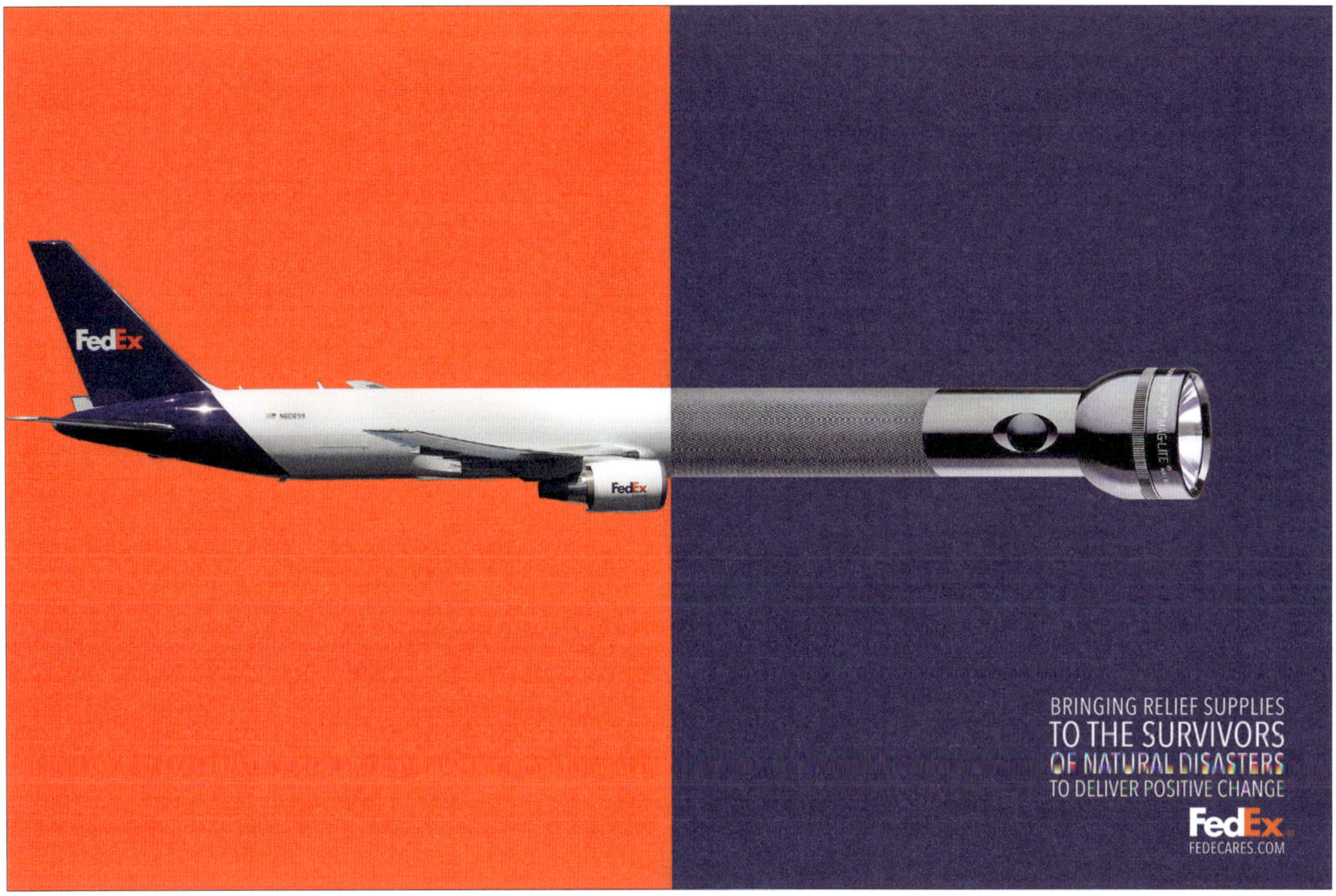

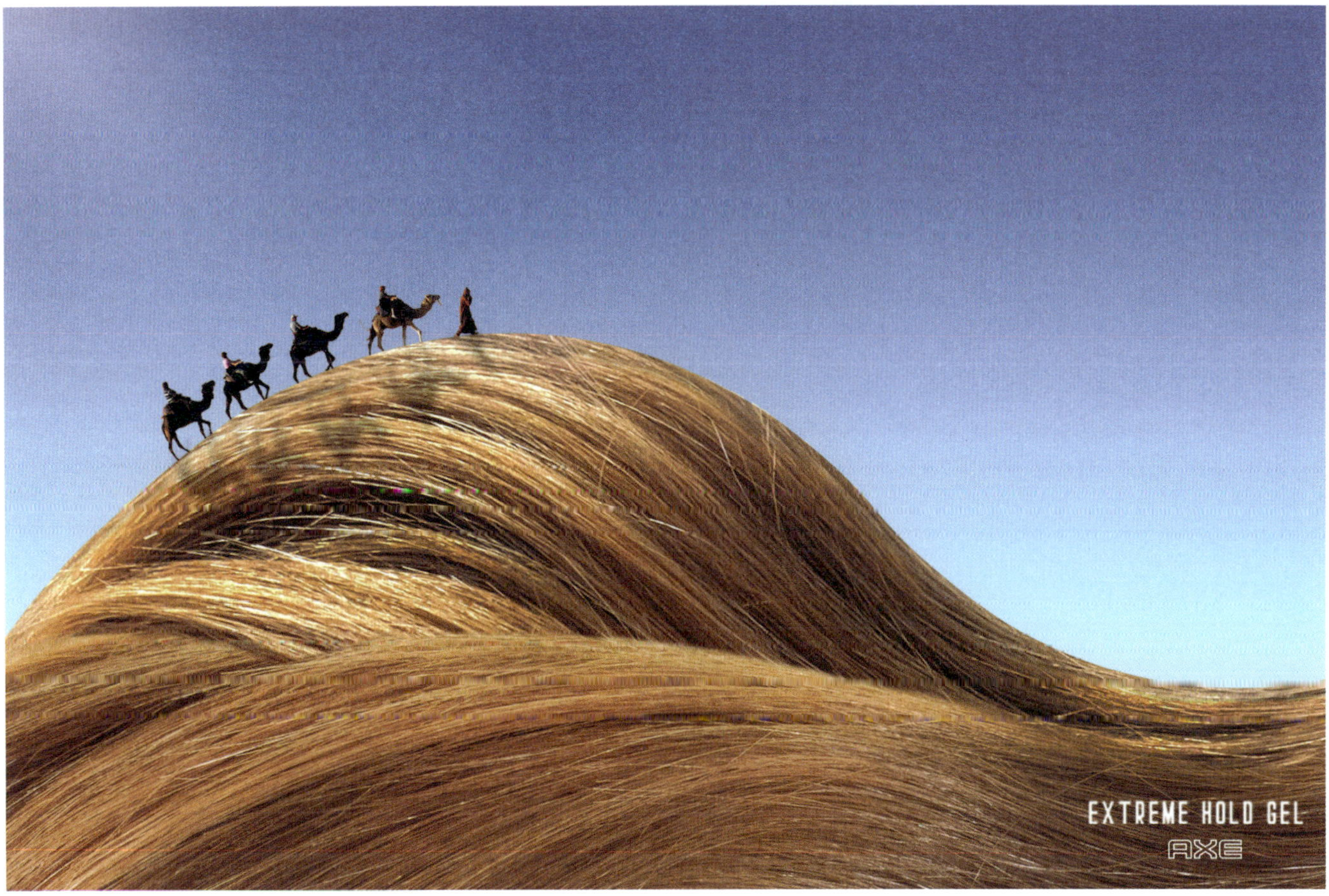

(Top) "Fed Ex Cares Campaign," New Talent Annual 2017, Gold-award winning student: Alexis Watson
(Bottom) "Extreme Hold," New Talent Annual 2020, Platinum-award winning student: Xinran Xiao

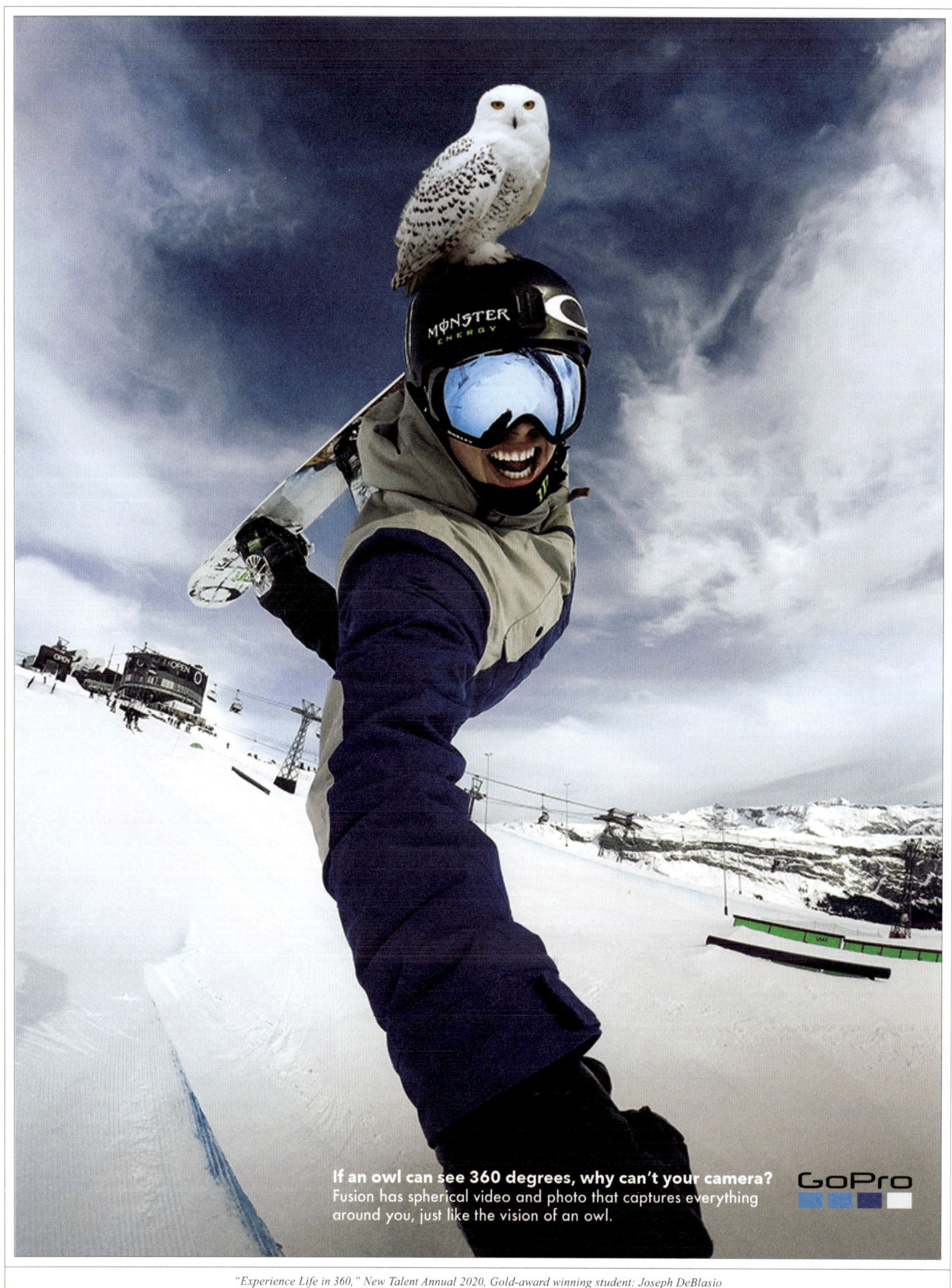

"Experience Life in 360," New Talent Annual 2020, Gold-award winning student: Joseph DeBlasio

SHE HAS ALWAYS BEEN HELPFUL AND INSPIRING. SHE HAS PUSHED ME TO MY FULL POTENTIAL AND IT'S SUCH A PLEASURE TO BE HER STUDENT.

Joyee Lin, *Platinum-winning Student, Syracuse University, Newhouse School*

And one was from Newhouse. We're the first undergraduate university in the United States ever to win. Only four other U.S. schools had won since the competition started in 2007. And the winning campaign was created in my Portfolio III course. Out of the art director / copywriter Newhouse student team who created this award-winning entry, the copywriter student Emily Alek and I went to Cannes, France to accept the award and to attend the famous weeklong Cannes Lions International Festival of Creativity.

All of the award-winning student work has been created in my and Kevin O'Neill's Portfolio courses. I teach Portfolio I every semester, and O'Neill teaches a section in the Fall. Portfolio II is taught by O'Neill and I teach Portfolio III. That way, the students experience different perspectives and different ways of learning. With my creative director / art director background, and O'Neill's creative director / copywriter background, we have created a robust Copywriting and Art Direction Sequence in the Advertising major here at Syracuse University Newhouse and have enjoyed seeing our students win awards for the campaigns they have worked so hard on.

Looking at the last three years in my Portfolio I courses, 100% of students reached award-winning work in Fall 2017, Spring 2018, Spring 2019, and Fall 2019. In Fall 2018 it was 82%. In my Portfolio III courses, 100% reached award-winning work in Fall 2017. In Spring 2018 it was 96%, Fall 2018 it was 80%, Spring 2019 it was 75%, and Fall 2019 it was 80%. We are still waiting on more award show results for Spring 2020.

This is a reflection of my strong visual solution advertising pedagogy. With these awards, the ad industry is communicating that our Newhouse creative advertising student work is excellent. It's no longer just the professor, or friends, or parents saying the student work is good, it's now the ad industry that has given it the stamp of approval.

And ad agencies have been known to recruit from these shows. Ad agency creative recruiters and creative directors are always incredibly impressed with seeing these awards in the Newhouse creative advertising students' portfolios when reviewing them for internships and jobs.

All of our creative advertising students have been placed into internships and/or jobs in 2016, 2017, 2018, and 2019, including two that chose to freelance and a small handful who chose grad school. The department's recent success in placing creative advertising students is partly the culmination of my five-year effort at re-imagining and re-engineering the curriculum emphasis in the department's Portfolio I and Portfolio III courses; my creation of a new student-accessible, 70 plus page internship database; my development of the Portfolio III Mentor Program; my comprehensive awards show and entry information research which I made available and encouraged creative advertising students to submit entries to; and my organizing and running the annual Newhouse Creative Advertising Portfolio Review in NYC/virtual, which I started and organized. Another part of the success is Kevin O'Neill's help in inviting some of the ad agencies who attend our Portfolio Review; excellent teaching in Portfolio I and II; and advice he gives our copywriter students, especially for my Portfolio III copywriters who need editing advice for their case study video scripts. Kevin has been a great partner in running our creative advertising program together.

Over the last five years, our creative advertising students from my and O'Neill's Portfolio courses are being placed for internships and jobs at ad agencies such as: 360i, 72andSunny, Anomaly, Apple, Arnold, BBDO, BBH, DDB, Digitas, Doner, Droga5, Edelman, FCB, Geometry, Goodby, Grey, Havas, Hill Holiday, Jack Morton, McCann, McKinney, Merkley+Partners, MullenLowe, Oberland, Ogilvy, Publicis, R/GA, Saatchi & Saatchi, Slack, Solve, TBWA Chiat Day, TBWA Raad Dubai, Terri & Sandy, Translation, VaynerMedia, VMLY&R, Walrus, Wieden+Kennedy, and Wunderman Thompson.

What kind of advice do you give to the class?
I tell the students that the best ways to stand out in an ad agency are to create outstanding, fresh ideas; put in the hours; ask Creative Directors if they need help on a project; try to get on any of the projects that allow for the kind of creativity that could lead to an award; promote diversity in your work, such as in casting; and you and your creative partner should each present equally. Presenting the work is key in getting noticed. Don't be the shy one and let your partner do all of the presenting. I also talk with the female students about some issues they might end up facing in the industry.

Can you name a few students who have gained success?
A number of our creative advertising students who have taken our Portfolio courses have already created industry-coveted Super Bowl spots and won top industry awards – both of which are very difficult to achieve over the course of an entire creative advertising career, much less so shortly after graduating. Some recent graduates find themselves working on Super Bowl ads and winning awards because they land at great agencies right out of school.

Some of my successful students include: Tan Erginay a Copywriter at Grey in NYC, who created Pringles Super Bowl spots in 2019 and 2020 and won Silver and Merit One Show Awards.
Brandon Holliday a copywriter at Johannes Leonardo in NYC, who won a D&AD Wood Pencil and One Show Awards.
Kate Sheehan and Alyssa Pauker, a copywriter / art director team at R/GA in NYC, who won a Gold Clio.
Jill Archibold and Zach Schweikert, an art director / copywriter team at VaynerMedia in NYC, worked on the highly discussed Planters Mr. Peanut campaign that aired before and during the Super Bowl with the passing of Mr. Peanut. And they've won Cannes Lions, One Show, and Clio Awards. When Archibold and Schweikert were students at Newhouse, I put them together as a creative team in my Portfolio III course, and they are still a team today.
Chase Condrone, a copywriter at McKinney in NC, worked on the Little Caesars' "Sliced Bread" commercial for the 2020 Super Bowl with his art director partner.
Emily Alek, a Jr copywriter, is at McCann in NYC and won Jay Chiat Awards. Also at McCann are copywriters Josh Race and Emma Bhayani, and designer Lindsay Weisleder.
Ryan Harper is an art director at Goodby and before that, he worked at BBDO in NYC.
Kate Degan and Doug Knopf, an art director / copywriter team at BBDO in NYC started working together as a team in my Portfolio III course. Also at BBDO in NYC, are Samantha Spellman and Sabrina Ghantous, art directors, and Evan Hohenwarter, copywriter.
Summer Schneider, Sr art director at Laundry Service in NYC.
Shelby Guller, a copywriter at Anomaly in LA, and previously at 72andSunny in LA.
At TBWA Chiat Day are, Laura Vancil, Jamie Wynn, Lexey Watson, and Erika Mack.
Edan Michener is a Designer at R/GA in Portland.
At FCB in NYC, copywriter Annie Turner, and art director / copywriter team Nicole Framm and Sophie Knochenhauer who also were a team in my Portfolio III course.
At Ogilvy, copywriters Andy Mendes and Karen Miranda.
Taylor Whitelow, copywriter at Cartwright in LA, and previously Jr copywriter at 72andSunny in LA.
Bryan Allman, copywriter at MullenLowe in NYC, and previously at Anomaly in NYC.
Diane Danneels, Jr art director at Grey in NYC.

Hannah Murphy, Jr art director at Publicis in NYC.
For in-house, Lucas Spain, copywriter at Apple, and Hairol Ma, copywriter at Slack.

Who is or was your greatest mentor?
When I started teaching at Syracuse University Newhouse five years ago, after being in the industry for 26 years, there were four creative advertising alumni who gave me feedback and advice on our program early on that helped me shape our Copywriting and Art Direction Sequence: Taras Wayner, CCO of Wunderman Thompson in NYC and SU VPA alumni; Tom Murphy, Co-CCO of McCann in NYC and SU VPA alumni; Ari Halper, CCO and Founder of Sauce Idea Lab in NYC (formerly CCO of FCB in NYC) and SU Newhouse alumni; and Deacon Webster, CCO and Founder of Walrus in NYC and SU Newhouse alumni. Each of them came to Newhouse to give a talk to our advertising students and faculty (Wayner came twice), reviewed student portfolios, gave a talk in my Portfolio III class, and answered student questions in the "Meet the Speaker" session. Their feedback on the portfolios helped me to shape and develop the program to get the students even more prepared for the industry.

Now, Wayner, Murphy, Halper, and Webster make up four of the eight members of the first Syracuse University Alumni Newhouse Creative Council that I created, after Wayner had initially thought of the idea. It is an aggregate of SU graduates who are leaders in the advertising agency creative departments, who collectively or individually will give industry feedback in two critical areas: (1) Advise SU Newhouse creative advertising faculty to facilitate students becoming better prepared to enter the industry and; (2) Provide creative and professional insights to help keep SU Newhouse with current curriculum that is on the cutting edge of the ad industry.

Who among your contemporaries today do you most admire?
I most admire Colleen DeCourcy, CCO and co-president of Wieden+Kennedy in Portland, for being a strong creative leader behind some of the most groundbreaking work in the industry. Her leadership embraces how brands can lead with purpose. While the typical leaders of creative advertising departments are mostly male, having a strong leader who is female is an excellent role model for all creatives, and especially female ones. She brings a much-needed diverse voice.

Some words of wisdom that DeCourcy said in a Zoom interview with Adweek in April that stuck with me was "The answer is not always going to be an ad." Focus on solving the problem and it might have the possibility to affect pop culture."

Is working in creative teams an important part of the process?
One thing I wish I had received through my undergraduate studies that would have better prepared me for my career in art direction, was working on a team with student copywriter(s) on advertising campaigns. This creative team experience is crucial for success in advertising as a creative. The synergy that develops between an art director and a copywriter inevitably yields more interesting and breakthrough ideas. Also, diverse teams create diverse ideas, and yet the creative departments in ad agencies still have a diversity problem.

I have chosen my students to work in art director/copywriter teams with diversity, talent, and work ethic standards in mind to set them up for vibrant synergistic thinking. If the teams start diverse in school, they could potentially get hired as diverse teams in the industry, thus helping increase the diversity of the workforce in the creative advertising departments. There have been several male/female teams hired from my Portfolio III pairings.

In the ad industry, gender-diverse creative teams are steadily becoming of greater importance as several large multinational corporation clients are now requiring their ad agencies to have 50/50 male and female creatives working on their accounts; some large and influential clients are now requiring that a certain percentage of their ad agencies' creative leadership be women; and some clients have gone on record stating that they refused business pitches from certain ad agencies because they did not have any female creative leadership on the team.

I also actively seek to establish racial, ethnic, and cultural diversity on the student creative teams. Studies have shown that creative teams with partners of diverse backgrounds tend to create more diverse, and potentially more breakthrough ideas.

Forming student creative teams based on these factors is a practice that I will continue to teach, advocate for, and employ in all of my current and future teaching and faculty responsibilities. In our ever-increasing globalized world, to not be constantly teaching, advocating for, and employing this diversity-promoting practice would, more narrowly, be putting all of our advertising students at a disadvantage while, more broadly, represent a failure to promote one of the most basic and longstanding tenets of higher education – to promote an awareness, understanding, and respect for the plethora of perspectives on human familial and social group norms.

When students do get hired as a creative team, they could stay together as a creative team for many years, and possibly for their entire careers. For a creative's career to advance, it is imperative to have an excellent creative partner, which can be hard to find if the ad agency arbitrarily assigns solo creatives their creative partners. And some creatives can be in the industry for years without ever finding a good creative partner.

It is often difficult to predict whether two creatives will work well together, so using Portfolio III as a venue for students to develop an understanding of their own work styles, creative processes, etc. as part of one (or more) creative teams can help them develop the discernment as to who they might potentially work most effectively with. Before the start of each semester, I spend time assessing and then pairing up students for my Portfolio III courses – trying to match-up talent, work ethic, and personalities, as well as, trying to make the teams ethnically and gender diverse. Since I taught many of these same students in prior sections of Portfolio I, I become fairly knowledgeable about these students' work styles, personalities, and talent. And for students whom I did not know as well, I reviewed their portfolios, set-up meetings with them, and spoke with Kevin O'Neill, to get his assessment on these students' talent, personalities, and work styles. I also ask the students to email me a list of students they would like to work with, which I also consider.

Since 2016, at least thirteen creative teams from my classes were hired. Eleven of those teams are male-female creative teams and all the teams were hired for internships or jobs by top ad agencies nationwide.

With the ad industry still being male-skewed in both creative leadership and in the assignment of more career-accelerating accounts, female creatives can potentially get some of these same benefits as male creatives get simply by teaming up with them. So by my teaming up female students with male students for art director / copywriter teams that could potentially get hired together as teams, it is in an incremental way to help level the playing field for our female creative students as they enter an industry that historically and, unfortunately, still currently presents significant career-advancement impediments and obstacles that male creatives do not encounter.

Mel Whites newhouse.syr.edu
See her Graphis Master Portfolio on graphis.com.

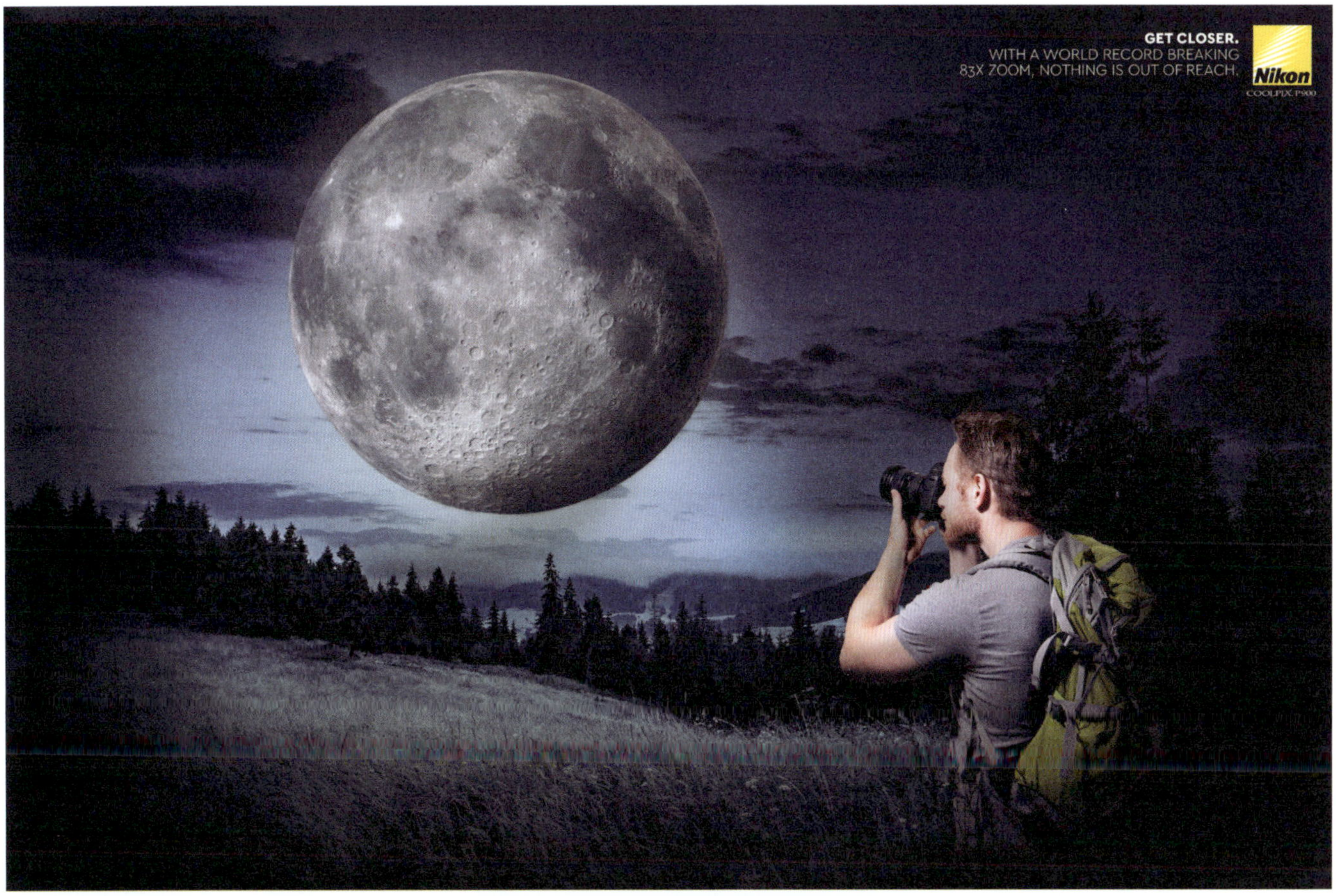

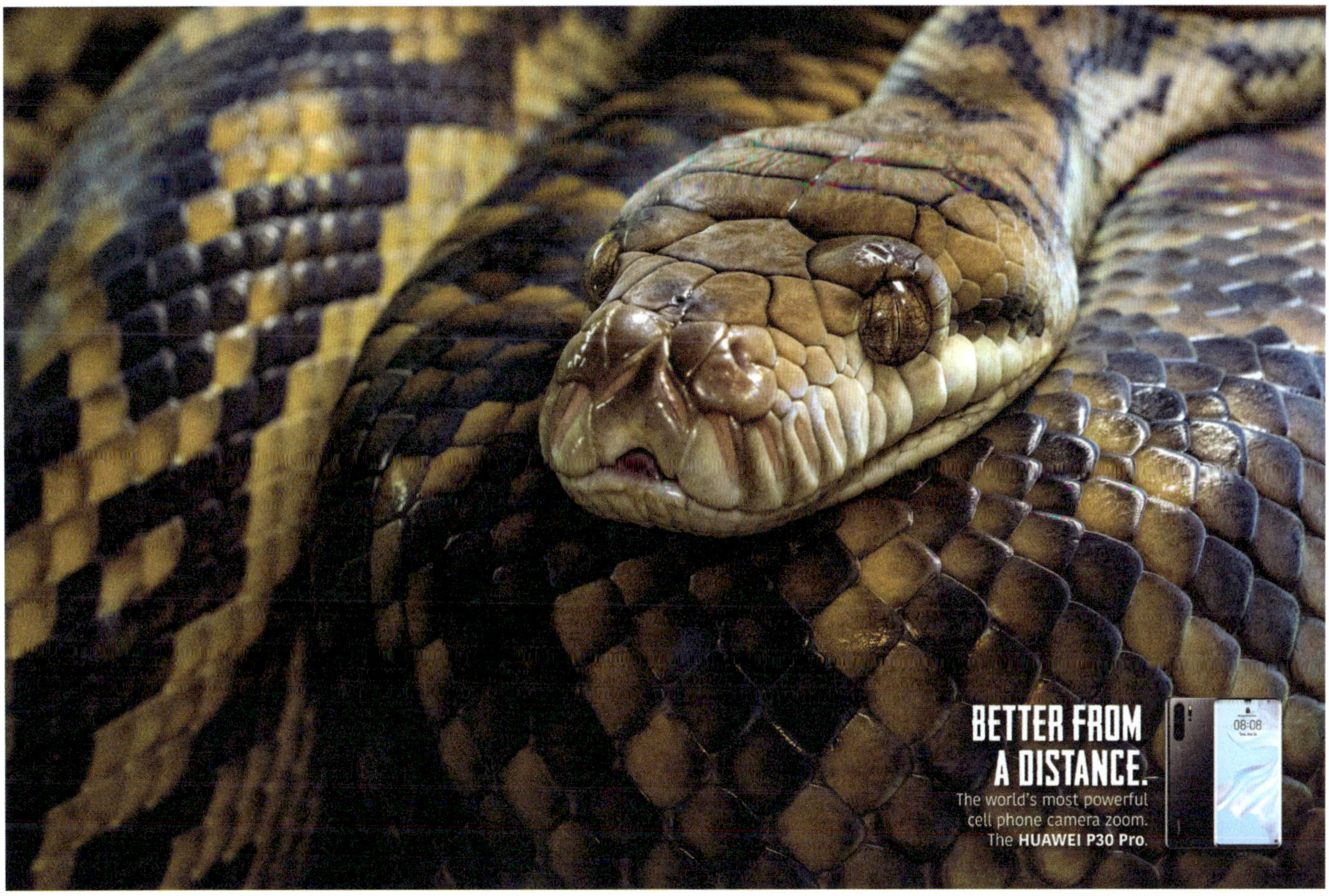

(Top) "Nikon COOLPIX P900 Digital Camera," New Talent Annual 2018, Gold-award winning student: Justina Hnatowicz
(Bottom) "Better From a Distance," New Talent Annual 2020, Gold-award winning students: Charley Karchin and Tom Ciaccio

MEL WHITE'S BRILLIANT RESULTS WITH STUDENTS IS ON PAR WITH THE ANSELMO'S, MARIUCCI'S, PULFUR'S, ETC. **B. Martin Pedersen,** *Designer*

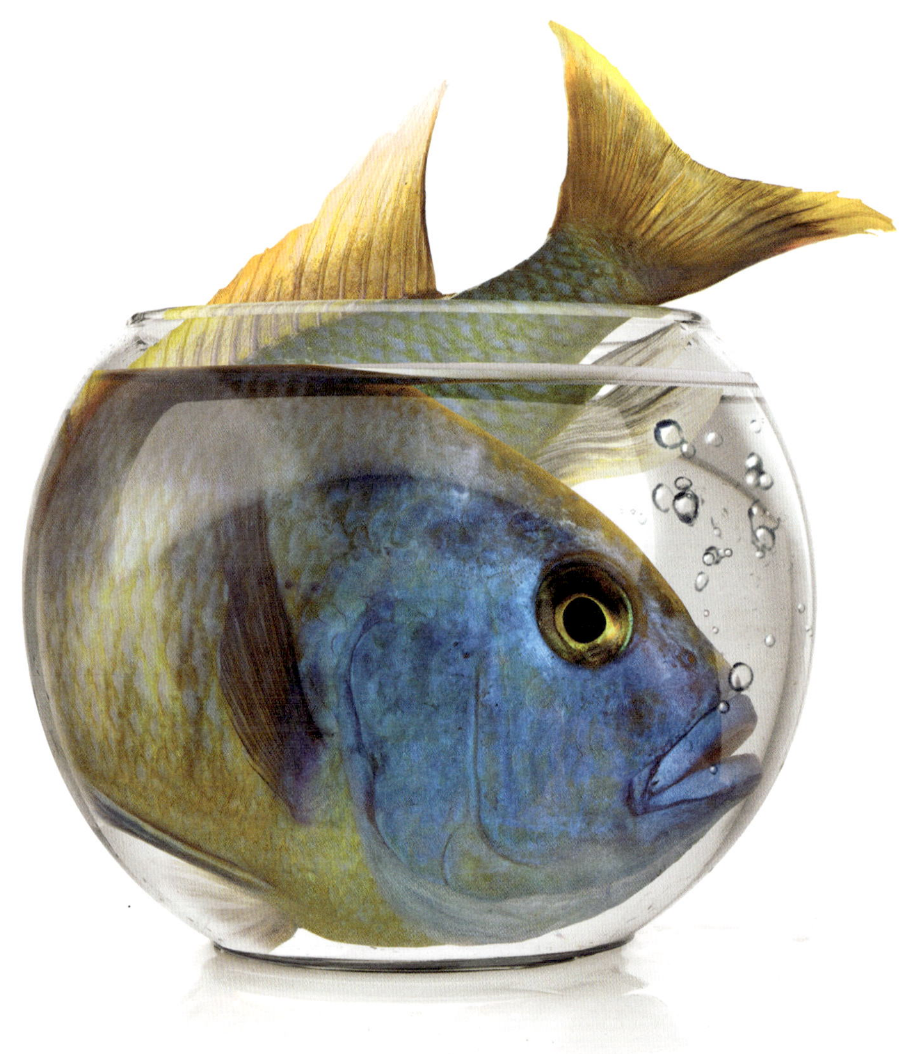

SHE IS THE MOST DEDICATED PROFESSOR.
SHE TOOK A SUCCESSFUL ADVERTISING PROGRAM
AND TURNED IT INTO A MODERN, MINI VERSION
OF THE REAL-LIFE INDUSTRY.

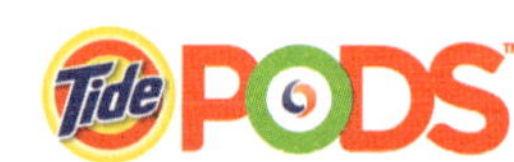

Summer Schneider, *Senior Art Director, Launch y Serv!c*

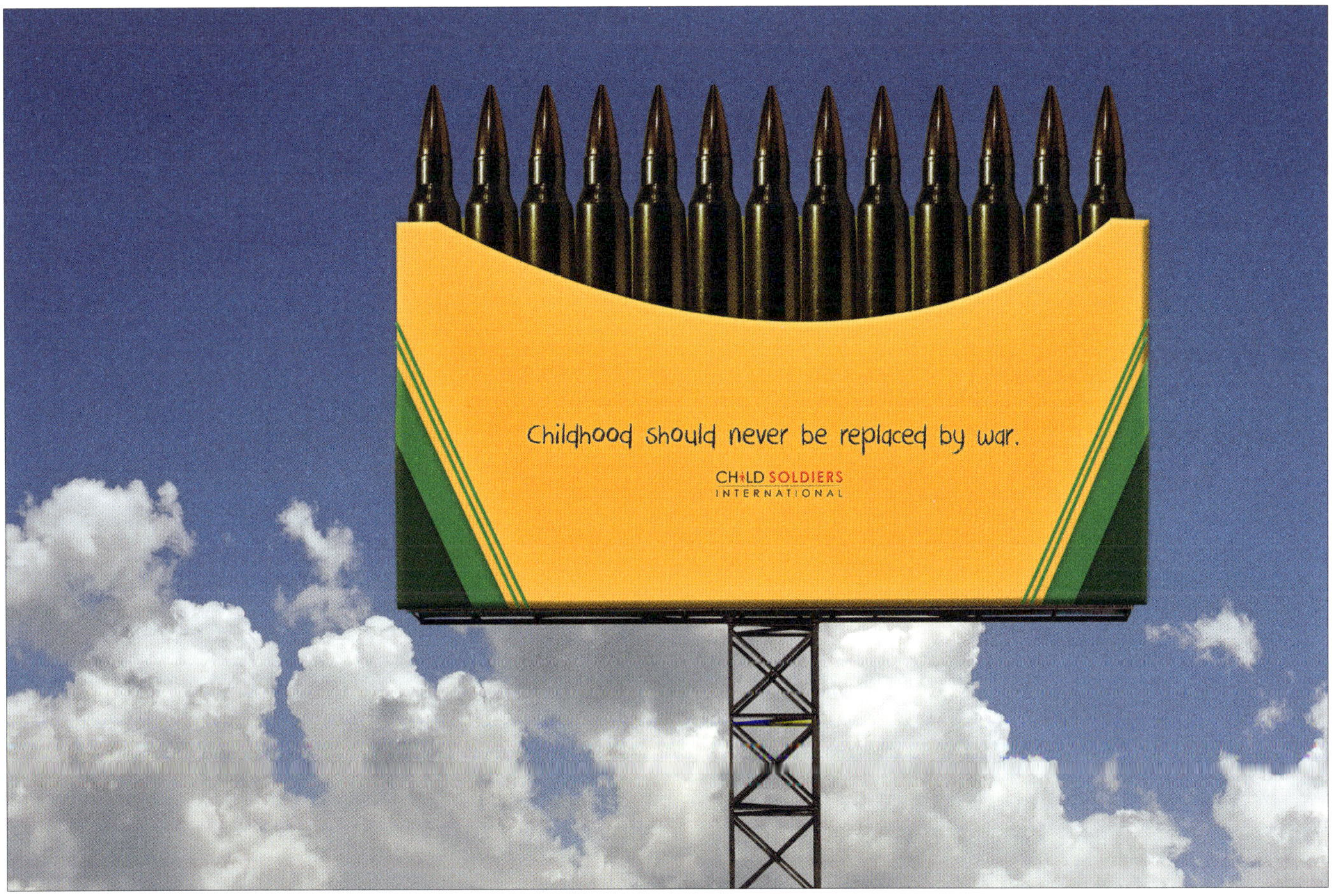

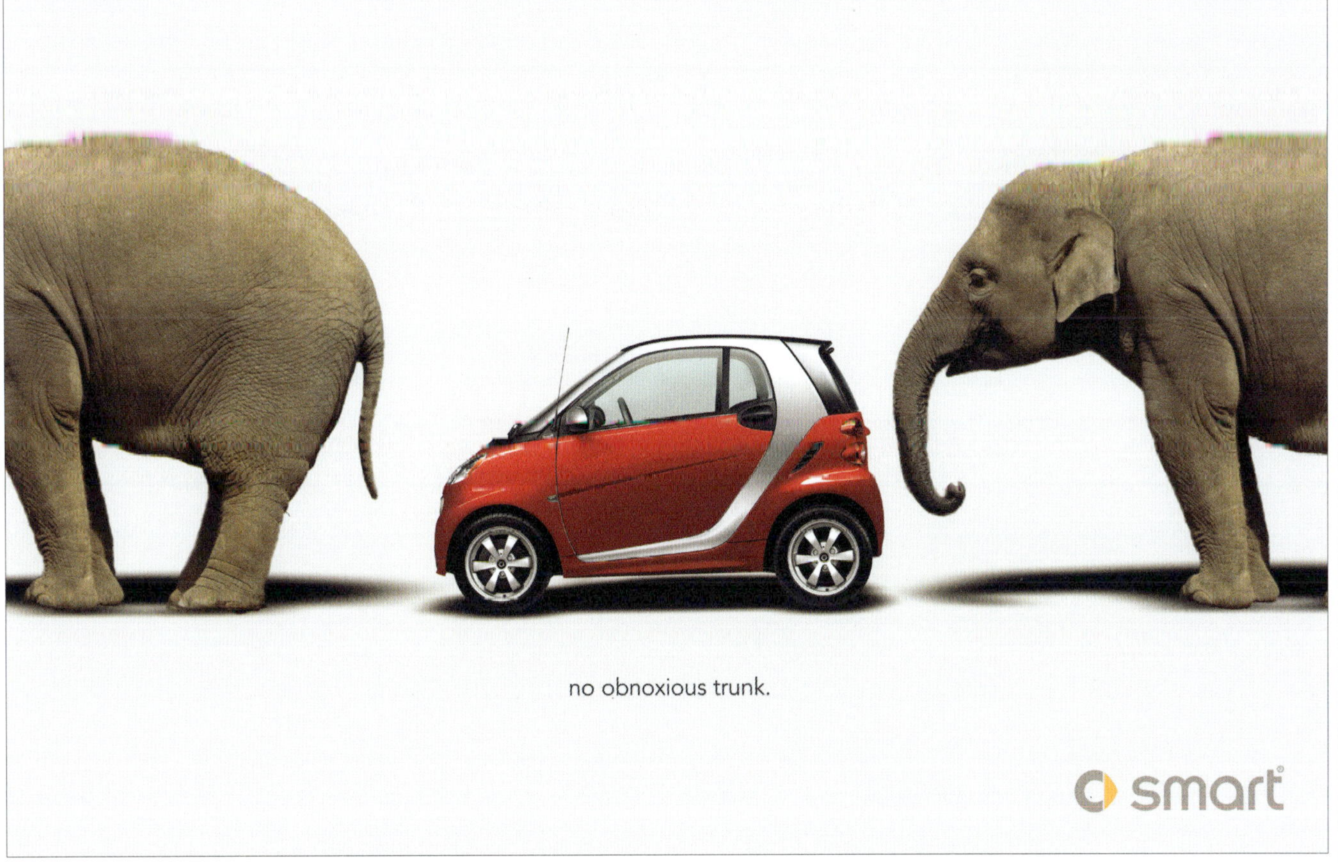

(Top) "Child Soldier Billboard," New Talent Annual 2018, Platinum-award winning student: Nicole Framm
(Bottom) "SmartCar," New Talent Annual 2018, Gold-award winning students: Alexis Watson and Spencer Kolbert

Graphis Books

POSTER

DESIGN

ADVERTISING

PHOTOGRAPHY

NUDES

TYPOGRAPHY

PROTEST POSTERS

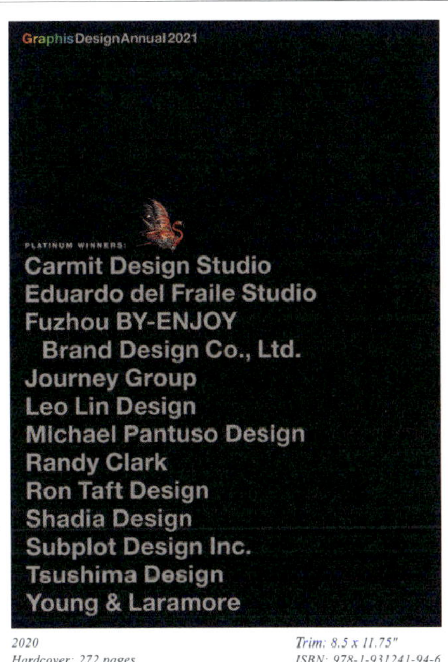

Design Annual 2021

2020
Hardcover: 272 pages
200-plus color illustrations
Trim: 8.5 x 11.75"
ISBN: 978-1-931241-94-6
US $90

Awards: This Annual awards 12 Platinum, 125 Gold, 317 Silver awards, and 241 Honorable Mentions for outstanding achievement in Design. **Platinum Winners:** Randy Clark, Eduardo del Fraile, Carmit Makler Haller, Young Huale, Journey Group, Leo Lin, Shadia Ohanessian, Michael Pantuso, Subplot Design, Ron Taft, Hajime Tsushima, and Young & Laramore. **Judges:** All work was judged by a panel of past Platinum and Gold winners, John Fairley, Gavin Hurrell, Erin Mutlu, Alvaro Perez, Diogo Gama Rocha, Jared Welle, and Yin Zhongjun. **Content:** Award-winning work from the judges, and full-page presentations of Platinum, and Gold-winning design work. Silver and Honorable Mentions are also presented, and a list of international design museums are included.

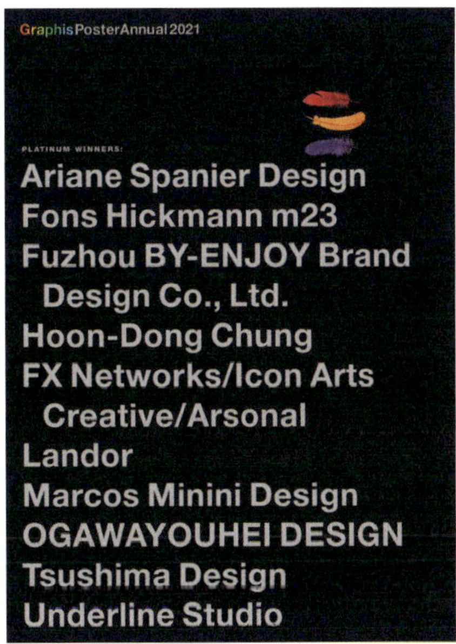

Poster Annual 2021

2020
Hardcover: 240 pages
200-plus color illustrations
Trim: 8.5 x 11.75"
ISBN: 978-1-931241-91-5
US $90

Awards: This year Graphis Awarded 10 Platinum, 94 Gold, 220 Silver awards and 171 Honorable Mentions for exemplary talent in poster design. **Platinum Winners:** Hoon-Dong Chung, FX Networks, Fons Hickmann, Young Huale, Landor, Marcos Minini, OGAWAYOUHEI Design, Ariane Spanier, Hajime Tsushima, and Underline Studio. **Judges:** All work was judged by a panel of past Platinum and Gold winners, Mann Lao (Chiii Design), Pekka Loiri, Jisuke Matsuda (Atelier Jisuke), Marcos Minini, Spencer Till (Lewis Communications) and Thomas Wilder (Collins). **Content:** Award-winning work from the judges, and full pages of Platinum, and Gold-winning posters. Silver and Honorable Mentions are presented, and a list of international poster museums are included.

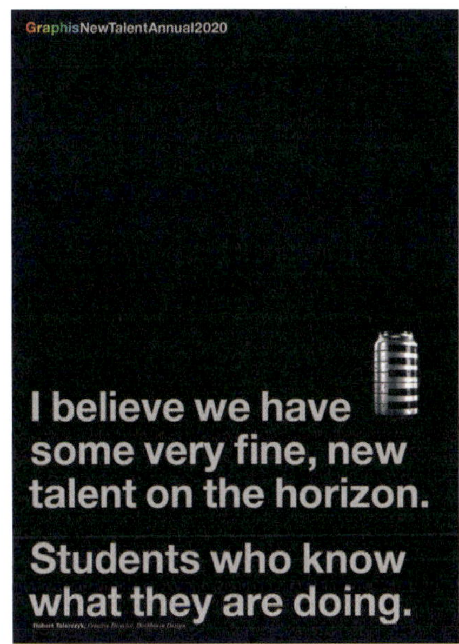

New Talent Annual 2020

2020
Hardcover: 272 pages
200-plus color illustrations
Trim: 8.5 x 11.75"
ISBN: 978-1-931241-86-1
US $90

This Annual presents work from award-winning instructors and students. **Platinum:** Advertising: Josh Ege, David Elizalde, Antonio Fragoso, Tu Phan, Vinny Tulley, and Mel White. Design: Peter Ahlberg, Nelson Carnicelli, Tina Fong, Seung-Min Han, Natasha Jen, Ken Koester, and Dong-Joo Park. Photo: Taylor Bareford. This year we awarded 19 Platinum, 179 Gold, and 359 Silver award-winning work from students whose professors have influenced them to create distinct and unique works. We award up to 500 Honorable Mentions, encouraging new talent to submit. All winners are equally presented and archived on our website. This book is a tool for teachers to raise their students' standards and gauge how their school measures up.

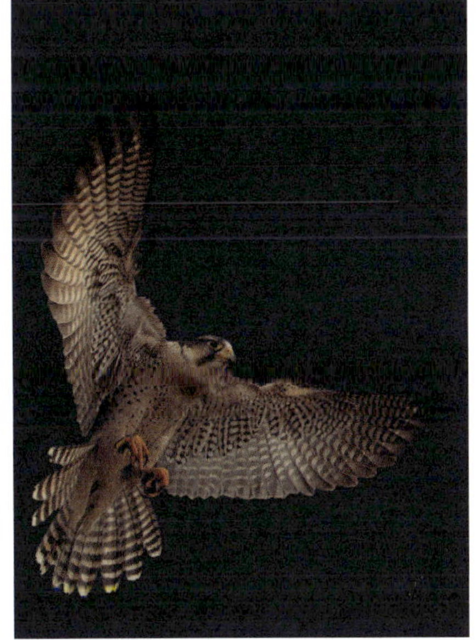

Photography Annual 2020

2020
Hardcover: 256 pages
200-plus color illustrations
Trim: 8.5 x 11.75"
ISBN: 978-1-931241-85-4
US $90

Awards: Graphis presents 12 Platinum, 94 Gold, 117 Silver Awards, and 65 Honorable Mentions in this annual.
Platinum Winners: Craig Cutler, Bruce DeBoer, Nicholas Duers, Nick Hall, Vincent Junier, Jonathan Knowles, McCandliss and Campbell, Lennette Newell, Joseph Saraceno, Howard Schatz, Michael Schoenfeld, Sarah Ward.
Judges: Work was judged by a panel of Photographers who had been past winners such as: Graphis Masters Athena Azevedo, Andreas Franke, and Ricardo de Vicq de Cumptich as well as Colin Faulkner and Frank P. Wartenberg.
Content: Photos from judges, and award-winning photographers. Also included is a retrospective on the past decade of winning photography, and a list of international photography museums.

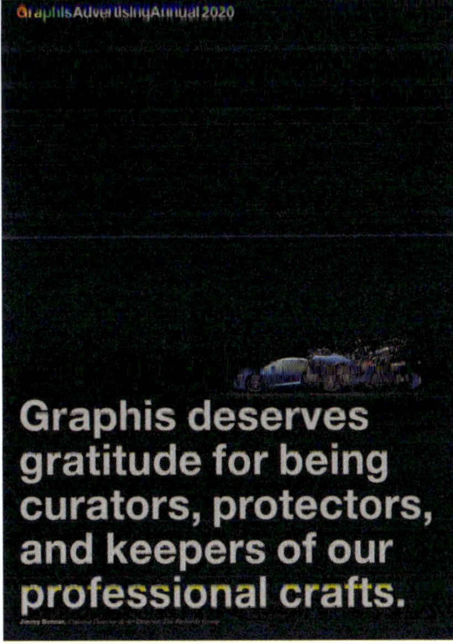

Advertising Annual 2020

2020
Hardcover: 224 pages
200-plus color illustrations
Trim: 8.5 x 11.75"
ISBN: 978-1-931241-83-0
US $90

Awards: 10 Platinum, 89 Gold, 59 Silver awards, totaling more than 180 winners, along with 22 Honorable Mentions.
Platinum Winners: ARSONAL, AUDI USA, Brunner, daDá, The Designory, Duncan Channon, Fabian Oetner, FBC Design, INNOCEAN USA, PPK,USA, and Shine United.
Judges: Benjamin Bailey of Doner, Jimmy Bonner of The Richards Group, Matt Herrmann of BVK, Jinsoo Jeon of BRAND DIRECTORS, John Peed of Cold Open, and Xosé Teiga of xosé teiga, studio.
Content: Designs by the judges and award-winning advertising agencies, Q&A's from Platinum-winning instructors, and a special feature on a decade of excellence in Advertising.

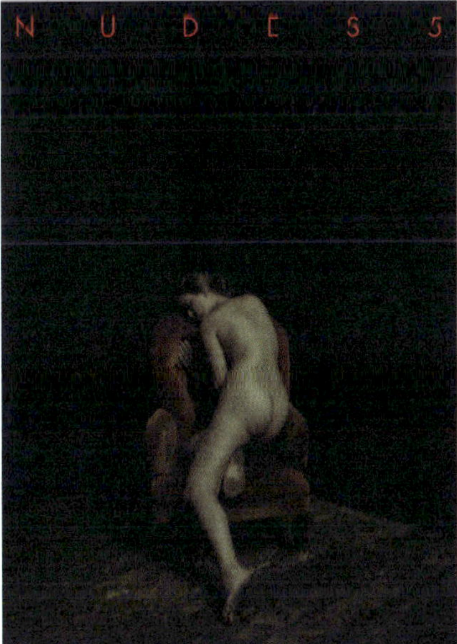

Nudes 5

2019
Hardcover: 256 pages
200-plus color illustrations
Trim: 10.06 x 13.41"
ISBN: 978-1-931241-84-7
US $90

The fifth volume in this series, Nudes 5 continues to present some of the most refined and creative nudes photography. Just as this genre helped elevate photography into a realm of fine art, one will find that many of the images on these pages deserve to be presented in museums. Award-winning Photographers include **Erik Almas, Rosanne Olson, Klaus Kampert, Howard Schatz, Phil Marco, Joel-Peter Witkin, Chris Budgeon**, among others.

Books are available at www.graphis.com/store

At $90 each, these books present award-winning talent. Become a Professional Member and get a copy for only $45.

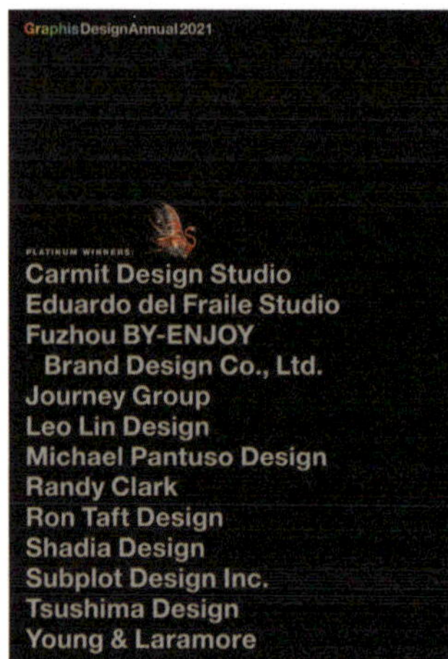

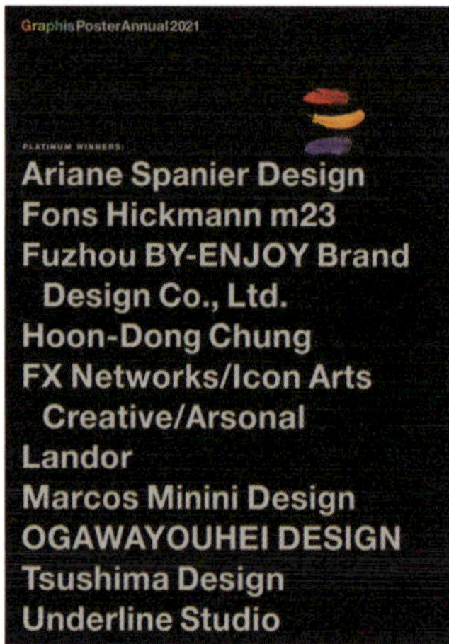

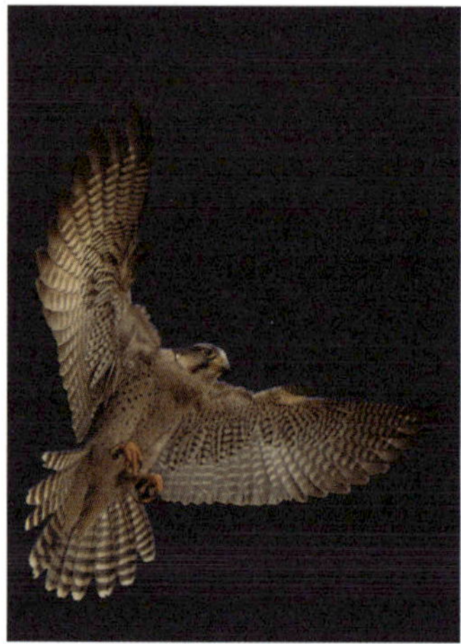

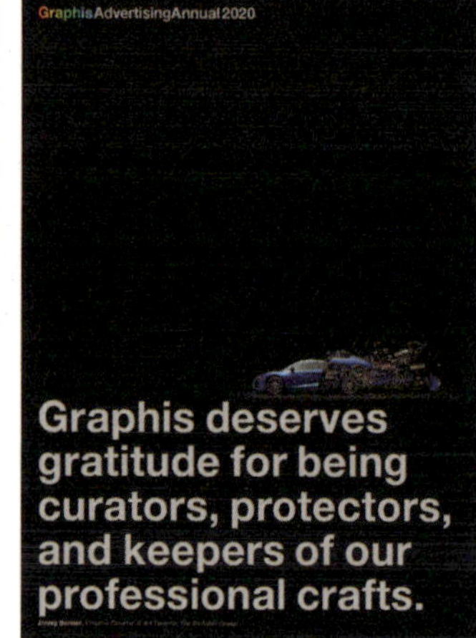

DESIGN ANNUAL 2021 PLATINUM WINNERS:

Carmit Design Studio
Eduardo del Fraile Studio
Fuzhou BY-ENJOY
  Brand Design Co., Ltd.
Journey Group
Leo Lin Design
Michael Pantuso Design
Randy Clark
Ron Taft Design
Shadia Design
Subplot Design Inc.
Tsushima Design
Young & Laramore

POSTER ANNUAL 2021 PLATINUM WINNERS:

Ariane Spanier Design
Fons Hickmann m23
Fuzhou BY-ENJOY Brand
  Design Co., Ltd.
Hoon-Dong Chung
FX Networks/Icon Arts
  Creative/Arsonal
Landor
Marcos Minini Design
OGAWAYOUHEI DESIGN
Tsushima Design
Underline Studio

PHOTOGRAPHY ANNUAL 2020 PLATINUM WINNERS:

Craig Cutler
Bruce DeBoer
Nicholas Duers
Nick Hall
Vincent Junier
Jonathan Knowles
McCandliss and Campbell
Lennette Newell
Joseph Saraceno
Howard Schatz
Michael Schoenfeld
Sarah Ward

ADVERTISING ANNUAL 2020 PLATINUM WINNERS:

ARSONAL
AUDI USA
Brunner
daDá
The Designory
Duncan Channon
Fabian Oefner
FBC Design
INNOCEAN USA
PPK, USA
Shine United

Books are available at www.graphis.com/store

EVERY DESIGNER, EVERY ART DIRECTOR SHOULD MEASURE EVERY EFFORT WITH A SINGLE QUESTION. "IS IT WORTHY OF GRAPHIS?"

Stan Richards, *Creative Director/Principal, The Richards Group, Design Annual 2010*

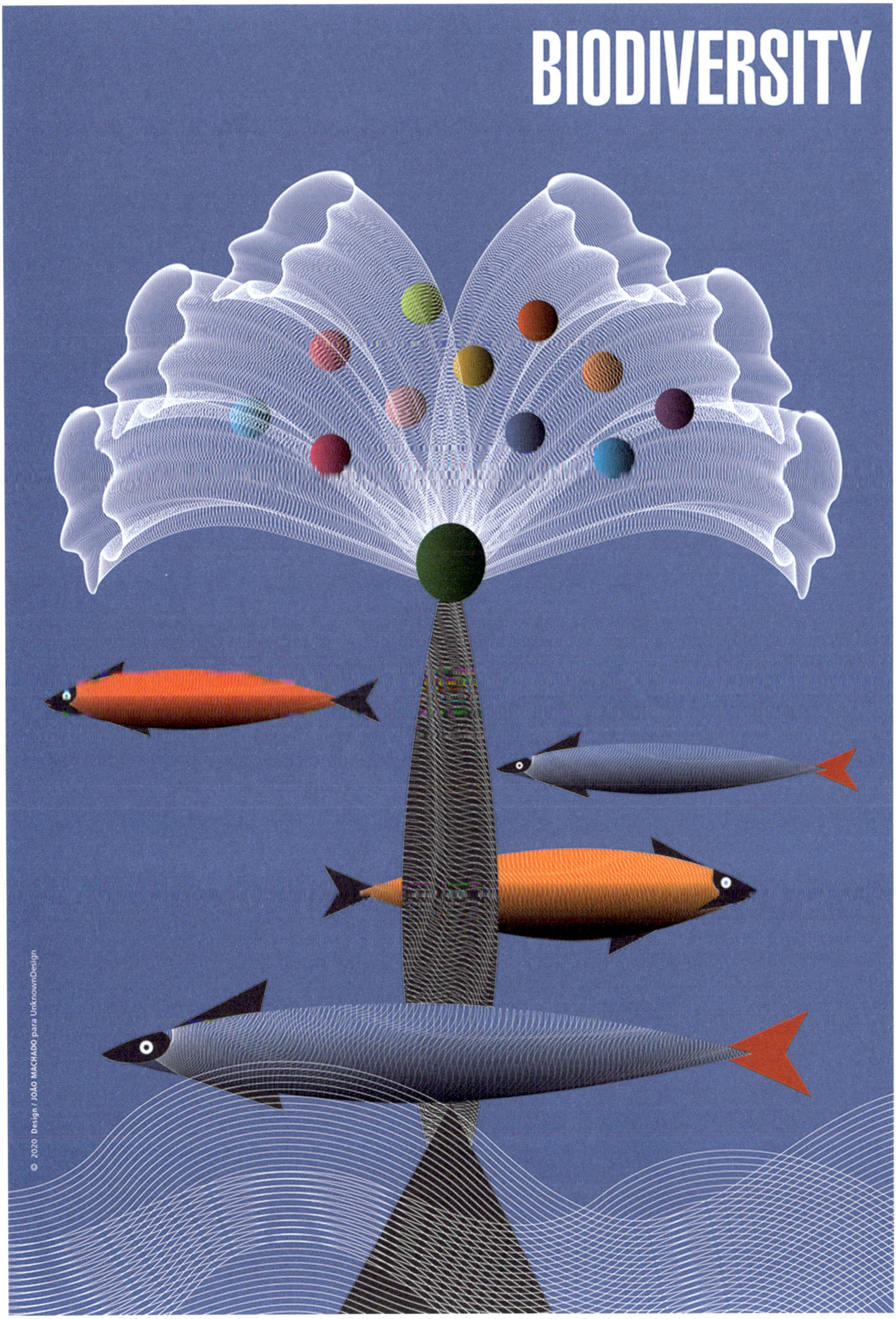

Designer: **João Machado** | Client: **Unknowndesign**

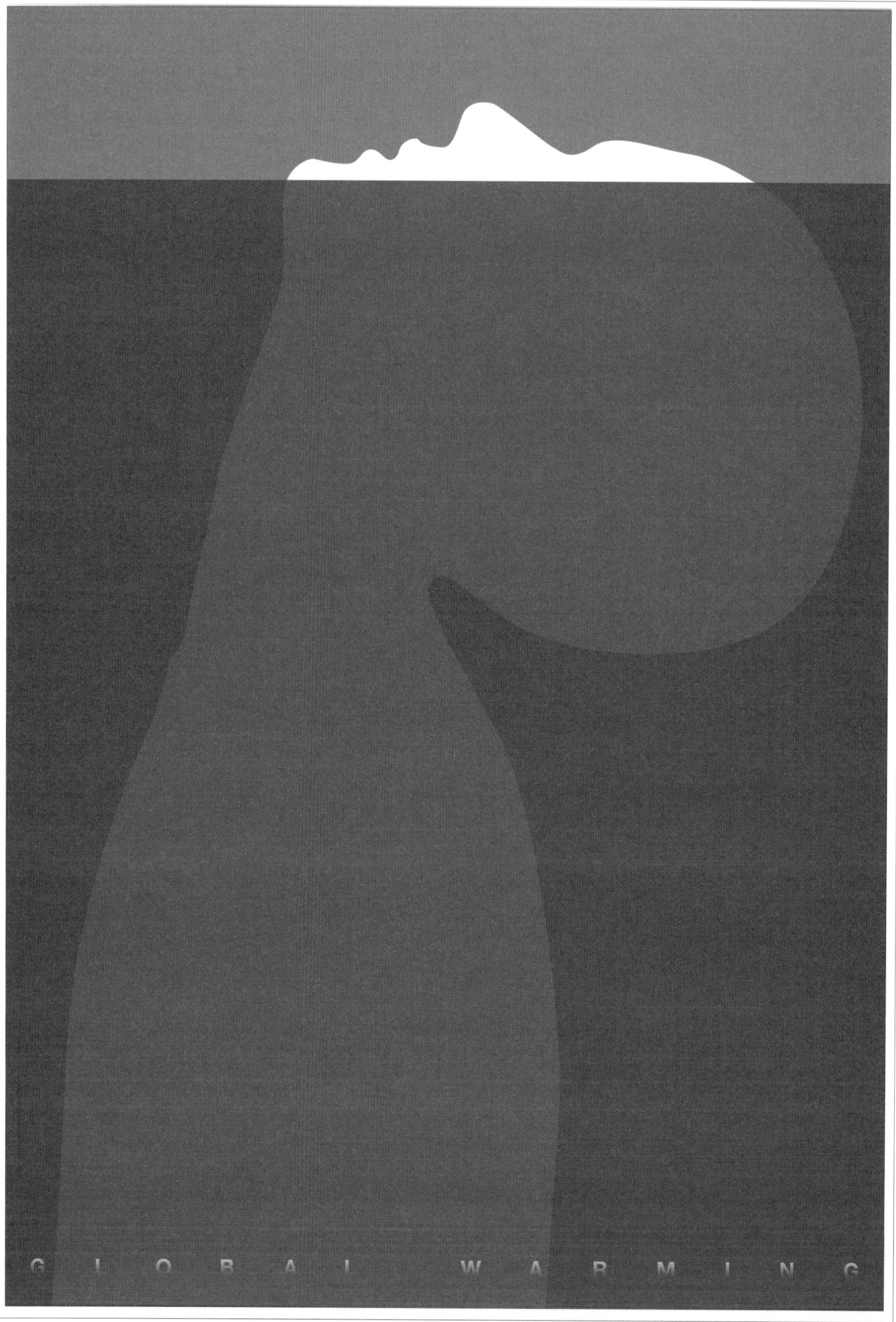

Designer: **Leo Lin** | Client: **Taiwan Poster Design Association**

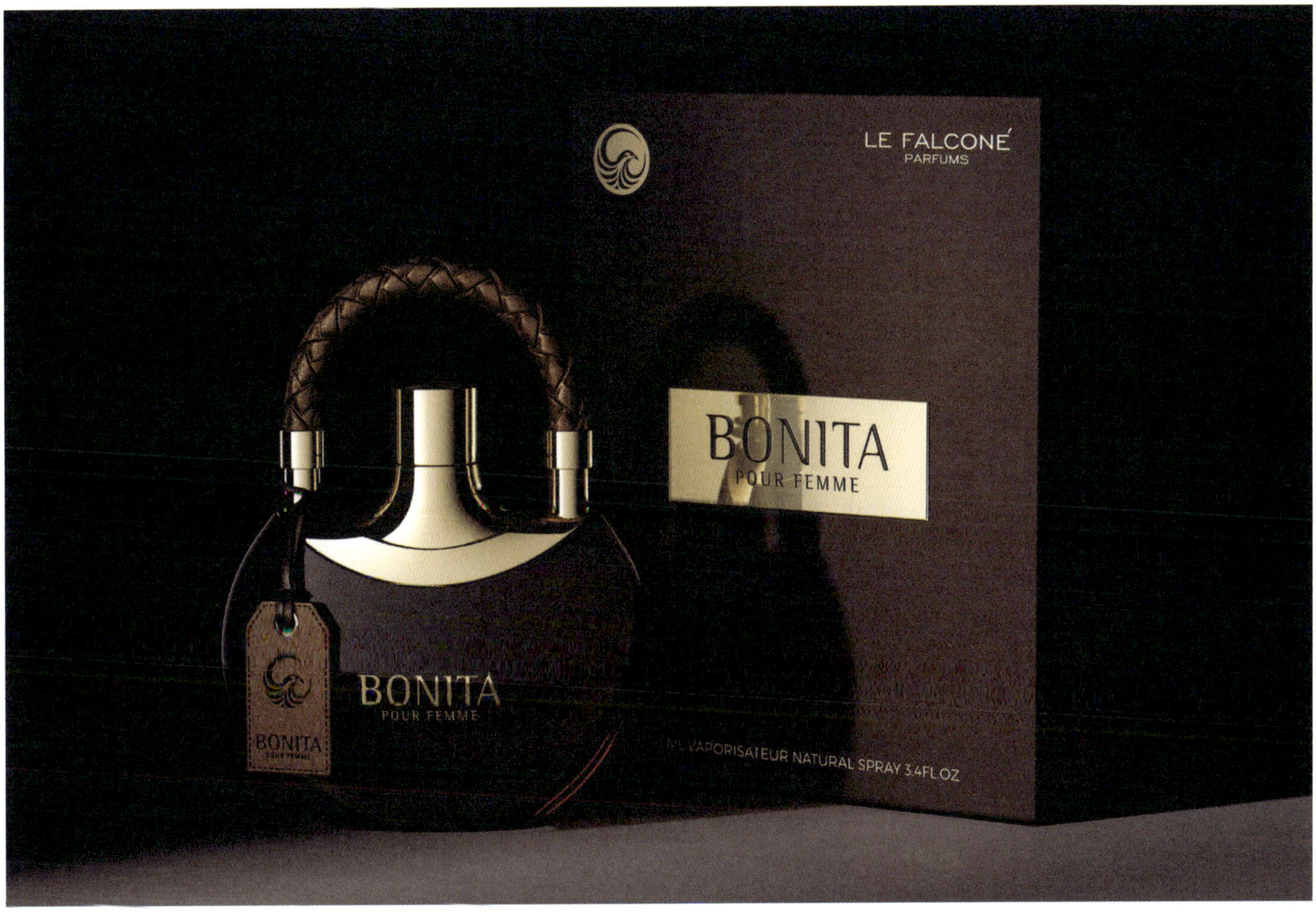

Agency: **Sol Benito** | Designer: **Vishal Vora, Janak Vora, Hardik Chudasama, Jyoti Pithwa** | Client: **Elite Brands**

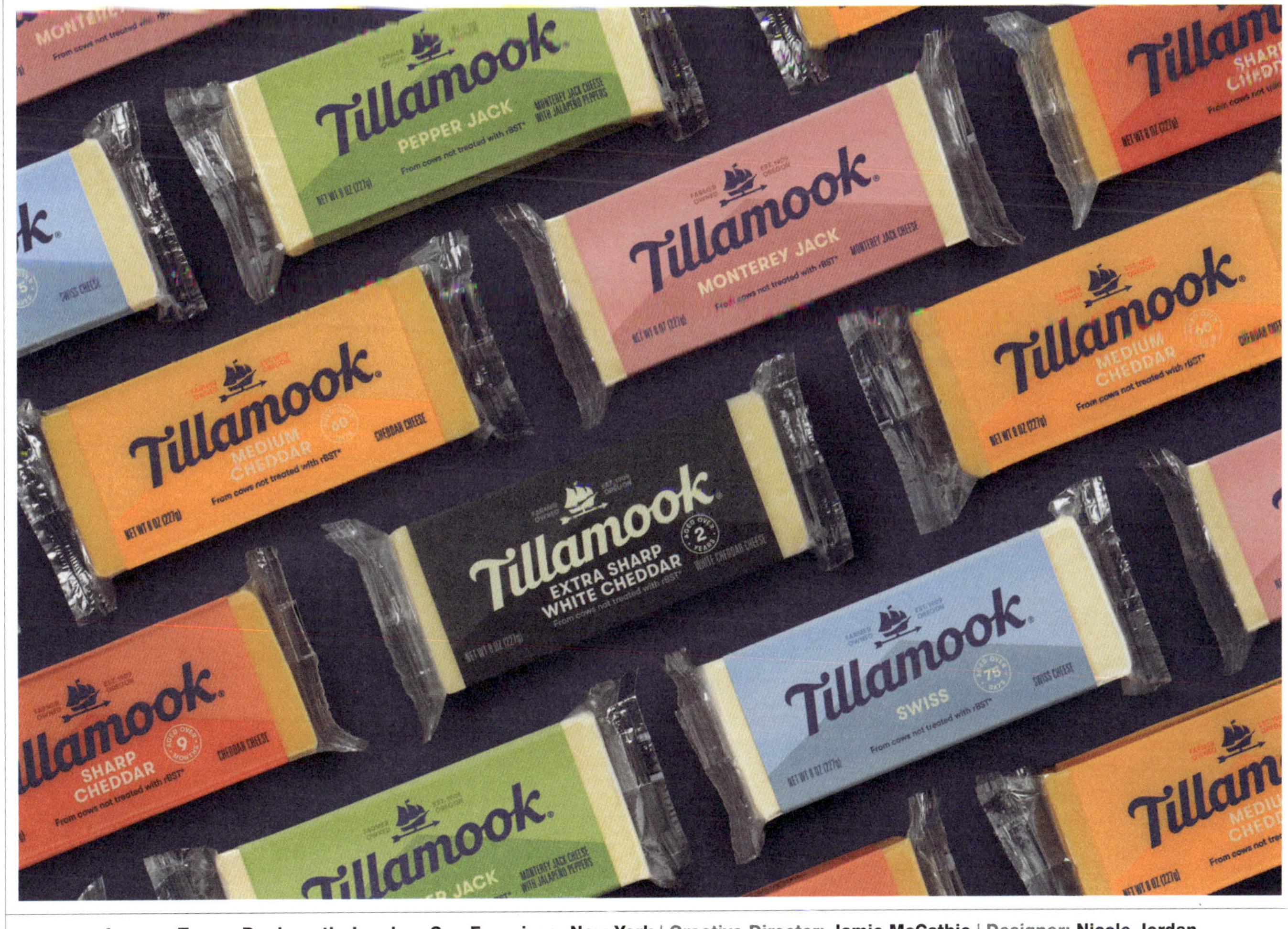

Agency: **Turner Duckworth: London, San Francisco, New York** | Creative Director: **Jamie McCathie** | Designer: **Nicole Jordan**
Lettering Artist: **Jeremy Mickel** | Copywriter: **Colin Corcoran** | Photographer: **Maren Caruso** | Client: **Tillamook**

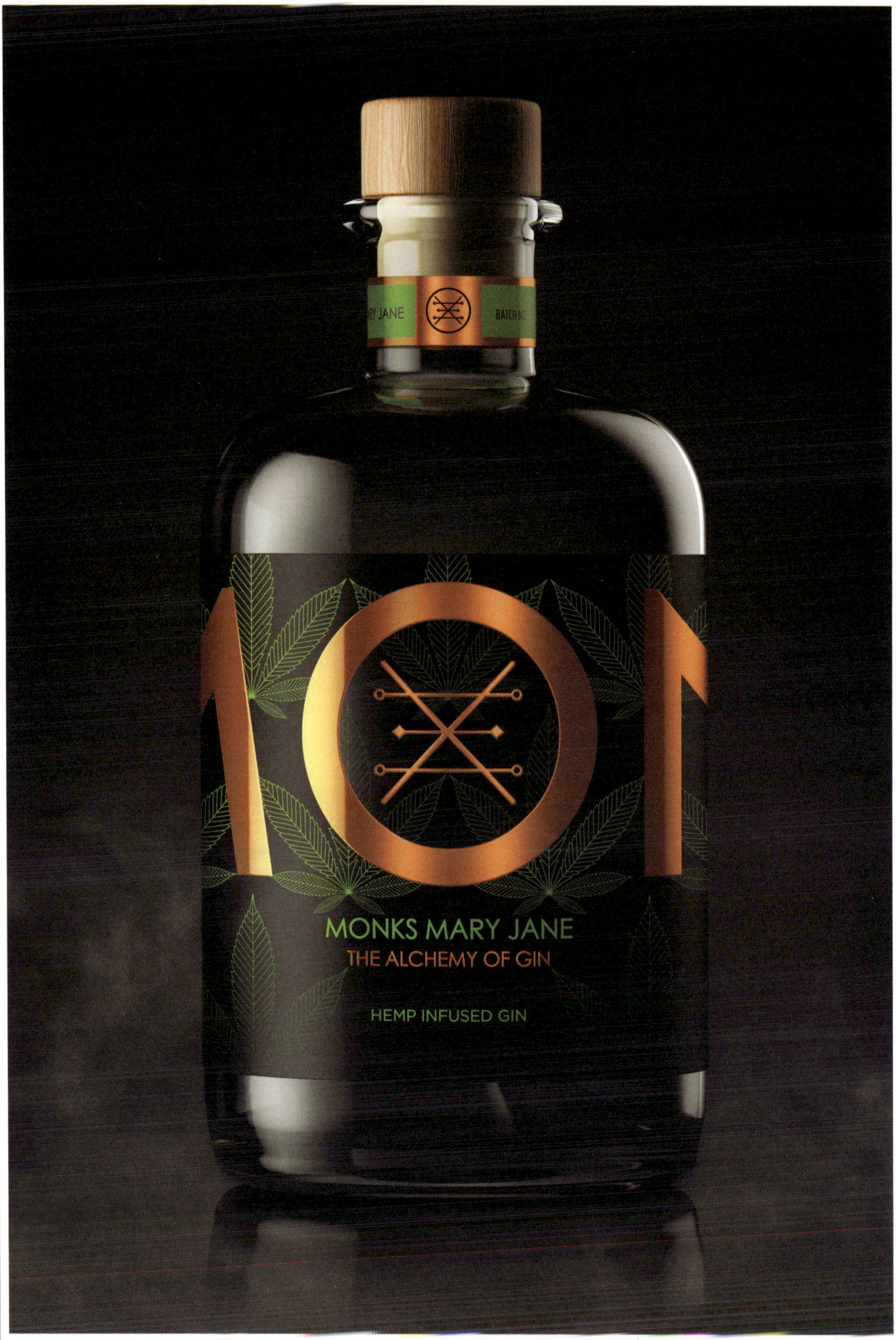

Agency: **Next** | Designer: **Michele Dush** | Client: **Monks**

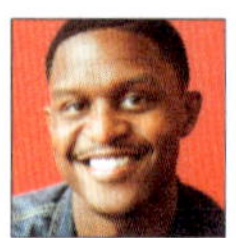

Quinnton Harris

Publicis Sapient Group Creative Director, Experience and co-leads of Global Computational Design, focusing on improving our design operation systems. He plays a critical role in accelerating CXO John Maeda's vision for fostering a more inclusive, multi-dimensional and cohesive Experience capability. ■ He also serves as Head of Experience for San Francisco. He also completed a short tenure as John Maeda's Chief of Staff, finding much success in pushing critical CXO initiatives, implementing systems for global collaboration, and enhancing internal communication strategies. ■ Harris recently led the #hellajuneteenth movement and got over 600 companies committed to observing Juneteenth as a paid holiday for its employees. Prior to joining Publicis Sapient, Quinnton was the inaugural Creative Director at Blavity, Inc. and before that, led design at Walker & Company Brands, a start-up consumer products and tech company notably acquired by Procter & Gamble. ■ He is an MIT alum, graduating with S.B. in Mechanical Engineering and dual minors in Architecture & Visual Arts.

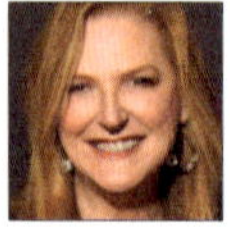

Patti Judd

Award-winning creative director, accomplished marketing and film executive, and co-founder of the San Diego International Film Festival, Patti recently joined Graphis as Chief Visionary Officer. A key initiative was forming the Graphis Industry Advisory Board to promote greater industry insights and connection globally. ■ Patti blends business savvy gained from 20+ years at her agency with the entertainment biz acumen garnered from working in music and film. Her studio, Judd Brand Media, champions her passion for creating innovative work receiving over 100 awards in design, advertising and marketing. Her work includes notable global brands such as WME, Disney, Mattel, Montreux Jazz Festival, Century 21, Aramark, Service America, Hilton, alongside numerous emerging brands, recording artists and filmmakers. ■ Her influence goes from helping launch a major live music venue, where she was a key player in it's growth to one of the top live jazz venues in the world, to co-founding the San Diego International Film Festival. She holds two executive producer credits for a children's TV series on Nickelodeon, and a feature film in association with the BBC which premiered at Sundance (acquired by Universal Pictures). Currently, she is in development as executive producer on an exciting new animated children's series. ■ Patti's nonprofit work includes being a foster youth board member, past president of an arts & culture board benefiting Balboa Park, the largest urban cultural park in the US. Recently, she was awarded as an Altruist Honoree by Modern Luxury magazine.

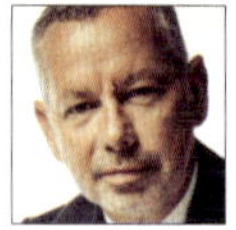

Duncan Milner

Born in Kingston, Jamaica, Duncan was drawn to the world of advertising, intrigued by the clash of art and commerce. This led to art school in Toronto, and the launch of his career at small, but creatively respected shops in San Diego, where his good work caught the eye of Chiat/Day. ■ Various roles in the Chiat/Day network included stints in the Toronto, St. Louis and New York offices on blue-chip brands like Nissan, Pepsi, Mars and Levi's. This led to Duncan being handpicked to co-found TBWA/Media Arts Lab where, as Chief Creative Officer, Duncan worked closely with Steve Jobs to help re-build the Apple brand, launching the iPod, iPhone, iPad, Apple Watch, and Apple TV. ■ Duncan's influence has been recognized at numerous awards shows including the iconic "Mac vs. PC" campaign, which was named Campaign of the Decade by Adweek, 2013 Cannes Press Grand Prix, 2014 Emmy Award for best commercial, and Apple's "Shot on iPhone 6" campaign that won the 2015 Cannes Grand Prix and Grand Clio for Outdoor. In 2015, he was named to Fast Company's Creative 50. In 2017, TBWA\Media Arts Lab and Apple were awarded the One Show's Penta pencil, recognizing the successful partnership and outstanding body of work between agency and client over 5-years. ■ Currently, Duncan consults with numerous brands and has also taken on a new role sharing his experience and the occasional funny story speaking at corporate events.

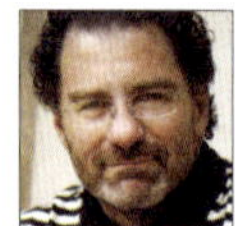

Michael Pantuso

As a multi-disciplined Graphic Designer and Artist, Michael Pantuso thrives at the intersection of creative thinking, artistic expression and strategically inspired ideas. Throughout his career, Michael has managed his own design practice, partnered in the branding agency IDEAS360°, and held positions inside TBWA Worldhealth (formerly CAHG) and Discover Financial. ■ Located in the Chicago area, Michael is focused on creating design and art for clients, collectors and organizations that make a social impact — these include charities, not-for-profits, NGOs, educational and arts bodies, social enterprises and for-profit businesses who want to do more good. Michael's practice creates all the usual outputs of a branding agency — design identities, advertising, social media, print literature, websites, email, e-newsletters, photography, etc... But he does so in the context of a bigger picture — a vision for what the brand is, and more importantly, what it can become. It's a passion that comes from a desire to make things better. ■ Michael's art is an extension of this passion but it's revealed and expressed in a more visceral way. One example of this can be seen through his "Mechanical Integration" work where he explores nature and humanity through a series of fine art illustrations that integrate natural life forms with the inner-workings of mechanical components. Part of this collection was recently celebrated as a solo exhibition which began in Paris, France followed by a tour of Europe that concluded in early 2020. Much of that work now remains in galleries and private collections.